Classic Ethics for the Modern Man

Andrew Lynn holds a Ph.D. in Renaissance literature from Cambridge University and has lectured in Western civilization in Beijing. He now practises law.

www.andrewlynn.com

Classic Ethics for the Modern Man

Andrew Lynn

HOWGILL HOUSE

Copyright © Andrew Lynn 2021

All rights reserved. No part of this book may be reproduced, stored in a retrieval system, or transmitted, in any form or by any means, electronic, mechanical, photocopying, recording or otherwise, without the prior permission of the copyright owner.

Published by Howgill House Books

First paperback edition 2021

ISBN 978-1-912360-24-6 (paperback)
ISBN 978-1-912360-23-9 (ebook)

To my son, Aristotle.

Contents

Introduction 1

1. Plato, The Republic & Phaedo 9

2. Aristotle, Nicomachean Ethics 35

3. The Stoics: Seneca, Epictetus, Marcus Aurelius 55

4. Boethius, The Consolation of Philosophy 91

5. Benedict de Spinoza, Ethics 103

6. David Hume, A Treatise on Human Nature 121

7.
Immanuel Kant, Groundwork of the Metaphysics of Morals
139

8. Friedrich Schiller, On Grace and Dignity 151

9. Søren Kierkegaard, Fear and Trembling 165

10. Arthur Schopenhauer, On Human Nature 189

11.
Friedrich Nietzsche, Beyond Good and Evil & The Genealogy of Morals
209

12. John Stuart Mill, On Liberty & Utilitarianism 227

Conclusion 253
Bibliography 257

INTRODUCTION

Once upon a time—way back when the Western world, in the sportiveness of its youth, shook its honeyed locks and gazed out smilingly across the sun-speckled Mediterranean—ethics was conceived to be, of its very nature, a healthy, life-affirming, and inherently joyous affair. In that age, as the philosophers strolled in the bustling agora or reclined in dappled olive groves, they spoke to one another of the 'good' man as the man who had cultivated in his inner being the cardinal virtues—justice, wisdom, courage, moderation—and who, as a natural consequence, lived life well. A man's job was first and foremost to get *himself* in order, these philosophers unhesitatingly affirmed, for this was the path to the personal excellence that constituted virtue, and it was through virtuous, well-balanced, and self-disciplined men that the state could be turned into an agent of human flourishing rather than an instrument of tyranny and oppression.

The West—or something that goes by its name—stumbles forward zombie-like to this day, but it has long been wracked by a moral sickness from within that renders it virtually unrecognisable from what it once was. In truth, the seeds of the disorder may have been there from the very beginning, blown many hundreds of years ago from the hardness of the desert, where the sun pounds mercilessly against the barren sands, into the heartlands of Europe, where they landed and took root in the soul of Western man. At first the thing seemed harmless—no more than a light delirium, which infected the mind and whispered, seductively, of a moral law that would be answerable to all man's doubts and misgivings. Bit by bit, however, the new dogma began to edge out the old wisdom, and the ancient virtues came to seem no longer quite so serviceable. What a struggle it was to live day-in, day-out, in pursuit of personal excellence! What a struggle to chase after the exquisite self-balance that seemed always to escape just beyond one's reach, like the horizon or the shimmering cusp of a rainbow! Let us speak instead, said Western man, not of *virtue* but of *duty*—and of a duty that, since it applies universally, applies to each of us equally. But as the years shaded into decades, and decades into centuries, human weakness took hold, and each man took to pointing his gnarled finger at the other to insist that the other was in the wrong. By now the mind-madness was complete: man was shrill and accusatory to the very same extent that he had become cretinous, dwarfish, and cloven-footed.

It is the underlying proposition of this book that what is commonly understood as ethics in the West has become dangerously one-sided. In the popular mind, the ethical life is to be lived by doing one's duty through acting in accordance with universalistic moral laws, and has little or nothing to do with cultivating a better self or in living the good life. This privileging of what is known as 'duty ethics' over 'virtue ethics' may seem to be nothing more than a quirk of intellectual or cultural history. In fact, the feverish pursuit of abstract moral universalism in place of an ethics of personal virtue has had profound consequences for the West.

First is the tendency towards moral posturing. When virtue corresponded to excellence, there was no place for this: what mattered was the crafting and cultivating of one's own character—something that could only with great difficulty be feigned. Once goodness was conceived of exclusively as adherence to a universal moral law, however, fakery became inevitable: for whereas one's character displays itself in the minutest of acts and in the face of the smallest of provocations, whether or not one abides by a rule is a matter of report and reputation. Two further co-morbidities, conformism and self-righteousness, follow naturally at its heels: conformism because the universality of the moral law is unlikely to be found, so it is thought, in the minority view; and self-righteousness because there is no easier way to associate oneself with the moral law than to be one of those shouting it out most loudly and most aggressively hunting down its infractors.

Second is the tendency to moralise what are in fact legitimate differences in views. When the virtuous life was conceived as the good life lived in pursuit of personal excellence, differences in the content of mens' views were secondary. When morality is determined by the dictates of a universal moral law, however, divergence from the orthodoxy comes to be seen as divergence from the good itself, and therefore as a kind of deficiency or even active immorality. Put slightly differently, the former approach conceives of difference as difference; the latter, as wrongdoing, wickedness, and sin. This moralising tendency strikes at our ability to take a step back and discuss our differences with cool heads and steady hearts; it makes us tetchy, ill-tempered, and accusatory.

Third is the self-defeating quality of a moral code that neglects the ethical mandate to work first on oneself. To arrogate to oneself the moral high ground, without having first gone through the long slow process of building and refining one's inner nature, might sometimes receive the approbation of the state or the masses, but rarely does it inspire or engage the community more broadly. True respect cannot be commanded; it can only be earned. If you are slovenly, appetitive, ill-disciplined or weak, you have no reason to expect to be listened to, however loudly you may shout.

This book sets out, by introducing several of the most enduringly relevant of the classic texts, to bring some balance back to our understanding of what ethics can be. It presents a tradition that has, in fact, been with us all along, although perhaps 'hidden in plain sight'—for virtue ethics, despite having been neglected for the better part of two centuries, has always been a fundamental part of the Western tradition. There is, as John Stuart Mill puts it, a 'Greek ideal of self-development' deriving from 'a conception of humanity as having its nature bestowed on it for other purposes than to be merely abnegated'; 'Pagan self-assertion,' he adds, 'is one of the elements of human worth, as well as Christian self-denial.'[1] This ideal is, however, one that has at times—and perhaps in recent years more than ever—been overwhelmed by the urge for abstract moralism and self-abnegation. Now, as the West seems to cringe in embarrassment at its own achievements and as much as at its own sins, is time for the corrective that this book, in small part, attempts.

Classic Ethics for the Modern Man opens by examining what the ancient Greeks advocated in their virtue ethics—the goals of personal excellence, inner harmony, and the pursuit of the good life through rational activity and contemplation. In selections from the *Republic* and *Phaedo*, Plato explores the idea of 'the good' in his notion of the 'just man' whose constituent elements of soul and body are rightly ordered in preparation for death. Aristotle, on the other hand, is this-worldly as always: for him, personal excellence is to be achieved by striving to realize the 'golden mean' of conduct that is found

---

1. John Stuart Mill, *On Liberty* (London: Longman, Green, Longman, Roberts & Green, 1864), 112.

at the mid-point between two vices; that is done, he explains in his *Nicomachean Ethics*, by habituating oneself to virtue. In each case, the focus remains on character: cultivating, refining, and sculpting from the raw material of a superior version of oneself.

From the ancient Greeks we turn to the Stoics of ancient Rome—Seneca, Epictetus, and Marcus Aurelius. The Stoics are the masters of precisely the kind of practical philosophy that has fallen out of favour and yet remains so necessary today. Seneca opens with his discussion of how a man's divine nature is most pronounced when he faces down fortune with a smile; he follows that with a detailed analysis of anger and the steps we can take to overcome it. Next comes Epictetus, who in selections from his *Enchiridion* (or 'Handbook') guides us in the art of self-mastery through an enumeration of specific mental techniques that can be employed to achieve it. The chapter ends with the *Meditations* of the one true philosopher king, the Emperor Marcus Aurelius, who wisely directs us towards a calm and measured understanding of our position in the universe and how best to cope with all that life may throw at us.

One of the most influential works of medieval philosophy is Boethius' *Consolations of Philosophy*. Boethius was a statesman who had been accused of treason, and he penned the *Consolations* while in prison in Pavia awaiting his execution. The work is a meditation on the vicissitudes of fortune and the inscrutability of God's providence. The life lived well cannot depend on fortune, suggests Boethius, or on anything external to man and outside his control; in fact, fortune brings its own inconveniences by making us more sensitive to trifling misfortunes and petty slights. Boethius marries classical precepts with Christian faith: seek the good in the action of one's virtues and trust in providence, he suggests—more we cannot ask, nor more do we really need.

The Renaissance is represented by Baruch Spinoza's

Ethics. In the *Ethics*, Spinoza deploys a minimalistic lapidary style to expand upon and develop the central insights of virtue ethics. For Spinoza, virtue is self-mastery, but it is also the power of self-actualisation and of action. His distinctive contribution is to appreciate the need to engage the emotions to heighten the power of our activity—and hence that which makes us virtuous.

From here we move forward to the eighteenth century. First in significance is Immanuel Kant, for it is Kant's hugely influential elaboration of the 'categorical imperative'—the proposition that you should only act on that maxim that you can at the same time will to be a universal law—that consolidated the hegemony of duty-based ethics over classical virtue ethics. Other eighteenth century thinkers are, however, less than categorical in agreeing with him on this. David Hume, on the one hand, addresses the fundamental 'is-ought' problem and suggests that we should look for the moral element not in abstract principle but in our empirical sentiments of approval and blame. Friedrich Schiller, on the other hand, considers that ethical conduct arises from the instincts of the 'noble soul', rather than from arid rules, and that virtue is not a form of self-abnegation but rather 'an inclination for duty'.

The towering figures of the nineteenth century propose new ways in which the character can be cultivated, deepened, and enlarged. For Søren Kierkegaard, the ethical stage is only one of life's stages, and not the last or the most profound—that is reserved to the religious stage, which is to be experienced as a deepening and intensification of our relationship with existence that can only be effected by way of an absurd 'leap of faith'. Arthur Schopenhauer, on the other hand, seeks to base his ethics on the operations of the universal 'Will'—the ceaseless struggle for existence that pulsates through all things—and the sympathy that is engendered when one grasps that all men find themselves in a common predicament, awaiting death like prisoners awaiting execution.

The rambunctious and ever-provocative Nietzsche comes next—raging (as only Nietzsche can rage) against the 'transvaluation of values' which has inverted the moral order so that the original notion of the 'good' (that which is noble and excellent) is now constituted as 'evil', while the morality of the herd (a slave morality proclaiming the meek as the inheritors of the earth) becomes the 'good'. Nietzsche grabs us by the lapels and urges us to re-think much of what we have taken for granted. He questions whether the old aristocratic morality, which elevated the powerful and the impulsive, was not perhaps preferable to the slave morality which insists that the poor, the weak, and the lowly alone are good. He asks whether our much vaunted social conscience is really high-minded altruism, or whether it stems from bug-eyed jealousy and a desire to show up others as bad. And he forces us to consider what consequences the 'dwarfing and levelling' of man will have for the future of mankind. There is almost nothing here that is tame and politically correct—and nothing that is not in equal measure engaging and thought-provoking.

The volume ends with John Stuart Mill. Mill is best known for his elucidation of the utilitarian 'greatest happiness principle', according to which actions are right as they tend to promote happiness, and wrong as they tend to produce the reverse of happiness. What is less well known is that Mill conceives of the pursuit of happiness squarely in the tradition of the virtue ethicists: for the happiness that is proper to man, he insists, must extend far beyond the pleasures of the sense to the pleasures of the intellect, the feelings, the imagination, and the moral sentiments—and even, in certain cases, to the enjoyment of virtue itself. In *On Liberty* (1859), Mill expressly invokes the spirit of the Greeks, as against the self-abnegation of religious fundamentalists, in advocating for the freedom to flourish. The tale of Western ethics comes, thus, full circle, and ends where it began—with the dream of excellence, virtue, and life well lived.

To take seriously the ethical thinking of these men—as practical guides for conduct rather than merely as texts of academic or historic interest—is no small thing. They conceive, collectively, of an ideal human condition: self-controlled (Plato), well-balanced (Aristotle), tolerant, detached, and present-focused (the Stoics), strong in faith (Boethius), urbane and convivial (Hume), universalistic (Kant), graceful and dignified (Schiller), deepened by experience (Kierkegaard), humane (Schopenhauer), aspirational (Nietzsche), and self-actualising (Mill). This is an ethical tradition that demands far more of its adherents than the mere imposition upon oneself, and more commonly upon others, of the dictates, prohibitions, and nay-saying of a moral law. The tradition does not demand a man have a religion, but neither is it incompatible with the religious view: it urges us, as have most of the great religious teachers, to 'first cast out the beam out of thine own eye'. Nor is the tradition incompatible with a heightened feeling of love towards one's fellow men: in fact, man can best love his fellow men, as Mill so cogently expressed, when each man strives to be a man worth loving. What lies at its heart is the notion that the ethical life involves making oneself better. There is a peculiar magic in taking responsibility for one's own existential condition; subtle changes occur as the world starts answering back. The point is to make a start. Fear not, then, and read on.

PLATO, THE REPUBLIC & PHAEDO

INTRODUCTION

If we were to boldly sum up what it is—in the Western tradition of ethical thinking—that has fallen away from our gaze, it would probably be this: the focus on cultivation of excellence.

The core concept is *aretê*. *Aretê* has often been translated as 'virtue', but 'excellence' is better, for anything that has a function has its corresponding *aretê* (or excellence) which is made manifest when it performs its functions well. For Socrates, eyes and knives could display *aretê* if they could see, or cut, well; Homer spoke of the *aretê* of horses that could run fast; and Thucydides found *aretê* in the fertility of the soil which yielded plentiful crops. *Aretê*, in short, is the quality that makes something good at doing what it is intended, by nature or design, to do.

Plato, who made *aretê* the keystone of a whole system of ethical philosophy, was born around 428-7BC into an aristocratic family during the early years of the Peloponnesian War. As a young man, he had associated with Socrates, who famously roamed the city of Athens challenging those he met to define and give an account of whatever particular excellence it was they were supposed to profess—with often mixed results. This manner of life was brought to an abrupt end when, in 404BC and after 27 years of war, Athens was taken by Sparta and handed over to an oligarchy of thirty, which included Plato's relatives Critias and Charmides. The oligarchy proceeded to murder roughly 1500 Athenians and drive others out of the city; within the space of a year, however, the thirty tyrants were overthrown and the democracy restored. Socrates—whose disciples had included Critias (Plato's cousin who spearheaded the tyranny) and Charmides (Plato's uncle)—was, under the restored democracy, prosecuted and sentenced to death on charges of impiety and corrupting the youth. After the death of Socrates, it appears that Plato travelled extensively in Greece and Italy, where he met with the Pythagorean philosophers who would influence his work, before returning to Athens to establish his Academy—the ancestor of the modern university.

The nature of the 'just man' is explored by Plato most fully in his *Republic*. Plato's *Republic* is, indeed, a work of ethical philosophy as much as it is a work of political philosophy: the state, in Plato's view, is as the man writ large—for, in the just man as in the just state, everything operates in its proper place; what is to be sought, whether in the individual or in the polity, is δίκη (*dike*)—a Greek term that is broader than what we understand as 'justice' and has been rendered in English as 'all-in rightness'. Plato's ethical ideal is, accordingly, one that is oriented primarily towards the perfectibility of the self through harmonious self-development and self-regulation rather than obedience to moral demands and commandments.

Once it understood that justice is δίκη (*dike*)—'all-in rightness' and everything in its proper place—then it is an straightforward matter for Plato to show that the just man will live well. Everything has its end or function and its own excellence, suggests Plato, and the soul's end or function is to 'superintend and command and deliberate' over the lower faculties; that being the case, the soul's excellence is justice, i.e. in maintaining all the elements of man's being in their proper place. The inner principles are three: a rational element (*nous*), a spirited element (*thumos*), and a desiring element (*epithumia*). In a well-governed soul, the rational element is the ruling principle, and is allied with the spirited element, so that both of them can keep guard over the desiring element, which in chasing after false pleasures exposes a man to internal disruption and weakens him as against his external enemies. Justice, like health, is the institution of a natural order.

The just man, says Plato, 'sets in order his own inner life, and is his own master and his own law' and it is through doing this that he unleashes his 'natural power' and becomes a more effective person. Conduct that preserves and enhances this harmonious condition is to be considered just and good action, and the knowledge that promotes it is to be considered wisdom; conversely, anything that impairs this condition is unjust action, and any of man's opinions that detract from should be recognised as ignorance. These principles give the just man a guide for future action and a method for deepening his wisdom as to the best way of living. By its nature, the just man's mode of being will tend towards a stable harmonious state, for 'virtue is one' but 'the forms of vice are innumerable'.

Plato is explicit that in the same way that living justly makes a man more capable, injustice, as a form of internal disequilibrium, robs him of his powers. Wherever injustice is found—whether in a city, an army, in a family or any other body—that body is rendered incapable of united action 'by reason of sedition and distraction'. Injustice is no less fatal when existing within a single person, 'in the first place rendering him incapable of action because he is not at unity with himself, and in the second place making him an enemy to himself and the just.' When one's being is disharmonious and self-divided, consistent and coordinated action will not be possible.

Often what is stressed in accounts of the ancient Greeks is their openness to rational inquiry. What is less widely recognised, although not necessarily of less value or significance, is the mystical quality that they bring to their speculations on man and his role in the universe. Plato is no exception. In his *Phaedo*, in particular, he depicts Socrates expounding on the proposition that philosophy is nothing less than 'the study of death'. Reality, for Plato, is constituted by unchangeable abstract 'ideas'—truth, beauty, goodness, et cetera—that underlie reality; man's earthly experience, in contrast, is compared to observing the shadows of puppets on the walls of a cave. It is the body—or rather the soul's attachment to the body—that, we are told in the *Phaedo*, not only pollutes and confuses the soul in its earthly existence, but also impedes its progress in the life hereafter. 'Why, because each pleasure and pain is a sort of nail which nails and rivets the soul to the body,' says Socrates in the *Phaedo*, 'until she becomes like the body, and believes that to be true which the body affirms to be true; and from agreeing with the body and having the same delights she is obliged to have the same habits and haunts, and is not likely ever to be pure at her departure to the world below, but is always infected by the body; and so she sinks into another body and there germinates and grows, and has therefore no part in the communion of the divine and pure and simple.' Plato's ethics are, for sure, very much 'this-worldly' in their focus on the cultivation of excellence and effectiveness; but we do him a disservice if we do not also recognise an 'otherworldly' orientation directed towards training the soul for greater insight during life, and greater preparedness in the face of death.

Plato's ethics has several attractions for the modern man. In the first place, he is one of the early exponents of the 'virtue ethics' that, it is suggested, puts in its rightful place the development and cultivation of character and personal excellence, rather than reducing ethics to observance of duties and rules (duty ethics) or assessment of the consequences of actions (consequentialism). Furthermore, Plato's speculative project is attractive in its breadth of scope: in making room for both rational inquiry and for flashes of intuitive insight, it embraces not only this-worldly matters but also reaches out to probe the most profound questions of life and death. Above all, Plato's conviction that absolutes exist—that there is such a thing as Justice, such a thing as Truth, such a thing as Goodness—provides a valuable counterpoint to the sterile and repetitive relativism of the post-modern orthodoxies that dominate the public discourse of the current era.

REPUBLIC

BOOK I

SOCRATES-THRASYMACHUS

Socrates:[1] Then I will repeat the question which I asked before, in order that our examination of the relative nature of justice and injustice may be carried on regularly. A statement was made that injustice is stronger and more powerful than justice, but now justice, having been identified with wisdom and virtue, is easily shown to be stronger than injustice, if injustice is ignorance; this can no longer be questioned by anyone. But I want to view the matter, Thrasymachus, in a different way:

1. *Republic*, V, 351a-354c.

You would not deny that a state may be unjust and may be unjustly attempting to enslave other states, or may have already enslaved them, and may be holding many of them in subjection?

Thrasymachus: True, he replied; and I will add the best and perfectly unjust state will be most likely to do so.

Socrates: I know, I said, that such was your position; but what I would further consider is, whether this power which is possessed by the superior state can exist or be exercised without justice.

Thrasymachus: If you are right in your view, and justice is wisdom, then only with justice; but if I am right, then without justice.

Socrates: I am delighted, Thrasymachus, to see you not only nodding assent and dissent, but making answers which are quite excellent.

Thrasymachus: That is out of civility to you, he replied.

Socrates: You are very kind, I said; and would you have the goodness also to inform me, whether you think that a state, or an army, or a band of robbers and thieves, or any other gang of evil-doers could act at all if they injured one another?

Thrasymachus: No indeed, he said, they could not.

Socrates: But if they abstained from injuring one another, then they might act together better?

Thrasymachus: Yes.

Socrates: And this is because injustice creates divisions and hatreds and fighting, and justice imparts harmony and friendship; is not that true, Thrasymachus?

Thrasymachus: I agree, he said, because I do not wish to quarrel with you.

Socrates: How good of you, I said; but I should like to know also whether injustice, having this tendency to arouse hatred, wherever existing, among slaves or among freemen, will not make them hate one another and set them at variance and render them incapable of common action?

Thrasymachus: Certainly.

Socrates: And even if injustice be found in two only, will they not quarrel and fight, and become enemies to one another and to the just.

Thrasymachus: They will.

Socrates: And suppose injustice abiding in a single person, would your wisdom say that she loses or that she retains her natural power?

Thrasymachus: Let us assume that she retains her power.

Socrates: Yet is not the power which injustice exercises of such a nature that wherever she takes up her abode, whether in a city, in an army, in a family, or in any other body, that body is, to begin with, rendered incapable of united action by reason of sedition and distraction; and does it not become its own enemy and at variance with all that opposes it, and with the just? Is not this the case?

Thrasymachus: Yes, certainly.

Socrates: And is not injustice equally fatal when existing in a single person; in the first place rendering him incapable of action because he is not at unity with himself, and in the second place making him an enemy to himself and the just? Is not that true, Thrasymachus?

Thrasymachus: Yes.

Socrates: And O my friend, I said, surely the gods are just?

Thrasymachus: Granted that they are.

Socrates: But if so, the unjust will be the enemy of the gods, and the just will be their friend?

Thrasymachus: Feast away in triumph, and take your fill of the argument; I will not oppose you, lest I should displease the company.

Socrates: Well then, proceed with your answers, and let me have the remainder of my repast. For we have already shown that the just are clearly wiser and better and abler than the unjust, and that the unjust are incapable of common action; nay more, that to speak as we did of men who are evil acting at any time vigorously together, is not strictly true, for if they had been perfectly evil, they would have laid hands upon one another; but it is evident that there must have been some remnant of justice in them, which enabled them to combine; if there had not been they would have injured one another as well as their victims; they were but half-villains in their enterprises; for had they been whole villains, and utterly unjust, they would have been utterly incapable of action. That, as I believe, is the truth of the matter, and not what you said at first. But whether the just have a better and happier life than the unjust is a further question which we also proposed to consider. I think that they have, and for the reasons which I have given; but still I should like to examine further, for no light matter is at stake, nothing less than the rule of human life.

Thrasymachus: Proceed.

Socrates: I will proceed by asking a question: Would you not say that a horse has some end?

Thrasymachus: I should.

Socrates: And the end or use of a horse or of anything would be that which could not be accomplished, or not so well accomplished, by any other thing?

Thrasymachus: I do not understand, he said.

Socrates: Let me explain: Can you see, except with the eye?

Thrasymachus: Certainly not.

Socrates: Or hear, except with the ear?

Thrasymachus: No.

Socrates: These then may be truly said to be the ends of these organs?

Thrasymachus: They may.

Socrates: But you can cut off a vine-branch with a dagger or with a chisel, and in many other ways?

Thrasymachus: Of course.

Socrates: And yet not so well as with a pruning-hook made for the purpose?

Thrasymachus: True.

Socrates: May we not say that this is the end of a pruning-hook?

Thrasymachus: We may.

Socrates: Then now I think you will have no difficulty in understanding my meaning when I asked the question whether the end of anything would be that which could not be accomplished, or not so well accomplished, by any other thing?

Thrasymachus: I understand your meaning, he said, and assent.

Socrates: And that to which an end is appointed has also an excellence? Need I ask again whether the eye has an end?

Thrasymachus: It has.

Socrates: And has not the eye an excellence?

Thrasymachus: Yes.

Socrates: And the ear has an end and an excellence also?

Thrasymachus: True.

Socrates: And the same is true of all other things; they have each of them an end and a special excellence?

Thrasymachus: That is so.

Socrates: Well, and can the eyes fulfil their end if they are wanting in their own proper excellence and have a defect instead?

Thrasymachus: How can they, he said, if they are blind and cannot see?

Socrates: You mean to say, if they have lost their proper excellence, which is sight; but I have not arrived at that point yet. I would rather ask the question more generally, and only enquire whether the things which fulfil their ends fulfil them by their own proper excellence, and fail of fulfilling them by their own defect?

Thrasymachus: Certainly, he replied.

Socrates: I might say the same of the ears; when deprived of their own proper excellence they cannot fulfil their end?

Thrasymachus: True.

Socrates: And the same observation will apply to all other things?

Thrasymachus: I agree.

Socrates: Well; and has not the soul an end which nothing else can fulfil? For example, to superintend and command and deliberate and the like. Are not these functions proper to the soul, and can they rightly be assigned to any other?

Thrasymachus: To no other.

Socrates: And is not life to be reckoned among the ends of the soul?

Thrasymachus: Assuredly, he said.

Socrates: And has not the soul an excellence also?

Thrasymachus: Yes.

Socrates: And can she or can she not fulfil her own ends when deprived of that excellence?

Thrasymachus: She cannot.

Socrates: Then an evil soul must necessarily be an evil ruler and superintendent, and the good soul a good ruler?

Thrasymachus: Yes, necessarily.

Socrates: And we have admitted that justice is the excellence of the soul, and injustice the defect of the soul?

Thrasymachus: That has been admitted.

Socrates: Then the just soul and the just man will live well, and the unjust man will live ill?

Thrasymachus: That is what your argument proves.

Socrates: And he who lives well is blessed and happy, and he who lives ill the reverse of happy?

Thrasymachus: Certainly.

Socrates: Then the just is happy, and the unjust miserable?

Thrasymachus: So be it.

Socrates: But happiness and not misery is profitable.

Thrasymachus: Of course.

Socrates: Then, my blessed Thrasymachus, injustice can never be more profitable than justice.

Thrasymachus: Let this, Socrates, he said, be your entertainment at the Bendidea.[2]

Socrates: For which I am indebted to you, I said, now that you have grown gentle towards me and have left off scolding. Nevertheless, I have not been well entertained; but that was my own fault and not yours. As an epicure snatches a taste of every dish which is successively brought to table, he not having allowed himself time to enjoy the one before, so have I gone from one subject to another without having discovered what I sought at first, the nature of justice. I left that enquiry and turned away to consider whether justice is virtue and wisdom or evil and folly; and when there arose a further question about the comparative advantages of justice and injustice, I could not refrain from passing on to that. And the result of the whole discussion has been that I know nothing at all. For I know not what justice is, and therefore I am not likely to know whether it is or is not a virtue, nor can I say whether the just man is happy or unhappy.

BOOK IV

SOCRATES-GLAUCON

Socrates:[3] And the individual will be acknowledged by us to be just in the same way in which the State is just?

Glaucon: That follows, of course.

Socrates: We cannot but remember that the justice of the

---

2. A Thracian festival held in honour of the goddess Bendis and celebrated with great revelry.
3. *Republic*, IV, 441d-445c.

State consisted in each of the three classes doing the work of its own class?

Glaucon: We are not very likely to have forgotten, he said.

Socrates: We must recollect that the individual in whom the several qualities of his nature do their own work will be just, and will do his own work?

Glaucon: Yes, he said, we must remember that too.

Socrates: And ought not the rational principle, which is wise, and has the care of the whole soul, to rule, and the passionate or spirited principle to be the subject and ally?

Glaucon: Certainly.

Socrates: And, as we were saying, the united influence of music and gymnastic will bring them into accord, nerving and sustaining the reason with noble words and lessons, and moderating and soothing and civilizing the wildness of passion by harmony and rhythm?

Glaucon: Quite true, he said.

Socrates: And these two, thus nurtured and educated, and having learned truly to know their own functions, will rule over the concupiscent, which in each of us is the largest part of the soul and by nature most insatiable of gain; over this they will keep guard, lest, waxing great and strong with the fullness of bodily pleasures, as they are termed, the concupiscent soul, no longer confined to her own sphere, should attempt to enslave and rule those who are not her natural-born subjects, and overturn the whole life of man?

Glaucon: Very true, he said.

Socrates: Both together will they not be the best defenders of the whole soul and the whole body against attacks from without; the one counselling, and the other fighting under his leader, and courageously executing his commands and counsels?

Glaucon: True.

Socrates: And he is to be deemed courageous whose spirit

retains in pleasure and in pain the commands of reason about what he ought or ought not to fear?

Glaucon: Right, he replied.

Socrates: And him we call wise who has in him that little part which rules, and which proclaims these commands; that part too being supposed to have a knowledge of what is for the interest of each of the three parts and of the whole?

Glaucon: Assuredly.

Socrates: And would you not say that he is temperate who has these same elements in friendly harmony, in whom the one ruling principle of reason, and the two subject ones of spirit and desire are equally agreed that reason ought to rule, and do not rebel?

Glaucon: Certainly, he said, that is the true account of temperance whether in the State or individual.

Socrates: And surely, I said, we have explained again and again how and by virtue of what quality a man will be just.

Glaucon: That is very certain.

Socrates: And is justice dimmer in the individual, and is her form different, or is she the same which we found her to be in the State?

Glaucon: There is no difference in my opinion, he said.

Socrates: Because, if any doubt is still lingering in our minds, a few commonplace instances will satisfy us of the truth of what I am saying.

Glaucon: What sort of instances do you mean?

Socrates: If the case is put to us, must we not admit that the just State, or the man who is trained in the principles of such a State, will be less likely than the unjust to make away with a deposit of gold or silver? Would any one deny this?

Glaucon: No one, he replied.

Socrates: Will the just man or citizen ever be guilty of sacrilege or theft, or treachery either to his friends or to his country?

Glaucon: Never.

Socrates: Neither will he ever break faith where there have been oaths or agreements?

Glaucon: Impossible.

Socrates: No one will be less likely to commit adultery, or to dishonour his father and mother, or to fall in his religious duties?

Glaucon: No one.

Socrates: And the reason is that each part of him is doing its own business, whether in ruling or being ruled?

Glaucon: Exactly so.

Socrates: Are you satisfied then that the quality which makes such men and such states is justice, or do you hope to discover some other?

Glaucon: Not I, indeed.

Socrates: Then our dream has been realised; and the suspicion which we entertained at the beginning of our work of construction, that some divine power must have conducted us to a primary form of justice, has now been verified?

Glaucon: Yes, certainly.

Socrates: And the division of labour which required the carpenter and the shoemaker and the rest of the citizens to be doing each his own business, and not another's, was a shadow of justice, and for that reason it was of use?

Glaucon: Clearly.

Socrates: But in reality justice was such as we were describing, being concerned, however, not with the outward man, but with the inward, which is the true self and concernment of man: for the just man does not permit the several elements within him to interfere with one another, or any of them to do the work of others—he sets in order his own inner life, and is his own master and his own law, and at peace with himself; and when he has bound together the three principles within him, which may be compared to the higher, lower, and middle notes of the scale, and the intermediate intervals—when he has bound all these together, and is no longer many, but has become one entirely temperate and perfectly adjusted nature, then he proceeds to act, if he has to act, whether in a matter of property, or in the treatment of the body, or in some affair of politics or private business; always thinking and calling that which preserves and co-operates with this harmonious condition, just and good action, and the knowledge which presides over it, wisdom, and that which at any time impairs this condition, he will call unjust action, and the opinion which presides over it ignorance.

Glaucon: You have said the exact truth, Socrates.

Socrates: Very good; and if we were to affirm that we had discovered the just man and the just State, and the nature of justice in each of them, we should not be telling a falsehood?

Glaucon: Most certainly not.

Socrates: May we say so, then?

Glaucon: Let us say so.

Socrates: And now, I said, injustice has to be considered.

Glaucon: Clearly.

Socrates: Must not injustice be a strife which arises among the three principles—a meddlesomeness, and interference, and rising up of a part of the soul against the whole, an assertion of unlawful authority, which is made by a rebellious subject against a true prince, of whom he is the natural vassal—what is all this confusion and delusion but injustice, and intemperance and cowardice and ignorance, and every form of vice?

Glaucon: Exactly so.

Socrates: And if the nature of justice and injustice be known, then the meaning of acting unjustly and being unjust, or, again, of acting justly, will also be perfectly clear?

Glaucon: What do you mean? he said.

Socrates: Why, I said, they are like disease and health; being in the soul just what disease and health are in the body.

Glaucon: How so? he said.
Socrates: Why, I said, that which is healthy causes health, and that which is unhealthy causes disease.
Glaucon: Yes.
Socrates: And just actions cause justice, and unjust actions cause injustice?
Glaucon: That is certain.
Socrates: And the creation of health is the institution of a natural order and government of one by another in the parts of the body; and the creation of disease is the production of a state of things at variance with this natural order?
Glaucon: True.
Socrates: And is not the creation of justice the institution of a natural order and government of one by another in the parts of the soul, and the creation of injustice the production of a state of things at variance with the natural order?
Glaucon: Exactly so, he said.
Socrates: Then virtue is the health and beauty and well-being of the soul, and vice the disease and weakness and deformity of the same?
Glaucon: True.
Socrates: And do not good practices lead to virtue, and evil practices to vice?
Glaucon: Assuredly.
Socrates: Still our old question of the comparative advantage of justice and injustice has not been answered: Which is the more profitable, to be just and act justly and practise virtue, whether seen or unseen of gods and men, or to be unjust and act unjustly, if only unpunished and unreformed?
Glaucon: In my judgment, Socrates, the question has now become ridiculous. We know that, when the bodily constitution is gone, life is no longer endurable, though pampered with all kinds of meats and drinks, and having all wealth and all power; and shall we be told that when the very

essence of the vital principle is undermined and corrupted, life is still worth having to a man, if only he be allowed to do whatever he likes with the single exception that he is not to acquire justice and virtue, or to escape from injustice and vice; assuming them both to be such as we have described?

Socrates: Yes, I said, the question is, as you say, ridiculous. Still, as we are near the spot at which we may see the truth in the clearest manner with our own eyes, let us not faint by the way.

Glaucon: Certainly not, he replied.

Socrates: Come up hither, I said, and behold the various forms of vice, those of them, I mean, which are worth looking at.

Glaucon: I am following you, he replied: proceed.

Socrates: I said, the argument seems to have reached a height from which, as from some tower of speculation, a man may look down and see that virtue is one, but that the forms of vice are innumerable. ...

PHAEDO

SOCRATES-CEBES

Socrates:[4] Then now let us return to the previous discussion. Is that idea or essence, which in the dialectical process we define as essence or true existence—whether essence of equality, beauty, or anything else—are these essences, I say, liable at times to some degree of change? Or are they each of them always what they are, having the same simple self-existent and unchanging forms, not admitting of variation at all, or in any way, or at any time?

4. *Phaedo*, 78c-84a.

Cebes: They must be always the same, Socrates, replied Cebes.

Socrates: And what would you say of the many beautiful—whether men or horses or garments or any other things which are named by the same names and may be called equal or beautiful—are they all unchanging and the same always, or quite the reverse? May they not rather be described as almost always changing and hardly ever the same, either with themselves or with one another?

Cebes: The latter, replied Cebes; they are always in a state of change.

Socrates: And these you can touch and see and perceive with the senses, but the unchanging things you can only perceive with the mind—they are invisible and are not seen?

Cebes: That is very true, he said.

Socrates: Well then, added Socrates, let us suppose that there are two sorts of existences—one seen, the other unseen.

Cebes: Let us suppose them.

Socrates: The seen is the changing, and the unseen is the unchanging?

Cebes: That may be also supposed.

Socrates: And, further, is not one part of us body, another part soul?

Cebes: To be sure.

Socrates: And to which class is the body more alike and akin?

Cebes: Clearly to the seen—no one can doubt that.

Socrates: And is the soul seen or not seen?

Cebes: Not by man, Socrates.

Socrates: And what we mean by 'seen' and 'not seen' is that which is or is not visible to the eye of man?

Cebes: Yes, to the eye of man.

Socrates: And is the soul seen or not seen?

Cebes: Not seen.

Socrates: Unseen then?

Cebes: Yes.

Socrates: Then the soul is more like to the unseen, and the body to the seen?

Cebes: That follows necessarily, Socrates.

Socrates: And were we not saying long ago that the soul when using the body as an instrument of perception, that is to say, when using the sense of sight or hearing or some other sense (for the meaning of perceiving through the body is perceiving through the senses)—were we not saying that the soul too is then dragged by the body into the region of the changeable, and wanders and is confused; the world spins round her, and she is like a drunkard, when she touches change?

Cebes: Very true.

Socrates: But when returning into herself she reflects, then she passes into the other world, the region of purity, and eternity, and immortality, and unchangeableness, which are her kindred, and with them she ever lives, when she is by herself and is not let or hindered; then she ceases from her erring ways, and being in communion with the unchanging is unchanging. And this state of the soul is called wisdom?

Cebes: That is well and truly said, Socrates, he replied.

Socrates: And to which class is the soul more nearly alike and akin, as far as may be inferred from this argument, as well as from the preceding one?

Cebes: I think, Socrates, that, in the opinion of every one who follows the argument, the soul will be infinitely more like the unchangeable—even the most stupid person will not deny that.

Socrates: And the body is more like the changing?

Cebes: Yes.

Socrates: Yet once more consider the matter in another light: when the soul and the body are united, then nature orders the soul to rule and govern, and the body to obey and serve. Now which of these two functions is akin to the divine? And which to the mortal? Does not the divine appear to you to be that which naturally orders and rules, and the mortal to be that which is subject and servant?

Cebes: True.

Socrates: And which does the soul resemble?

Cebes: The soul resembles the divine, and the body the mortal—there can be no doubt of that, Socrates.

Socrates: Then reflect, Cebes. Of all which has been said is not this the conclusion: that the soul is in the very likeness of the divine, and immortal, and intellectual, and uniform, and indissoluble, and unchangeable; and that the body is in the very likeness of the human, and mortal, and unintellectual, and multiform, and dissoluble, and changeable? Can this, my dear Cebes, be denied?

Cebes: It cannot.

Socrates: But if it be true, then is not the body liable to speedy dissolution? And is not the soul almost or altogether indissoluble?

Cebes: Certainly.

Socrates: And do you further observe, that after a man is dead, the body, or visible part of him, which is lying in the visible world, and is called a corpse, and would naturally be dissolved and decomposed and dissipated, is not dissolved or decomposed at once, but may remain for some time, nay even for a long time, if the constitution be sound at the time of death, and the season of the year favourable? For the body when shrunk and embalmed, as the manner is in Egypt, may remain almost entire through infinite ages; and even in decay, there are still some portions, such as the bones and ligaments, which are practically indestructible. Do you agree?

Cebes: Yes.

Socrates: And is it likely that the soul, which is invisible, in passing to the place of the true Hades, which like her is invisible, and pure, and noble, and on her way to the good and wise God, whither, if God will, my soul is also soon to go—that the soul, I repeat, if this be her nature and origin, will be blown away and destroyed immediately on quitting the body, as the many say? That can never be, my dear Simmias and Cebes. The truth rather is, that the soul which is pure at departing and draws after her no bodily taint, having never voluntarily during life had connection with the body, which she is ever avoiding, herself gathered into herself; and making such abstraction her perpetual study—which means that she has been a true disciple of philosophy; and therefore has in fact been always engaged in the practice of dying? For is not philosophy the study of death?

Cebes: Certainly.

Socrates: That soul, I say, herself invisible, departs to the invisible world—to the divine and immortal and rational: thither arriving, she is secure of bliss and is released from the error and folly of men, their fears and wild passions and all other human ills, and for ever dwells, as they say of the initiated, in company with the gods. Is not this true, Cebes?

Cebes: Yes, said Cebes, beyond a doubt.

Socrates: But the soul which has been polluted, and is impure at the time of her departure, and is the companion and servant of the body always, and is in love with and fascinated by the body and by the desires and pleasures of the body, until she is led to believe that the truth only exists in a bodily form, which a man may touch and see and taste, and use for the purposes of his lusts—the soul, I mean, accustomed to hate and fear and avoid the intellectual principle, which to the bodily eye is dark and invisible, and can be attained only by philosophy—do you suppose that such a soul will depart pure and unalloyed?

Cebes: Impossible, he replied.

Socrates: She is held fast by the corporeal, which the continual association and constant care of the body have wrought into her nature.

Cebes: Very true.

Socrates: And this corporeal element, my friend, is heavy and weighty and earthy, and is that element of sight by which a soul is depressed and dragged down again into the visible world, because she is afraid of the invisible and of the world below—prowling about tombs and sepulchres, near which, as they tell us, are seen certain ghostly apparitions of souls which have not departed pure, but are cloyed with sight and therefore visible.

Cebes: That is very likely, Socrates.

Socrates: Yes, that is very likely, Cebes; and these must be the souls, not of the good, but of the evil, which are compelled to wander about such places in payment of the penalty of their former evil way of life; and they continue to wander until, through the craving after the corporeal which never leaves them, they are imprisoned finally in another body. And they may be supposed to find their prisons in the same natures which they have had in their former lives.

Cebes: What natures do you mean, Socrates?

Socrates: What I mean is that men who have followed after gluttony, and wantonness, and drunkenness, and have had no thought of avoiding them, would pass into asses and animals of that sort. What do you think?

Cebes: I think such an opinion to be exceedingly probable.

Socrates: And those who have chosen the portion of injustice, and tyranny, and violence, will pass into wolves, or into hawks and kites—whither else can we suppose them to go?

Cebes: Yes, said Cebes; with such natures, beyond question.

Socrates: And there is no difficulty, he said, in assigning to all of them places answering to their several natures and propensities?

Cebes: There is not, he said.

Socrates: Some are happier than others; and the happiest both in themselves and in the place to which they go are those who have practised the civil and social virtues which are called temperance and justice, and are acquired by habit and attention without philosophy and mind.

Cebes: Why are they the happiest?

Socrates: Because they may be expected to pass into some gentle and social kind which is like their own, such as bees or wasps or ants, or back again into the form of man, and just and moderate men may be supposed to spring from them.

Cebes: Very likely.

Socrates: No one who has not studied philosophy and who is not entirely pure at the time of his departure is allowed to enter the company of the gods, but the lover of knowledge only. And this is the reason, Simmias and Cebes, why the true votaries of philosophy abstain from all fleshly lusts, and hold out against them and refuse to give themselves up to them—not because they fear poverty or the ruin of their families, like the lovers of money, and the world in general; nor like the lovers of power and honour, because they dread the dishonour or disgrace of evil deeds.

Cebes: No, Socrates, that would not become them, said Cebes.

Socrates: No indeed, he replied; and therefore they who have any care of their own souls, and do not merely live moulding and fashioning the body, say farewell to all this; they will not walk in the ways of the blind; and when philosophy offers them purification and release from evil, they feel that they ought not to resist her influence, and whither she leads they turn and follow.

Cebes: What do you mean, Socrates?

Socrates: I will tell you, he said. The lovers of knowledge are conscious that the soul was simply fastened and glued to the body—until philosophy received her, she could only view real existence through the bars of a prison, not in and through herself; she was wallowing in the mire of every sort of ignorance, and by reason of lust had become the principal accomplice in her own captivity. This was her original state; and then, as I was saying, and as the lovers of knowledge are well aware, philosophy, seeing how terrible was her confinement, of which she was to herself the cause, received and gently comforted her and sought to release her, pointing out that the eye and the ear and the other senses are full of deception, and persuading her to retire from them, and abstain from all but the necessary use of them, and be gathered up and collected into herself, bidding her trust in herself and her own pure apprehension of pure existence, and to mistrust whatever comes to her through other channels and is subject to variation; for such things are visible and tangible, but what she sees in her own nature is intelligible and invisible. And the soul of the true philosopher thinks that she ought not to resist this deliverance, and therefore abstains from pleasures and desires and pains and fears, as far as she is able; reflecting that when a man has great joys or sorrows or fears or desires, he suffers from them, not merely the sort of evil which might be anticipated—as for example, the loss of his health or property which he has sacrificed to his lusts—but an evil greater far, which is the greatest and worst of all evils, and one of which he never thinks.

Cebes: What is it, Socrates? said Cebes.

Socrates: The evil is that when the feeling of pleasure or pain is most intense, every soul of man imagines the objects of this intense feeling to be then plainest and truest: but this is not so, they are really the things of sight.

Cebes: Very true.

Socrates: And is not this the state in which the soul is most enthralled by the body?

Cebes: How so?

Socrates: Why, because each pleasure and pain is a sort of nail which nails and rivets the soul to the body, until she becomes like the body, and believes that to be true which the body affirms to be true; and from agreeing with the body and having the same delights she is obliged to have the same habits and haunts, and is not likely ever to be pure at her departure to the world below, but is always infected by the body; and so she sinks into another body and there germinates and grows, and has therefore no part in the communion of the divine and pure and simple.

Cebes: Most true, Socrates, answered Cebes.

Socrates: And this, Cebes, is the reason why the true lovers of knowledge are temperate and brave; and not for the reason which the world gives.

Cebes: Certainly not.

ARISTOTLE, NICOMACHEAN ETHICS

INTRODUCTION

Approached with an open and probing mind, Aristotle's *Ethics* is nothing less than transformative. It could very well be said, of course, that his fundamental view of the topic is one held by many other ethical thinkers of his day and beyond: namely, that the key question for the ethicist is how to live the good life by cultivating virtue as a form of excellence (*arête*). Aristotle's contribution is of particular value, though, in the practical guidance that he provides in his *Ethics*: he gives not only the principle (the 'golden mean') by which we can identify the virtues, but also the methods by which we can realize those virtues, as an everyday matter, in our own lives. His *Ethics* should be the first port of call for those who recognise our need to reestablish a code for living that puts man's character back at the heart of things.

Aristotle was born in 384 BC at Stagira in Greece. The son of a court physician to the King of Macedonia, at the age of seventeen he went to Athens in order to pursue his education in Plato's Academy. After spending the best part of two decades studying in Plato's school, Aristotle left Athens at around the time of Plato's death in 347 BC, disappointed with the direction in which the Academy was heading, and travelled to Asia Minor where he met and married his wife Pythias. Invited back to Macedonia by King Philip II in 342 BC, he spent several years as tutor to the young Alexander the Great. In around 335 BC, Aristotle finally returned to Athens, where he established his own philosophical school, the Lyceum. It was an immensely fruitful time for him: he authored works on a wide range of topics, from physics and biology to logic and metaphysics, from astronomy and mathematics to rhetoric and ethics. When in 323 BC Alexander died, however, Athens soon became the site of an anti-Macedonian revolt which resulted in Aristotle being falsely indicted on charges of impiety. Mindful, no doubt, of what had happened when Socrates had faced similar allegations, Aristotle fled into exile, where he died the following year.

Aristotle's fundamental insight is that moral virtue is neither purely an inborn competence nor a purely acquired learning, but an *ethos* (habit) that arises out of an innate potentiality when that potentiality is regularly exercised in practice. States of character, he says, are the products of their related activities, and correspond to the differences between such activities. The virtue of courage is an obvious example: it is by doing the acts that we do in the presence of danger—by being habituated to fear and confidence—that we become brave or cowardly. The same is true of temperance: it is through behaving as we do in provoking circumstances that we become temperate or irascible, as the case may be. All virtues are, in fact, habituated this way; that is why, in Aristotle's view, the formation of the correct habits from childhood not only makes no small difference between men—it makes *all* the difference.

How, then, should we act in order to cultivate the habits that are commensurate with virtuous states of character? What we are looking for, says Aristotle, are not precise instructions, but principles that can be adapted to the circumstances in which we find ourselves. The answer, he suggests, lies in the recognition that, in matters of human conduct, 'it is in the nature of things to be destroyed by defect and excess'. This leads to the famous doctrine of the 'golden mean': namely, that the ethical virtues are found at the mean between the extremes of excess and deficiency. Courage, for example, is found at the mean between cowardice (fearing everything) and rashness (fearing nothing); temperance, similarly, is found at the mean between self-indulgence (indulging in all pleasures and abstaining from none) and boorishness (shunning every pleasure). Magnificence, says Aristotle, is the virtue of spending appropriately to one's situation, and is found as the mean between vulgarity and niggardliness, while good temper is the virtue of being angry at the right things and with the right people and at the right times. That being said, it will not always be the middle path that is to be preferred, because it may be that we are temperamentally inclined towards one of the two extremes, whether as a result of a general human inclination, or a particular personal one. In that case, we would do well to bend ourselves in the opposite direction from that of our natural inclination, as we straighten a bent stick by bending it the opposite way. What is important is the particular conduct being fitting to the doer and the circumstances in which that act is done, rather than the observance of rigid and invariable rules.

Habituating ourselves to virtue can be made easier by bearing in mind two matters in particular. First, we should understand that virtue cannot be disassociated from our feelings of pleasure and pain. It is in our nature, as humans, that pleasure and pain are engaged whenever we come to take action. The virtuous man, then, does not only habituate himself to virtuous conduct, but also conditions himself to finding pleasure in it. So, for example, the truly temperate man does not only habituate himself to temperance, he also attempts to find pleasure in self-restraint; likewise, the courageous man likewise does not only habituate himself to courage, but also obtains joy through facing danger. Second, making virtue a habit may be difficult at the outset, but it becomes progressively easier, since the more we exercise virtue, the more deeply ingrained it becomes. It is by habitually standing our ground that we become brave, suggests Aristotle, and being brave in turn makes it easier for us to stand our ground; it is by abstaining from pleasure we become temperate, and the more temperate we become the easier it is to abstain from pleasure. Through these two principles, then, Aristotle in effect provides us with a definite formula for the cultivation of virtue: we are enjoined both to find ways to derive pleasure from virtue, and to inculcate it through regular practice.

Aristotle sketch of the 'high-minded' man gives us a concrete example of life lived in broadly in accordance with virtue. The high-minded man is a man, says Aristotle, who both thinks himself worthy of great things, and is in fact worthy of them: he is the sort of man to confer benefits on others, but is ashamed of receiving them; he is dignified towards people who enjoy high position and good fortune, but unassuming towards those of the lower classes; he asks for nothing, or scarcely anything, but is willing to give help readily; he is slow to act except where honour or great work is at stake; he is open in his hate and his love, is free of speech, and is given to telling the truth; he is unable to make his life revolve around another, unless it be a friend; he is not given to admiration, for nothing to him is great; he is not mindful of wrongs, for it is no part of the proud man to have a long memory; he is not a gossip, for he cares not to be praised nor for others to be blamed; he is one who will possess beautiful and profitless things rather than profitable and useful ones, for this is more proper to a character that suffices to itself; he walks with a slow step, and speaks with a deep voice and level utterance, for a man who takes few things seriously is not likely to be hurried, nor is the man who thinks nothing great likely to be excited.

The end of life, over and above the particular virtues, must, says Aristotle, be that which we choose for its own sake rather than for the sake of something else. Wealth, fame, honour, friendship, reward—these may all be desirable, but they are desirable because they allow us to obtain other things that we want: wealth, for example, allows us to obtain the goods that we desire or the leisure to enjoy them; honour helps us to obtain the respect of those whose respect we value. What is left as an 'end in itself', when other options have been eliminated, is happiness, for happiness alone is sought after for its own sake and no other.

What, though, is happiness? Aristotle is keen to emphasise that the happiness to which he refers has nothing to do with lazy pleasures and idle amusements: it must be an activity rather than a disposition (otherwise it could belong to someone who was asleep throughout his life and 'living the life of a plant'), and it must be more than relaxation or amusement (for relaxation and amusement are not ends in themselves). Instead, he says, happiness is virtuous activity; in fact, as the best thing in us, it must be activity in accordance with the highest virtue.

The best activity of man—activity in accordance with man's highest virtue—is the exercise of contemplative reason. This activity alone is loved for its own sake—for nothing is gained from it over and above the act of contemplation itself. It is also the most continuous and the most self-sufficient of activities, since it can be carried on unceasingly and without the need for anything more than the bare necessities of life. It is the most proper thing for man, and that which is proper to each thing is, says Aristotle, by nature best and most pleasant. Above all, it is the authoritative and better part of man; the closest thing in him to the divine; and, through it, man's one hope of making himself immortal.

Bertrand Russell has said that there is, in Aristotle's ethics, an 'emotional poverty' and 'almost complete lack of what may be called benevolence or philanthropy.'[1] Of course, for Aristotle that is exactly the point: ethics is concerned with the cultivation of character and the coordination of human activity in the pursuit of excellence, rather than in passionate displays of altruism or sentimental do-goodism. In fact, it could well be argued that the fundamental weakness of the Western moral imagination lies precisely in the fatal detachment of popular ethics from the focus on making a man the best he can be—it is this, arguably, that has led to moral imperatives based excessively on the desire of do-gooders to *feel* good, by demonstrating their moral credentials, rather than on their desire to *be* good. It is wrong to assume that Aristotle has no interest in doing well by one's fellow men; in fact, he has every interest in it. But for him, healthy moral conduct vis-à-vis others is properly incidental to the full and proper self-realisation of a man's better self. Aristotle's proud or 'high-minded' man, for example, would—if any such could be found—be a great credit to the society in which he lived simply because he has an overabundance of strength and a contempt for pettiness and triviality. In the end, posterity will have the last word as to whether it is Aristotle or Russell who has offered the better view; perhaps, indeed, it already has.

---

[1]. Bertrand Russell, *History of Western Philosophy* (London: Routledge, 2000), 195.

Book 2

1. MORAL VIRTUE IS ACQUIRED BY THE REPETITION OF THE CORRESPONDING ACTS

Excellence, then, being of these two kinds, intellectual and moral, intellectual excellence owes its birth and growth mainly to instruction, and so requires time and experience, while moral excellence is the result of habit or custom ('ethos'), and has accordingly in our language received a name formed by a slight change from 'ethos'.

From this it is plain that none of the moral excellences or virtues is implanted in us by nature; for that which is by nature cannot be altered by training. For instance, a stone naturally tends to fall downwards, and you could not train it to rise upwards, though you tried to do so by throwing it up ten thousand times, nor could you train fire to move downwards, nor accustom anything which naturally behaves in one way to behave in any other way.

The virtues, then, come neither by nature nor against nature, but nature gives the capacity for acquiring them, and this is developed by training.

Again, where we do things by nature we get the power first, and put this power forth in act afterwards: as we plainly see in the case of the senses; for it is not by constantly seeing and hearing that we acquire those faculties, but, on the contrary, we had the power first and then used it, instead of acquiring the power by the use. But the virtues we acquire by doing the acts, as is the case with the arts too. We learn an art by doing that which we wish to do when we have learned it; we become builders by building, and harpers by harping. And so by doing just acts we become just, and by doing acts of temperance and courage we become temperate and courageous.

This is attested, too, by what occurs in states; for the

legislators make their citizens good by training; i.e. this is the wish of all legislators, and those who do not succeed in this miss their aim, and it is this that distinguishes a good from a bad constitution.

Again, both the moral virtues and the corresponding vices result from and are formed by the same acts; and this is the case with the arts also. It is by harping that good harpers and bad harpers alike are produced: and so with builders and the rest; by building well they will become good builders, and bad builders by building badly. Indeed, if it were not so, they would not want anybody to teach them, but would all be born either good or bad at their trades. And it is just the same with the virtues also. It is by our conduct in our intercourse with other men that we become just or unjust, and by acting in circumstances of danger, and training ourselves to feel fear or confidence, that we become courageous or cowardly. So, too, with our animal appetites and the passion of anger; for by behaving in this way or in that on the occasions with which these passions are concerned, some become temperate and gentle, and others profligate and ill-tempered. In a word, acts of any kind produce habits or characters of the same kind.

Hence we ought to make sure that our acts be of a certain kind; for the resulting character varies as they vary. It makes no small difference, therefore, whether a man be trained from his youth up in this way or in that, but a great difference, or rather all the difference.

2. THESE ACTS MUST BE SUCH AS REASON PRESCRIBES; THEY CAN'T BE DEFINED EXACTLY, BUT MUST BE NEITHER TOO MUCH NOR TOO LITTLE

But our present inquiry has not, like the rest, a merely speculative aim; we are not inquiring merely in order to know what excellence or virtue is, but in order to become good; for otherwise it would profit us nothing. We must ask therefore about these acts, and see of what kind they are to be; for, as we said, it is they that determine our habits or character.

First of all, then, that they must be in accordance with right reason is a common characteristic of them, which we shall here take for granted, reserving for future discussion the question what this right reason is, and how it is related to the other excellences.

But let it be understood, before we go on, that all reasoning on matters of practice must be in outline merely, and not scientifically exact: for, as we said at starting, the kind of reasoning to be demanded varies with the subject in hand; and in practical matters and questions of expediency there are no invariable laws, any more than in questions of health.

And if our general conclusions are thus inexact, still more inexact is all reasoning about particular cases; for these fall under no system of scientifically established rules or traditional maxims, but the agent must always consider for himself what the special occasion requires, just as in medicine or navigation.

But though this is the case we must try to render what help we can.

First of all, then, we must observe that, in matters of this sort, to fall short and to exceed are alike fatal. This is plain (to illustrate what we cannot see by what we can see) in the case of strength and health. Too much and too little exercise alike destroy strength, and to take too much meat and drink, or to take too little, is equally ruinous to health, but the fitting amount produces and increases and preserves them. Just so, then, is it with temperance also, and courage, and the other virtues. The man who shuns and fears everything and never makes a stand, becomes a coward; while the man who fears nothing at all, but will face anything, becomes foolhardy. So, too, the man who takes his fill of any kind of pleasure, and abstains from none, is a profligate, but the man who shuns all (like him whom we call a 'boor') is devoid of sensibility.

Thus temperance and courage are destroyed both by excess and defect, but preserved by moderation.

But habits or types of character are not only produced and preserved and destroyed by the same occasions and the same means, but they will also manifest themselves in the same circumstances. This is the case with palpable things like strength. Strength is produced by taking plenty of nourishment and doing plenty of hard work, and the strong man, in turn, has the greatest capacity for these. And the case is the same with the virtues: by abstaining from pleasure we become temperate, and when we have become temperate we are best able to abstain. And so with courage: by habituating ourselves to despise danger, and to face it, we become courageous; and when we have become courageous, we are best able to face danger.

Book 4

3. OF HIGH-MINDEDNESS

High-mindedness would seem from its very name ('megalopsychia') to have to do with great things; let us first ascertain what these are.

It will make no difference whether we consider the quality itself, or the man who exhibits the quality.

By a high-minded man we seem to mean one who claims much and deserves much: for he who claims much without deserving it is a fool; but the possessor of a virtue is never foolish or silly. The man we have described, then, is high-minded.

He who deserves little and claims little is temperate or modest, but not high-minded: for high-mindedness—or greatness of soul—implies greatness, just as beauty implies stature; small men may be neat and well proportioned, but cannot be called beautiful.

He who claims much without deserving it is vain (though not every one who claims more than he deserves is vain).

He who claims less than he deserves is little-minded, whether his deserts be great or moderate, or whether they be small and he claims still less: but the fault would seem to be greatest in him whose deserts are great; for what would he do if his deserts were less than they are?

The high-minded man, then, in respect of the greatness of his deserts occupies an extreme position, but in that he behaves as he ought, observes the mean; for he claims that which he deserves, while all the others claim too much or too little.

If, therefore, he deserves much and claims much, and most of all deserves and claims the greatest things, there will be one thing with which he will be especially concerned. For desert has reference to external good things. Now, the greatest of external good things we may assume to be that which we render to the Gods as their due, and that which people in high stations most desire, and which is the prize appointed for the noblest deeds. But the thing that answers to this description is honour, which, we may safely say, is the greatest of all external goods. Honours and dishonours, therefore, are the field in which the high-minded man behaves as he ought.

And indeed we may see, without going about to prove it, that honour is what high-minded men are concerned with; for it is honour that they especially claim and deserve.

The little-minded man falls short, whether we compare his claims with his own deserts or with what the high-minded man claims for himself.

The vain or conceited man exceeds what is due to himself, though he does not exceed the high-minded man in his claims.

But the high-minded man, as he deserves the greatest things, must be a perfectly good or excellent man; for the better man always deserves the greater things, and the best possible man the greatest possible things. The really high-minded man, therefore, must be a good or excellent man. And indeed greatness in every virtue or excellence would seem to be necessarily implied in being a high-minded or great-souled man.

It would be equally inconsistent with the high-minded man's character to run away swinging his arms, and to commit an act of injustice; for what thing is there for love of which he would do anything unseemly, seeing that all things are of little account to him?

Survey him point by point and you will find that the notion of a high-minded man that is not a good or excellent man is utterly absurd. Indeed, if he were not good, he could not be worthy of honour; for honour is the prize of virtue, and is rendered to the good as their due.

High-mindedness, then, seems to be the crowning grace, as it were, of the virtues; it makes them greater, and cannot exist without them. And on this account it is a hard thing to be truly high-minded; for it is impossible without the union of all the virtues.

The high-minded man, then, exhibits his character especially in the matter of honours and dishonours and at great honour from good men he will be moderately pleased, as getting nothing more than his due, or even less; for no honour can be adequate to complete virtue; but nevertheless he will accept it, as they have nothing greater to offer him. But honour from ordinary men and on trivial grounds he will utterly despise; for that is not what he deserves. And dishonour likewise he will make light of; for he will never merit it.

But though it is especially in the matter of honours, as we have said, that the high-minded man displays his character, yet he will also observe the mean in his feelings with regard to wealth and power and all kinds of good and evil fortune, whatever may befall him, and will neither be very much exalted by prosperity, nor very much cast down by adversity; seeing that not even honour affects him as if it were a very important thing. For power and wealth are desirable for honour's sake (at least, those who have them wish to gain honour by them). But he who thinks lightly of honour must think lightly of them also.

And so high-minded men seem to look down upon everything.

But the gifts of fortune also are commonly thought to contribute to high-mindedness. For those who are well born are thought worthy of honour, and those who are powerful or wealthy; for they are in a position of superiority, and that which is superior in any good thing is always held in greater honour. And so these things do make people more high-minded in a sense; for such people find honour from some. But in strictness it is only the good man that is worthy of honour, though he that has both goodness and good fortune is commonly thought to be more worthy of honour. Those, however, who have these good things without virtue, neither have any just claim to great things, nor are properly to be called high-minded; for neither is possible without complete virtue.

But those who have these good things readily come to be supercilious and insolent. For without virtue it is not easy to bear the gifts of fortune becomingly; and so, being unable to bear them, and thinking themselves superior to everybody else, such people look down upon others, and yet themselves do whatever happens to please them. They imitate the high-minded man without being really like him, and they imitate him where they can; that is to say, they do not exhibit virtue in their acts, but they look down upon others. For the high-minded man never looks down upon others without justice (for he estimates them correctly), while most men do so for quite irrelevant reasons.

The high-minded man is not quick to run into petty dangers, and indeed does not love danger, since there are few things that he much values; but he is ready to incur a great danger, and whenever he does so is unsparing of his life, as a thing that is not worth keeping at all costs.

It is his nature to confer benefits, but he is ashamed to receive them; for the former is the part of a superior, the latter of an inferior. And when he has received a benefit, he is apt to confer a greater in return; for thus his creditor will become his debtor and be in the position of a recipient of his favour.

It seems, moreover, that such men remember the benefits which they have conferred better than those which they have received (for the recipient of a benefit is inferior to the benefactor, but such a man wishes to be in the position of a superior), and that they like to be reminded of the one, but dislike to be reminded of the other; and this is the reason why we read that Thetis would not mention to Zeus the services she had done him, and why the Lacedaemonians, in treating with the Athenians, reminded them of the benefits received by Sparta rather than of those conferred by her.

It is characteristic of the high-minded man, again, never or reluctantly to ask favours, but to be ready to confer them, and to be lofty in his behaviour to those who are high in station and favoured by fortune, but affable to those of the middle ranks; for it is a difficult thing and a dignified thing to assert superiority over the former, but easy to assert it over the latter. A haughty demeanour in dealing with the great is quite consistent with good breeding, but in dealing with those of low estate is brutal, like showing off one's strength upon a cripple.

Another of his characteristics is not to rush in wherever honour is to be won, nor to go where others take the lead, but to hold aloof and to shun an enterprise, except when great honour is to be gained, or a great work to be done—not to do many things, but great things and notable.

Again, he must be open in his hate and in his love (for it is cowardly to dissemble your feelings and to care less for truth than for what people will think of you), and he must be open in word and in deed (for his consciousness of superiority makes him outspoken, and he is truthful except in so far as he adopts an ironical tone in his intercourse with the masses), and he must be unable to fashion his life to suit another, except he be a friend; for that is servile: and so all flatterers or hangers on of great men are of a slavish nature, and men of low natures become flatterers.

Nor is he easily moved to admiration; for nothing is great to him.

He readily forgets injuries; for it is not consistent with his character to brood on the past, especially on past injuries, but rather to overlook them.

He is no gossip; he will neither talk about himself nor about others; for he cares not that men should praise him, nor that others should be blamed (though, on the other hand, he is not very ready to bestow praise); and so he is not apt to speak evil of others, not even of his enemies, except with the express purpose of giving offence.

When an event happens that cannot be helped or is of slight importance, he is the last man in the world to cry out or to beg for help; for that is the conduct of a man who thinks these events very important.

He loves to possess beautiful things that bring no profit, rather than useful things that pay; for this is characteristic of the man whose resources are in himself.

Further, the character of the high-minded man seems to require that his gait should be slow, his voice deep, his speech measured; for a man is not likely to be in a hurry when there are few things in which he is deeply interested, nor excited when he holds nothing to be of very great importance: and these are the causes of a high voice and rapid movements.

This, then, is the character of the high-minded man.

But he that is deficient in this quality is called little-minded; he that exceeds, vain or conceited.

Now these two also do not seem to be bad—for they do no harm—though they are in error.

For the little-minded man, though he deserves good things, deprives himself of that which he deserves, and so seems to be the worse for not claiming these good things, and for misjudging himself; for if he judged right he would desire what he deserves, as it is good. I do not mean to say that such people seem to be fools, but rather too retiring. But a misjudgment of this kind does seem actually to make them worse; for men strive for that which they deserve, and shrink from noble deeds and employments of which they think themselves unworthy, as well as from mere external good things.

But vain men are fools as well as ignorant of themselves, and make this plain to all the world; for they undertake honourable offices for which they are unfit, and presently stand convicted of incapacity; they dress in fine clothes and put on fine airs and so on; they wish everybody to know of their good fortune; they talk about themselves, as if that were the way to honour.

But little-mindedness is more opposed to high-mindedness than vanity is; for it is both commoner and worse.

High-mindedness, then, as we have said, has to do with honour on a large scale.

BOOK 10

7. OF THE SPECULATIVE LIFE AS HAPPINESS IN THE HIGHEST SENSE

But if happiness be the exercise of virtue, it is reasonable to suppose that it will be the exercise of the highest virtue; and that will be the virtue or excellence of the best part of us.

Now, that part or faculty—call it reason or what you will—which seems naturally to rule and take the lead, and to apprehend things noble and divine—whether it be itself divine, or only the divinest part of us—is the faculty the exercise of which, in its proper excellence, will be perfect happiness.

That this consists in speculation or contemplation we have already said.

This conclusion would seem to agree both with what we have said above, and with known truths.

This exercise of faculty must be the highest possible; for the reason is the highest of our faculties, and of all knowable things those that reason deals with are the highest.

Again, it is the most continuous; for speculation can be carried on more continuously than any kind of action whatsoever.

We think too that pleasure ought to be one of the ingredients of happiness; but of all virtuous exercises it is allowed that the pleasantest is the exercise of wisdom. At least philosophy is thought to have pleasures that are admirable in purity and steadfastness; and it is reasonable to suppose that the time passes more pleasantly with those who possess, than with those who are seeking knowledge.

Again, what is called self-sufficiency will be most of all found in the speculative life. The necessaries of life, indeed, are needed by the wise man as well as by the just man and the rest; but, when these have been provided in due quantity, the just man further needs persons towards whom, and along with whom, he may act justly; and so does the temperate and the courageous man and the rest; while the wise man is able to speculate even by himself, and the wiser he is the more is he able to do this. He could speculate better, we may confess, if he had others to help him, but nevertheless he is more self-sufficient than anybody else.

Again, it would seem that this life alone is desired solely for its own sake; for it yields no result beyond the contemplation, but from the practical activities we get something more or less besides action.

Again, happiness is thought to imply leisure; for we toil in order that we may have leisure, as we make war in order that we may enjoy peace. Now, the practical virtues are exercised either in politics or in war; but these do not seem to be leisurely occupations.

War, indeed, seems to be quite the reverse of leisurely; for no one chooses to fight for fighting's sake, or arranges a war for that purpose: he would be deemed a bloodthirsty villain who should set friends at enmity in order that battles and slaughter might ensue.

But the politician's life also is not a leisurely occupation, and, beside the practice of politics itself, it brings power and honours, or at least happiness, to himself and his fellow-citizens, which is something different from politics; for we who are asking what happiness is also ask what politics is, evidently implying that it is something different from happiness.

If, then, the life of the statesman and the soldier, though they surpass all other virtuous exercises in nobility and grandeur, are not leisurely occupations, and aim at some ulterior end, and are not desired merely for themselves, but the exercise of the reason seems to be superior in seriousness (since it contemplates truth), and to aim at no end beside itself, and to have its proper pleasure (which also helps to increase the exercise), and further to be self-sufficient, and leisurely, and inexhaustible (as far as anything human can be), and to have all the other characteristics that are ascribed to happiness, it follows that the exercise of reason will be the complete happiness of man, i.e. when a complete term of days is added;

for nothing incomplete can be admitted into our idea of happiness.

But a life which realized this idea would be something more than human; for it would not be the expression of man's nature, but of some divine element in that nature—the exercise of which is as far superior to the exercise of the other kind of virtue, as this divine element is superior to our compound human nature.

If then reason be divine as compared with man, the life which consists in the exercise of reason will also be divine in comparison with human life. Nevertheless, instead of listening to those who advise us as men and mortals not to lift our thoughts above what is human and mortal, we ought rather, as far as possible, to put off our mortality and make every effort to live in the exercise of the highest of our faculties; for though it be but a small part of us, yet in power and value it far surpasses all the rest.

And indeed this part would even seem to constitute our true self, since it is the sovereign and the better part. It would be strange, then, if a man were to prefer the life of something else to the life of his true self.

Again, we may apply here what we said above—for every being that is best and pleasantest which is naturally proper to it. Since, then, it is the reason that in the truest sense is the man, the life that consists in the exercise of the reason is the best and pleasantest for man—and therefore the happiest.

THE STOICS: SENECA, EPICTETUS, MARCUS AURELIUS

Introduction

The ethical thinking of the Stoics is among the most profound and practical in the Western tradition. It is pre-eminently a philosophy for 'men in the world'—men whose lives require them to be active, independent, and mindful of their personal, professional, and public duties—and among the Stoics are found not only philosophers in the strict sense (Zeno and Diogenes) but also statesmen (Cato and Seneca) and even an emperor (Marcus Aurelius). It has been said that Stoicism appealed particularly to rulers: 'nearly all the successors of Alexander—we may say the principal kings in existence in the generations following Zeno—professed themselves Stoics.'[1] It could equally be said that Stoicism is a philosophy uniquely well adapted to times of civilisational disorder and decay: Seneca lived under the tyrant Nero, who ordered him to take

1. Gilbert Murray, *Humanist Essays* (London: Routledge, 1964), 148.

his own life; Epictetus was a slave and a cripple who, having earned his freedom shortly after Nero's death, fled to Greece when Domitian banished philosophers from Rome; and Marcus Aurelius, the last emperor of the *Pax Romana*, spent much of his life fighting the Parthians and the Germanic tribes who threatened the Empire from the north and east. It is no surprise that Stoicism has much to offer those who find themselves placed, whether by choice or by fate, in challenging circumstances.

The selections introduced below are from three of the most influential of the Stoic philosophers: the Roman statesman Lucius Annaeus Seneca or Seneca the Younger (better known simply as 'Seneca'), the Greek ex-slave Epictetus, and the Roman emperor Marcus Aurelius Antoninus Augustus ('Marcus Aurelius'). The first of these, Seneca, was born in Córdoba in Hispania in around 4 BC into a wealthy equestrian family. Having been trained at Rome in rhetoric and philosophy (and briefly exiled under the Emperor Claudius), he became a tutor and later advisor to Nero, providing guidance to the emperor in the first five years of his reign, before falling out of favour and being forced to commit suicide under suspicion of having been complicit in an assassination conspiracy. As a philosopher, Seneca penned over a dozen essays and a hundred and twenty-four letters dealing with moral and ethical issues; as a dramatist, he is best known for tragic plays such as *Medea*, *Thyestes*, and *Phaedra*. Epictetus was born around 55 AD at Hierapolis, Phrygia (in present day Turkey), and although he spent his youth as a slave in Rome, his wealthy master allowed him to study philosophy under Musonius Rufus. Having obtained his freedom in around 68 AD, Epictetus began to teach philosophy first in Rome and then, after the Emperor Domitian banished all philosophers from that city, in Greece. Eminent people sought to converse with him, and the Emperor Hadrian considered him a friend; his work—which included the *Discourses* and the shorter, more practical *Enchiridion* ('handbook')—was compiled from lecture notes by his pupil Arrian. Marcus Aurelius, the last of the Stoic philosophers in our selection, was a Roman Emperor. Born in 121 AD, he was co-ruler of the empire with his adoptive brother, Lucius Verus, from 161 AD until Verus's death in 169 AD, after which he ruled alone for the next eleven years. Known as the last of the 'good emperors', his reign was troubled by attacks from the Parthians in the east and the German tribes in the north, as well as an outburst of the plague. His *Meditations*—the work for which he is now best known—was written (in Greek) during the final years of his military campaigns.

Seneca's goals are among the loftiest of the three: he gives advice that is intended to bring out 'the god in man'. Indeed, in one of his moral letters to Lucilius, he expressly states as much: we each have a holy spirit—be it conceived of as a higher self or literally as an aspect of the godhead—that dwells within us as our guardian and marks our good and our bad deeds, suggests Seneca, and it is this spirit that we manifest 'when we are unterrified in the midst of dangers, untouched by desires, happy in adversity, peaceful amid the storm'.[2] What Seneca advocates for is, in essence, an ethic of self-mastery and imperviousness to the vicissitudes of fortune. When fortune is vanquished in any combat, he says, the reward will be greater than any earthly honours—for a man will obtain 'virtue, steadfastness of soul, and a peace that is won for all time'.[3]

If self-mastery is what allows a man to access the higher part of himself, its opposite is the kind of mental, emotional and moral weakness that renders us slaves to our own passions and baser desires. For Seneca, it is a man's own personal virtue—his own relentless focus on the betterment of his character—that

2. Epistle 41.
3. Epistle 78.

forms the necessary basis for any 'other-directed' moral conduct. This is most clearly seen in his view of slavery. 'Slaves!' he exclaims in outrage at the presumption that one man should have, by accident of birth or fortune, total power over another as his chattel. 'Show me a man who is not a slave; one is a slave to lust, another to greed, another to ambition, and all men are slaves to fear.' What good Stoic, asks Seneca, could possibly consider slavery to be any more shameful than a man's enslavement to his own desires? And what good Stoic could not be aware of the human tendency to be made furious by whatever does not answer our whims? 'No, they are our fellow-slaves, if one reflects that Fortune has equal rights over slaves and free men alike.'[4]

It is one thing to talk about self-mastery, and another to know how to achieve it. The Stoics, however, were nothing if not practical philosophers, and Seneca was no exception. One method he promotes is asceticism: although the first stages of abstinence, he admits, are tiresome, sooner or later the organs of appetite decline in strength and cravings die down, and there is nothing harsh in doing without things for which your cravings have ceased. Another approach is to foster only the most wholesome of intellectual and social influences: crowds are to be avoided ('there is no person who does not make some vice attractive to us, or stamp it upon us, or taint us unconsciously therewith'), and teachers are to be carefully selected from the great souls of the past as well as the exemplary men of the present.[5] Perhaps most distinctively Senecan, however, is his insistence that we remember that death haunts us at all times; it is our constant companion and ultimate bedfellow. Live life, then, not graspingly as if each day *is* our last day, but bearing in mind that any day *could be* our last day—for it is on account of our proper relationship with

4. Epistle 47.
5. Epistle 7.

death that we best know how to live. 'The story of the Spartan lad has been preserved: taken captive while still a stripling, he kept crying in his Doric dialect, "I will not be a slave!" and he made good his word; for the very first time he was ordered to perform a menial and degrading service—and the command was to fetch a chamber-pot—he dashed out his brains against the wall.'[6]

Seneca is emphatic about the role that our free choice plays in self-regulation. His essay, 'De Ira' (Of Anger), masterfully anatomises that emotion. What we call 'anger', he says, passes (like other emotions) through three stages: first, an involuntary reaction to whatever it is that affects us; second, a voluntary mental reflection in the nature of a 'wish' (though not an obvious one) along the lines of 'it is my duty to avenge myself, because I have been injured,' or 'it is right that this man should be punished, because he has committed a crime'; third, the spiralling of the emotion out of control. Sandwiched in the middle of this process is a deliberate mental act—one that may, indeed, appear to be entirely justified—by which we in fact license and give way to our feelings. If we can pause at this moment and exercise our free will in an act of self-restraint, we can break the chains that bind us and obtain the inner freedom without which all other freedoms lose their lustre.

The *Enchiridion* (or 'handbook') is a manual of Stoic advice. Although attributed to Epictetus, it was in fact compiled by Epictetus' pupil and disciple, Arrian, from the record of his master's teachings that Arrian later published, in fuller form, as the *Discourses*. The *Enchiridion* remains today one of the first ports of call for those interested in deepening their knowledge of Stoic philosophy. There is probably no other work in the Stoic tradition—with the possible exception of the *Meditations*

---

6. Epistle 77.

of Marcus Aurelius—that so neatly encapsulates the ethical thinking of the Stoics and its direct practical application.

The core teaching of the *Enchiridion* is that we need to be clear what is in our power and what lies outside it. Within our power are our opinions, our aims, our desires, and our aversions; out of our power are body, property, reputation, and office. If we take for our own only what really belongs to us as our own, then we will be able to live freely and without compulsion or harm. If, however, we wrongly consider that we are able to control matters that are outside our power—if, in the words of the *Enchiridion*, we 'attribute freedom to things by nature dependent'—then we will be thwarted at every turn. This understanding allows us to choose our goals wisely: we should restrain both desire and aversion for the things outside our control, since these can neither be obtained nor avoided at will. It also allows us to adopt the best mental posture towards whatever it is that happens to us in life: only those things that are under our control should have value for us; anything beyond this should be accorded no real weight.

The *Enchiridion* suggests several mental attitudes for the wise Stoic to adopt. First and foremost, take no pride or pleasure in any excellence other than your own: since such excellence does not belong to you, it can be lost or taken away, so to consider it your own is the surest route to disappointment. Wish things to happen as they do happen: if you go to the bathhouse, be clear with yourself beforehand what is likely to go along with that—'some persons pouring out, others pushing in, others scolding, others pilfering'. Begin with little things: 'Is a little oil spilt or a little wine stolen? Say to yourself, "This is the price paid for peace and tranquility; and nothing is to be had for nothing."' Above all, remember at all times that you always have the power to construe accidents and events in such way as to extract the fullest benefit, and least detriment, from them; it is your views of things, and not the things in themselves, that disturb you. In particular, refrain from adding your own negative judgment. If anyone bathes hastily, do not say he does ill, but hastily; if anyone drinks much wine, do not say he does ill but that he drinks a great deal. Everything has two handles: one by which it may be tolerated; another by which it cannot. It behoves a man to lay hold of things in the manner that makes them bearable.

The last of our Stoics, the emperor Marcus Aurelius, penned his *Meditations* while he was on campaign in the Roman province of Pannonia, near modern-day Austria and Hungary—a land of gloomy forest, gigantic oaks, and birds with feathers that 'shine like fires at night'. To the analytical and practical insights of Seneca and Epictetus, Marcus Aurelius added his own distinct vision of man's role and position in the universe. When we are vexed at anything, he says, the soul of man does violence to itself; it 'becomes an abscess, and, as it were, a tumour on the universe.' In reality, a man's life is a very circumscribed thing: we are best served by focussing on the present moment, rather than letting the mind scout ahead to think upon the various troubles that may come in the future. Whole generations have come and gone and been entirely forgotten. Life itself is nothing less than change and all things have their natural limit.

Stoicism, as we have suggested, has often been considered a philosophy designed for difficult times: indeed, it came into being in the third century BC, when the classical world had been thrown into disarray after the death of Alexander, and it reached its consummation with Marcus Aurelius shortly before the Roman Empire, hemmed in by barbarian tribes, would begin its long slow decline. It was in these circumstances that an ethic of self-control, tranquility in adversity, and coming to terms with one's own death took on a particular resonance and appeal. Whether or not our own era affords a similar example of civilisational decline is something that can only be determined by the course of history. In any event, the revival of interest in Stoicism shows that increasing numbers of men are finding inspiration and solace from these works. Stoicism is, and will remain, one of the most powerful practical philosophies that the West has produced: it is a philosophy that, properly understood and implemented, allows its adherents to resist—if necessary to the death—those forces that seek their subjugation and their humiliation. *Fortune may, admittedly, take away my status, my profession, my livelihood, my friends, and even my life,* comes the Stoic's voice, hauntingly, from ancient times, *but neither it, nor you, will ever take my dignity—and you will never make me a slave.*

Seneca, Moral Letters

XLI. On the God within Us

1. You are doing an excellent thing, one which will be wholesome for you, if, as you write me, you are persisting in your effort to attain sound understanding; it is foolish to pray for this when you can acquire it from yourself. We do not need to uplift our hands towards heaven, or to beg the keeper of a temple to let us approach his idol's ear, as if in this way our prayers were more likely to be heard. God is near you, he is with you, he is within you.

2. This is what I mean, Lucilius: a holy spirit indwells within us, one who marks our good and bad deeds, and is our guardian. As we treat this spirit, so are we treated by it. Indeed, no man can be good without the help of God. Can one rise superior to fortune unless God helps him to rise? He it is that gives noble and upright counsel. In each good man:

A god doth dwell, but what god know we not.[7]

3. If ever you have come upon a grove that is full of ancient trees which have grown to an unusual height, shutting out a view of the sky by a veil of pleached and intertwining branches, then the loftiness of the forest, the seclusion of the spot, and your marvel at the thick unbroken shade in the midst of the open spaces, will prove to you the presence of deity. Or if a cave, made by the deep crumbling of the rocks, holds up a mountain on its arch, a place not built with hands but hollowed out into such spaciousness by natural causes, your soul will be deeply moved by a certain intimation of the existence of God. We worship the sources of mighty rivers; we erect altars at places where great streams burst suddenly from hidden sources; we adore springs of hot water as divine, and consecrate certain pools because of their dark waters or their immeasurable depth.

4. If you see a man who is unterrified in the midst of dangers, untouched by desires, happy in adversity, peaceful amid the storm, who looks down upon men from a higher plane, and views the gods on a footing of equality, will not a feeling of reverence for him steal over you? Will you not say: 'This quality is too great and too lofty to be regarded as resembling this petty body in which it dwells? A divine power has descended upon that man.'

5. When a soul rises superior to other souls, when it is under control, when it passes through every experience as if it were of small account, when it smiles at our fears and at our prayers, it is stirred by a force from heaven. A thing like this cannot stand upright unless it be propped by the divine. Therefore, a greater part of it abides in that place from whence it came down to earth. Just as the rays of the sun do indeed touch the earth, but still abide at the source from which they are sent; even so the

---

7. Virgil, *Aeneid*, XIII: 352.

great and hallowed soul, which has come down in order that we may have a nearer knowledge of divinity, does indeed associate with us, but still cleaves to its origin; on that source it depends, thither it turns its gaze and strives to go, and it concerns itself with our doings only as a being superior to ourselves.

6. What, then, is such a soul? One which is resplendent with no external good, but only with its own. For what is more foolish than to praise in a man the qualities which come from without? And what is more insane than to marvel at characteristics which may at the next instant be passed on to someone else? A golden bit does not make a better horse. The lion with gilded mane, in process of being trained and forced by weariness to endure the decoration, is sent into the arena in quite a different way from the wild lion whose spirit is unbroken; the latter, indeed, bold in his attack, as nature wished him to be, impressive because of his wild appearance—and it is his glory that none can look upon him without fear—is favoured in preference to the other lion, that languid and gilded brute.

7. No man ought to glory except in that which is his own. We praise a vine if it makes the shoots teem with increase, if by its weight it bends to the ground the very poles which hold its fruit; would any man prefer to this vine one from which golden grapes and golden leaves hang down? In a vine the virtue peculiarly its own is fertility; in man also we should praise that which is his own. Suppose that he has a retinue of comely slaves and a beautiful house, that his farm is large and large his income; none of these things is in the man himself; they are all on the outside.

8. Praise the quality in him which cannot be given or snatched away, that which is the peculiar property of the man. Do you ask what this is? It is soul, and reason brought to perfection in the soul. For man is a reasoning animal.

Therefore, man's highest good is attained, if he has fulfilled the good for which nature designed him at birth.

9. And what is it which this reason demands of him? The easiest thing in the world—to live in accordance with his own nature. But this is turned into a hard task by the general madness of mankind; we push one another into vice. And how can a man be recalled to salvation, when he has none to restrain him, and all mankind to urge him on? Farewell.

SENECA, DE IRA ('OF ANGER')

BOOK ONE

I.

You have demanded of me, Novatus, that I should write how anger may be soothed, and it appears to me that you are right in feeling especial fear of this passion, which is above all others hideous and wild: for the others have some alloy of peace and quiet, but this consists wholly in action and the impulse of grief, raging with an utterly inhuman lust for arms, blood and tortures, careless of itself provided it hurts another, rushing upon the very point of the sword, and greedy for revenge even when it drags the avenger to ruin with itself. Some of the wisest of men have in consequence of this called anger a short madness: for it is equally devoid of self-control, regardless of decorum, forgetful of kinship, obstinately engrossed in whatever it begins to do, deaf to reason and advice, excited by trifling causes, awkward at perceiving what is true and just, and very like a falling rock which breaks itself to pieces upon the very thing which it crushes. That you may know that they whom anger possesses are not sane, look at their appearance; for as there are distinct symptoms which mark madmen, such as a bold and menacing air, a gloomy brow, a stern face, a hurried walk, restless hands, changed colour, quick and strongly-drawn breathing; the signs of angry men, too, are the same: their eyes blaze and sparkle, their whole face is a deep red with the blood which boils up from the bottom of their heart, their lips quiver, their teeth are set, their hair bristles and stands on end, their breath is laboured and hissing, their joints crack as they twist them about, they groan, bellow, and burst into scarcely intelligible talk, they often clap their hands together and stamp on the ground with their feet, and their whole body is highly-strung and plays those tricks which mark a distraught mind, so as to furnish an ugly and shocking picture of self-perversion and excitement. You cannot tell whether this vice is more execrable or more disgusting. Other vices can be concealed and cherished in secret; anger shows itself openly and appears in the countenance, and the greater it is, the more plainly it boils forth. Do you not see how in all animals certain signs appear before they proceed to mischief, and how their entire bodies put off their usual quiet appearance and stir up their ferocity? Boars foam at the mouth and sharpen their teeth by rubbing them against trees, bulls toss their horns in the air and scatter the sand with blows of their feet, lions growl, the necks of enraged snakes swell, mad dogs have a sullen look—there is no animal so hateful and venomous by nature that it does not, when seized by anger, show additional fierceness. I know well that the other passions can hardly be concealed, and that lust, fear, and boldness give signs of their presence and may be discovered beforehand, for there is no one of the stronger passions that does not affect the countenance: what then is the difference between them and anger? Why, that the other passions are visible, but that this is conspicuous. ...

VII.

May it not be that, although anger be not natural, it may be right to adopt it, because it often proves useful? It rouses the spirit and excites it; and courage does nothing grand in war without it, unless its flame be supplied from this source; this is the goad which stirs up bold men and sends them to encounter perils. Some therefore consider it to be best to control anger, not to banish it utterly, but to cut off its extravagances, and force it to keep within useful bounds, so as to retain that part of it without which action will become languid and all strength and activity of mind will die away.

In the first place, it is easier to banish dangerous passions than to rule them; it is easier not to admit them than to keep them in order when admitted; for when they have established themselves in possession of the mind they are more powerful than the lawful ruler, and will in no wise permit themselves to be weakened or abridged. In the next place, Reason herself, who holds the reins, is only strong while she remains apart from the passions; if she mixes and befouls herself with them she becomes no longer able to restrain those whom she might once have cleared out of her path; for the mind, when once excited and shaken up, goes whither the passions drive it. There are certain things whose beginnings lie in our own power, but which, when developed, drag us along by their own force and leave us no retreat. Those who have flung themselves over a precipice have no control over their movements, nor can they stop or slacken their pace when once started, for their own headlong and irremediable rashness has left no room for either reflexion or remorse, and they cannot help going to lengths which they might have avoided. So, also, the mind, when it has abandoned itself to anger, love, or any other passion, is unable to check itself: its own weight and the downward tendency of vices must needs carry the man off and hurl him into the lowest depth. ...

Book Two

I.

My first book, Novatus, had a more abundant subject, for carriages roll easily downhill; now we must proceed to drier matters. The question before us is whether anger arises from deliberate choice or from impulse, that is, whether it acts of its own accord or like the greater part of those passions which spring up within us without our knowledge. It is necessary for our debate to stoop to the consideration of these matters, in order that it may afterwards be able to rise to loftier themes; for likewise in our bodies the parts which are first set in order are the bones, sinews, and joints, which are by no means fair to see, albeit they are the foundation of our frame and essential to its life: next to them come the parts of which all beauty of face and appearance consists; and after these, colour, which above all else charms the eye, is applied last of all, when the rest of the body is complete. There is no doubt that anger is roused by the appearance of an injury being done; but the question before us is whether anger straightway follows the appearance, and springs up without assistance from the mind, or whether it is roused with the sympathy of the mind. Our (the Stoics') opinion is that anger can venture upon nothing by itself without the approval of mind, for to conceive the idea of a wrong having been done, to long to avenge it, and to join the two propositions, that we ought not to have been injured and that it is our duty to avenge our injuries, cannot belong to a mere impulse which is excited without our consent. That impulse is a simple act; this is a complex one, and composed of several parts. The man understands something to have happened; he becomes indignant thereat; he condemns the deed; and he avenges it. All these things cannot be done without his mind agreeing to those matters which touched him.

II.

Whither, say you, does this inquiry tend? That we may know what anger is: for if it springs up against our will, it never will yield to reason, because all the motions which take place without our volition are beyond our control and unavoidable, such as shivering when cold water is poured over us, or shrinking when we are touched in certain places. Men's hair rises up at bad news, their faces blush at indecent words, and they are seized with dizziness when looking down a precipice; and as it is not in our power to prevent any of these things, no reasoning can prevent their taking place. But anger can be put to flight by wise maxims; for it is a voluntary defect of the mind, and not one of those things which are evolved by the conditions of human life, and which, therefore, may happen even to the wisest of us. Among these and in the first place must be ranked that thrill of the mind which seizes us at the thought of wrongdoing. We feel this even when witnessing the mimic scenes of the stage, or when reading about things that happened long ago. We often feel angry with Clodius for banishing Cicero, and with Antonius for murdering him. Who is not indignant with the wars of Marius, the proscriptions of Sulla? Who is not enraged against Theodotus and Achillas and the boy king who dared to commit a more than boyish crime? Sometimes songs excite us, and quickened rhythm and the martial noise of trumpets; so, too, shocking pictures and the dreadful sight of tortures, however well deserved, affect our minds. Hence it is that we smile when others are smiling, that a crowd of mourners makes us sad, and that we take a glowing interest in another's battles; all of which feelings are not anger, any more than that which clouds our brow at the sight of a stage shipwreck is sadness, or what we feel, when we read how Hannibal after Cannae beset the walls of Rome, can be called fear. All these are emotions of minds which are loath to be moved, and are not passions, but rudiments which may grow into passions. So, too, a soldier starts at the sound of a trumpet, although he may be dressed as a civilian and in the midst of a profound peace, and camp horses prick up their ears at the clash of arms. It is said that Alexander, when Xenophantus was singing, laid his hand upon his weapons.

III.

None of these things which casually influence the mind deserve to be called passions: the mind, if I may so express it, rather suffers passions to act upon itself than forms them. A passion, therefore, consists not in being affected by the sights which are presented to us, but in giving way to our feelings and following up these chance promptings: for whoever imagines that paleness, bursting into tears, lustful feelings, deep sighs, sudden flashes of the eyes, and so forth, are signs of passion and betray the state of the mind, is mistaken, and does not understand that these are merely impulses of the body. Consequently, the bravest of men often turns pale while he is putting on his armour; when the signal for battle is given, the knees of the boldest soldier shake for a moment; the heart even of a great general leaps into his mouth just before the lines clash together, and the hands and feet even of the most eloquent orator grow stiff and cold while he is preparing to begin his speech. Anger must not merely move, but break out of bounds, being an impulse: now, no impulse can take place without the consent of the mind, for it cannot be that we should deal with revenge and punishment without the mind being cognisant of them. A man may think himself injured, may wish to avenge his wrongs, and then may be persuaded by some reason or other to give up his intention and calm down: I do not call that anger, it is an emotion of the mind which is under the control of reason. Anger is that which goes beyond reason and carries her away with it: wherefore the first confusion of a man's mind when struck by what seems an injury is no more anger than the apparent injury itself; it is the subsequent mad rush, which not only receives the impression of the apparent injury, but acts upon it as true, that is anger, being an exciting of the mind to revenge, which proceeds from choice and deliberate resolve. There never has been any doubt that fear produces flight, and anger a rush forward; consider, therefore, whether you suppose that anything can be either sought or avoided without the participation of the mind.

IV.

Furthermore, that you may know in what manner passions begin and swell and gain spirit, learn that the first emotion is involuntary, and is, as it were, a preparation for a passion, and a threatening of one. The next is combined with a wish, though not an obstinate one, as, for example, 'It is my duty to avenge myself, because I have been injured,' or 'It is right that this man should be punished, because he has committed a crime.' The third emotion is already beyond our control, because it overrides reason, and wishes to avenge itself, not if it be its duty, but whether or no. We are not able by means of reason to escape from that first impression on the mind, any more than we can escape from those things which we have mentioned as occurring to the body: we cannot prevent other people's yawns temping us to yawn; we cannot help winking when fingers are suddenly darted at our eyes. Reason is unable to overcome these habits, which perhaps might be weakened by practice and constant watchfulness; they differ from an emotion which is brought into existence and brought to an end by a deliberate mental act. ...

Epictetus, The Enchiridion

I.

There are things which are within our power, and there are things which are beyond our power. Within our power are opinion, aim, desire, aversion, and, in one word, whatever affairs are our own. Beyond our power are body, property, reputation, office, and, in one word, whatever are not properly our own affairs.

Now the things within our power are by nature free, unrestricted, unhindered; but those beyond our power are weak, dependent, restricted, alien. Remember, then, that if you attribute freedom to things by nature dependent, and take what belongs to others for your own, you will be hindered, you will lament, you will be disturbed, you will find fault both with Gods and men. But if you take for your own only that which is your own, and view what belongs to others just as it really is, then no one will ever compel you, no one will restrict you, you will find fault with no one, you will accuse no one, you will do nothing against your will; no one will hurt you, you will not have an enemy, nor will you suffer any harm.

Aiming therefore at such great things, remember that you must not allow yourself any inclination, however slight, towards the attainment of the others; but that you must entirely quit some of them, and for the present postpone the rest. But if you would have these, and possess power and wealth likewise, you may miss the latter in seeking the former; and you will certainly fail of that by which alone happiness and freedom are procured.

Seek at once, therefore, to be able to say to every unpleasing semblance, 'You are but a semblance and by no means the real thing.' And then examine it by those rules which you have, and first and chiefly, by this: whether it concerns the things which are within our own power, or those which are not; and if it concerns anything beyond our power, be prepared to say that it is nothing to you.

II.

Remember that desire demands the attainment of that of which you are desirous; and aversion demands the avoidance of that to which you are averse; that he who fails of the object of his desires, is disappointed; and he who incurs the object of his aversion, is wretched. If, then, you shun only those undesirable things which you can control, you will never incur anything which you shun. But if you shun sickness, or death, or poverty, you will run the risk of wretchedness. Remove aversion, then, from all things that are not within our power, and transfer it to things undesirable, which are within our power. But for the present altogether restrain desire: for if you desire any of the things *not* within our own power, you must necessarily be disappointed; and you are not yet secure of those which *are* within our power, and so are legitimate objects of desire. Where it is practically necessary for you to pursue or avoid anything, do even this with discretion, and gentleness, and moderation.

III.

With regard to whatever objects either delight the mind, or contribute to use, or are tenderly beloved, remind yourself of what nature they are, beginning with the merest trifles: if you have a favourite cup, that it is a cup of which you are fond, for thus, if it is broken, you can bear it; if you embrace your child, or your wife, that you embrace a mortal, and thus, if either of them dies, you can bear it.

IV.

When you set about any action, remind yourself of what nature the action is. If you are going to bathe, represent to yourself the incidents usual in the bath: some persons pouring out, others pushing in, others scolding, others pilfering. And thus you will more safely go about this action if you say to yourself, 'I will now go to bathe, and keep my own will in harmony with nature.' And so with regard to every other action. For thus, if any impediment arises in bathing, you will be able to say, 'It was not only to bathe that I desired, but to keep my will in harmony with nature; and I shall not keep it thus if I am out of humour at things that happen.'

V.

Men are disturbed not by things, but by the views which they take of things. Thus death is nothing terrible, else it would have appeared so to Socrates. But the terror consists in our notion of death, that it is terrible. When, therefore, we are hindered, or disturbed, or grieved, let us never impute it to others, but to ourselves; that is, to our own views. It is the action of an uninstructed person to reproach others for his own misfortunes; of one entering upon instruction, to reproach himself; and of one perfectly instructed, to reproach neither others nor himself.

VI.

Be not elated at any excellence not your own. If a horse should be elated, and say, 'I am handsome,' it might be endurable. But when you are elated, and say, 'I have a handsome horse,' know that you are elated only on the merit of the horse. What, then, is your own? The use of the phenomena of existence. So that when you are in harmony with nature in this respect, you will be elated with some reason; for you will be elated at some good of your own.

VII.

As in a voyage, when the ship is at anchor, if you go on shore to get water, you may amuse yourself with picking up a shellfish or a truffle in your way; but your thoughts ought to be bent towards the ship, and perpetually attentive, lest the captain should call; and then you must leave all these things, that you may not have to be carried on board the vessel, bound like a sheep. Thus likewise in life, if, instead of a truffle or shellfish, such a thing as a wife or a child be granted you, there is no objection; but if the captain calls, run to the ship, leave all these things, and never look behind. But if you are old, never go far from the ship, lest you should be missing when called for.

VIII.

Demand not that events should happen as you wish; but wish them to happen as they do happen, and you will go on well.

IX.

Sickness is an impediment to the body, but not to the will, unless itself pleases. Lameness is an impediment to the leg, but not to the will; and say this to yourself with regard to everything that happens. For you will find it to be an impediment to something else, but not truly to yourself.

X.

Upon every accident, remember to turn towards yourself and inquire what faculty you have for its use. If you encounter a handsome person, you will find continence the faculty needed; if pain, then fortitude; if reviling, then patience. And when thus habituated, the phenomena of existence will not overwhelm you.

XI.

Never say of anything, 'I have lost it'; but, 'I have restored it.' Has your child died? It is restored. Has your wife died? She is restored. Has your estate been taken away? That likewise is restored. 'But it was a bad man who took it.' What is it to you, by whose hands He who gave it hath demanded it again? While He permits you to possess it, hold it as something not your own; as do travellers at an inn.

XII.

If you would improve, lay aside such reasonings as these: 'If I neglect my affairs, I shall not have a maintenance; if I do not punish my servant, he will be good for nothing.' For it were better to die of hunger, exempt from grief and fear, than to live in affluence with perturbation; and it is better that your servant should be bad than you unhappy.

Begin therefore with little things. Is a little oil spilt or a little wine stolen? Say to yourself, 'This is the price paid for peace and tranquility; and nothing is to be had for nothing.' And when you call your servant, consider that it is possible he may not come at your call; or, if he does, that he may not do what you wish. But it is not at all desirable for him, and very undesirable for you, that it should be in his power to cause you any disturbance.

XIII.

If you would improve, be content to be thought foolish and dull with regard to externals. Do not desire to be thought to know anything; and though you should appear to others to be somebody, distrust yourself. For be assured, it is not easy at once to keep your will in harmony with nature, and to secure externals; but while you are absorbed in the one, you must of necessity neglect the other.

XIV.

If you wish your children, and your wife, and your friends, to live forever, you are foolish; for you wish things to be in your power which are not so; and what belongs to others, to be your own. So likewise, if you wish your servant to be without fault, you are foolish; for you wish vice not to be vice, but something else. But if you wish not to be disappointed in your desires, that is in your own power. Exercise, therefore, what is in your power. A man's master is he who is able to confer or remove whatever that man seeks or shuns. Whoever then would be free, let him wish nothing, let him decline nothing, which depends on others; else he must necessarily be a slave.

XV.

Remember that you must behave as at a banquet. Is anything brought round to you? Put out your hand, and take a moderate share. Does it pass by you? Do not stop it. Is it not yet come? Do not yearn in desire towards it, but wait till it reaches you. So with regard to children, wife, office, riches; and you will some time or other be worthy to feast with the Gods. And if you do not so much as take the things which are set before you, but are able even to forego them, then you will not only be worthy to feast with the Gods, but to rule with them also. For, by thus doing, Diogenes and Heraclitus, and others like them, deservedly became divine, and were so recognized.

XVI.

When you see anyone weeping for grief, either that his son has gone abroad, or that he has suffered in his affairs, take care not to be overcome by the apparent evil. But discriminate, and be ready to say, 'What hurts this man is not this occurrence itself—for another man might not be hurt by it—but the view he chooses to take of it.' As far as conversation goes, however, do not disdain to accommodate yourself to him, and if need be, to groan with him. Take heed, however, not to groan inwardly too.

XVII.

Remember that you are an actor in a drama of such sort as the author chooses. If short, then in a short one; if long, then in a long one. If it be his pleasure that you should act a poor man, see that you act it well; or a cripple, or a ruler, or a private citizen. For this is your business, to act well the given part; but to choose it belongs to another.

XVIII.

When a raven happens to croak unluckily, be not overcome by

appearances, but discriminate, and say, 'Nothing is portended to me; but either to my paltry body, or property, or reputation, or children, or wife. But to me all portents are lucky, if I will. For whatsoever happens, it belongs to me to derive advantage therefrom.'

XIX.

You can be unconquerable if you enter into no combat in which it is not in your own power to conquer. When, therefore, you see anyone eminent in honours or power, or in high esteem on any other account, take heed not to be bewildered by appearances and to pronounce him happy; for if the essence of good consists in things within our own power, there will be no room for envy or emulation. But, for your part, do not desire to be a general, or a senator, or a consul, but to be free; and the only way to this is a disregard of things which lie not within our own power.

XX.

Remember that it is not he who gives abuse or blows who affronts; but the view we take of these things as insulting. When, therefore, anyone provokes you, be assured that it is your own opinion which provokes you. Try, therefore, in the first place, not to be bewildered by appearances. For if you once gain time and respite, you will more easily command yourself.

XXI.

Let death and exile, and all other things which appear terrible, be daily before your eyes, but death chiefly; and you will never entertain any abject thought, nor too eagerly covet anything.

XXII.

If you have an earnest desire towards philosophy, prepare yourself from the very first to have the multitude laugh and sneer, and say, 'He is returned to us a philosopher all at once'; and 'Whence this supercilious look?' Now for your part, do not have a supercilious look indeed; but keep steadily to those things which appear best to you, as one appointed by God to this particular station. For remember that, if you are persistent, those very persons who at first ridiculed, will afterwards admire you. But if you are conquered by them, you will incur a double ridicule.

XXIII.

If you ever happen to turn your attention to externals, for the pleasure of anyone, be assured that you have ruined your scheme of life. Be contented, then, in everything, with being a philosopher; and, if you wish to seem so likewise to anyone, appear so to yourself, and it will suffice you.

XXIV.

Let not such considerations as these distress you: 'I shall live in discredit, and be nobody anywhere.' For if discredit be an evil, you can no more be involved in evil through another, than in baseness. Is it any business of yours, then, to get power, or to be admitted to an entertainment? By no means. How, then, after all, is this discredit? And how is it true that you will be nobody anywhere, when you ought to be somebody in those things only which are within your own power, in which you may be of the greatest consequence? 'But my friends will be unassisted.' What do you mean by unassisted? They will not have money from you; nor will you make them Roman citizens.

Who told you, then, that these are among the things within our own power; and not rather the affairs of others? And who can give to another the things which he himself has not? 'Well, but get them, then, that we too may have a share.' If I can get them with the preservation of my own honour, and fidelity, and self-respect, show me the way, and I will get them; but if you require me to lose my own proper good, that you may gain what is no good, consider how unreasonable and foolish you are. Besides, which would you rather have, a sum of money, or a faithful and honourable friend? Rather assist me, then, to gain this character, than require me to do those things by which I may lose it. Well, but my country, say you, as far as depends upon me, will be unassisted. Here again, what assistance is this you mean? It will not have porticos nor baths of your providing? And what signifies that? Why, neither does a smith provide it with shoes, nor a shoemaker with arms. It is enough if every one fully performs his own proper business. And were you to supply it with another faithful and honourable citizen, would not he be of use to it? Yes. Therefore neither are you yourself useless to it. 'What place then,' say you, 'shall I hold in the state?' Whatever you can hold with the preservation of your fidelity and honour. But if, by desiring to be useful to that, you lose these, how can you serve your country, when you have become faithless and shameless?

XXV.

Is anyone preferred before you at an entertainment, or in courtesies, or in confidential intercourse? If these things are good, you ought to rejoice that he has them; and if they are evil, do not be grieved that you have them not. And remember that you cannot be permitted to rival others in externals without using the same means to obtain them. For how can he, who will not haunt the door of any man, will not attend him, will not praise him, have an equal share with him who does these things? You are unjust, then, and unreasonable, if you are unwilling to pay the price for which these things are sold, and would have them for nothing. For how much are lettuces sold? An obolus, for instance. If another, then, paying an obolus takes the lettuces, and you, not paying it, go without them, do not imagine that he has gained any advantage over you. For as he has the lettuces, so you have the obolus which you did not give. So, in the present case, you have not been invited to such a person's entertainment, because you have not paid him the price for which a supper is sold. It is sold for praise; it is sold for attendance. Give him, then, the value, if it be for your advantage. But if you would at the same time not pay the one, and yet receive the other, you are unreasonable and foolish. Have you nothing, then, in place of the supper? Yes, indeed you have: not to praise him whom you do not like to praise; not to bear the insolence of his lackeys.

XXVI.

The will of Nature may be learned from things upon which we are all agreed. As, when our neighbour's boy has broken a cup, or the like, we are ready at once to say, 'These are casualties that will happen.' Be assured, then, that when your own cup is likewise broken, you ought to be affected just as when another's cup was broken. Now apply this to greater things. Is the child or wife of another dead? There is no one who would not say, 'This is an accident of mortality.' But if anyone's own child happens to die, it is immediately, 'Alas! How wretched am I!' It should be always remembered how we are affected on hearing the same thing concerning others.

XXVII.

As a mark is not set up for the sake of missing the aim, so neither does the nature of evil exist in the world.

XXVIII.

If a person had delivered up your body to some passer-by, you would certainly be angry. And do you feel no shame in delivering up your own mind to any reviler, to be disconcerted and confounded?

XXIX.

In every affair consider what precedes and follows, and then undertake it. Otherwise you will begin with spirit indeed, careless of the consequences, and when these are developed, you will shamefully desist. 'I would conquer at the Olympic Games.' But consider what precedes and follows, and, then, if it be for your advantage, engage in the affair. You must conform to rules, submit to a diet, refrain from dainties; exercise your body, whether you choose it or not, at a stated hour, in heat and cold; you must drink no cold water, and sometimes no wine. In a word, you must give yourself up to your trainer as to a physician. Then, in the combat, you may be thrown into a ditch, dislocate your arm, turn your ankle, swallow abundance of dust, receive stripes; and, after all, lose the victory. When you have reckoned up all this, if your inclination still holds, set about the combat. Otherwise, take notice, you will behave like children who sometimes play wrestlers, sometimes gladiators; sometimes blow a trumpet, and sometimes act a tragedy, when they happen to have seen and admired these shows. Thus you too will be at one time a wrestler, at another a gladiator; now a philosopher, now an orator; but nothing in earnest. Like an

ape you mimic all you see, and one thing after another is sure to please you; but is out of favour as soon as it becomes familiar. For you have never entered upon anything considerately, nor after having surveyed and tested the whole matter; but carelessly, and with a half-way zeal. Thus some, when they have seen a philosopher, and heard a man speaking like Euphrates—though indeed who can speak like him?—have a mind to be philosophers too. Consider first, man, what the matter is, and what your own nature is able to bear. If you would be a wrestler, consider your shoulders, your back, your thighs; for different persons are made for different things. Do you think that you can act as you do and be a philosopher? That you can eat, drink, be angry, be discontented, as you are now? You must watch, you must labour, you must get the better of certain appetites; must quit your acquaintances, be despised by your servant, be laughed at by those you meet; come off worse than others in everything, in offices, in honors, before tribunals. When you have fully considered all these things, approach, if you please; if, by parting with them, you have a mind to purchase serenity, freedom, and tranquility. If not, do not come hither; do not, like children, be now a philosopher, then a publican, then an orator, and then one of Caesar's officers. These things are not consistent. You must be one man either good or bad. You must cultivate either your own Reason or else externals; apply yourself either to things within or without you; that is, be either a philosopher, or one of the mob.
...

MARCUS AURELIUS, MEDITATIONS

BOOK ONE

I.

Begin the morning by saying to yourself, I shall meet with the busybody, the ungrateful, arrogant, deceitful, envious, unsocial. All these things happen to them by reason of their ignorance of what is good and evil. But I who have seen the nature of the good that it is beautiful, and of the bad that it is ugly, and the nature of him who does wrong, that it is akin to me; not only of the same blood or seed, but that it participates in the same intelligence and the same portion of the divinity, I can neither be injured by any of them, for no one can fix on me what is ugly, nor can I be angry with my kinsman, nor hate him. For we are made for cooperation, like feet, like hands, like eyelids, like the rows of the upper and lower teeth. To act against one another, then, is contrary to nature; and it is acting against one another to be vexed and to turn away. ...

V.

Every moment think steadily as a Roman and a man to do what you have in hand with perfect and simple dignity, and feeling of affection, and freedom, and justice, and to give yourself relief from all other thoughts. And you will give yourself relief if you do every act of your life as if it were the last, laying aside all carelessness and passionate aversion from the commands of reason, and all hypocrisy, and self-love, and discontent with the portion which has been given to you. You see how few the things are, the which if a man lays hold of, he is able to live a life which flows in quiet, and is like the existence of the gods;

for the gods on their part will require nothing more from him who observes these things. ...

XVI.

The soul of man does violence to itself, first of all, when it becomes an abscess, and, as it were, a tumour on the universe, so far as it can. For to be vexed at anything which happens is a separation of ourselves from nature, in some part of which the natures of all other things are contained. In the next place, the soul does violence to itself when it turns away from any man, or even moves towards him with the intention of injuring, such as are the souls of those who are angry. In the third place, the soul does violence to itself when it is overpowered by pleasure or by pain. Fourthly, when it plays a part, and does or says anything insincerely and untruly. Fifthly, when it allows any act of its own and any movement to be without an aim, and does anything thoughtlessly and without considering what it is, it being right that even the smallest things be done with reference to an end; and the end of rational animals is to follow the reason and the law of the most ancient city and polity.

BOOK EIGHT

XXXVI.

Do not disturb yourself by thinking of the whole of your life. Let not your thoughts at once embrace all the various troubles which you may expect to befall you; but on every occasion ask yourself, 'What is there in this which is intolerable and past bearing?', for you will be ashamed to confess. In the next place remember that neither the future nor the past pains you, but only the present. But this is reduced to a very little, if you only circumscribe it, and chide your mind if it is unable to hold out against even this. ...

XLVII.

If you are pained by any external thing, it is not this thing that disturbs you, but your own judgment about it. And it is in your power to wipe out this judgment now. But if anything in your own disposition gives you pain, who hinders you from correcting your opinion? And even if you are pained because you are not doing some particular thing which seems to you to be right, why do you not rather act than complain? But some insuperable obstacle is in the way? Do not be grieved then, for the cause of its not being done depends not on you. But it is not worthwhile to live if this cannot be done? Take your departure then from life contentedly, just as he dies who is in full activity, and well pleased too with the things which are obstacles. ...

XLIX.

Say nothing more to yourself than what the first appearances report. Suppose that it has been reported to you that a certain person speaks ill of you. This has been reported; but that you have been injured, that has not been reported. I see that my child is sick. I do see; but that he is in danger, I do not see. Thus then always abide by the first appearances, and add nothing yourself from within, and then nothing happens to you. Or rather add something like a man who knows everything that happens in the world.

L.

A cucumber is bitter—throw it away. There are briars in the road—turn aside from them. This is enough. Do not add: And why were such things made in the world? For you will be ridiculed by a man who is acquainted with nature, as you would be ridiculed by a carpenter and shoemaker if you did find fault because you see in their workshop shavings and cuttings from the things which they make. And yet they have places into which they can throw these shavings and cuttings, and the universal nature has no external space; but the wondrous part of her art is that though she has circumscribed herself, everything within her which appears to decay and to grow old and to be useless she changes into herself, and again makes other new things from these very same, so that she requires neither substance from without nor wants a place into which she may cast that which decays. She is content then with her own space, and her own matter, and her own art.

Book Eleven

XVIII.

If any have offended against you, consider first: what is my relation to men, and that we are made for one another; and in another respect I was made to be set over them, as a ram over the flock or a bull over the herd. But examine the matter from first principles, from this. If all things are not mere atoms, it is nature which orders all things: if this is so, the inferior things exist for the sake of the superior, and these for the sake of one another.

Second, consider what kind of men they are at table, in bed, and so forth; and particularly, under what compulsions in respect of opinions they are; and as to their acts, consider with what pride they do what they do.

Third, that if men do rightly what they do, we ought not to be displeased: but if they do not right, it is plain that they do so involuntarily and in ignorance. For as every soul is unwillingly deprived of the truth, so also is it unwillingly deprived of the power of behaving to each man according to his deserts. Accordingly, men are pained when they are called unjust, ungrateful, and greedy, and in a word wrongdoers to their neighbours.

Fourth, consider that you also do many things wrong, and that you are a man like others; and even if you do abstain from certain faults, still you have the disposition to commit them, though either through cowardice, or concern about reputation, or some such mean motive, you do abstain from such faults.

Fifth, consider that you do not even understand whether men are doing wrong or not, for many things are done with a certain reference to circumstances. And in short, a man must learn a great deal to enable him to pass a correct judgment on another man's acts.

Sixth, consider when you are much vexed or grieved, that man's life is only a moment, and after a short time we are all laid out dead.

Seventh, that it is not men's acts which disturb us, for those acts have their foundation in men's ruling principles, but it is our own opinions which disturb us. Take away these opinions then, and resolve to dismiss your judgment about an act as if it were something grievous, and your anger is gone. How then shall I take away these opinions? By reflecting that no wrongful act of another brings shame on you: for unless that which is shameful is alone bad, you also must of necessity do many things wrong, and become a robber and everything else.

Eighth, consider how much more pain is brought on us by the anger and vexation caused by such acts than by the acts themselves, at which we are angry and vexed.

Ninth, consider that a good disposition is invincible if it be genuine, and not an affected smile and acting a part. For what will the most violent man do to you, if you continue to be of a kind disposition towards him, and if, as opportunity offers, you gently admonish him and calmly correct his errors at the very time when he is trying to do you harm, saying, 'Not so, my child: we are constituted by nature for something else; I shall certainly not be injured, but you are injuring yourself, my child.' And show him with gentle tact and by general principles that this is so, and that even bees do not do as he does, nor any animals which are formed by nature to be gregarious. And you must do this neither with any double meaning nor in the way of reproach, but affectionately and without any rancour in your soul; and not as if you were lecturing him, nor yet that any bystander may admire, but either when he is alone, and if others are present.

Remember these nine rules, as if you had received them as a gift from the Muses, and begin at last to be a man while you live. But you must equally avoid nattering men and being vexed at them, for both are unsocial and lead to harm. And let this truth be present to you in the excitement of anger, that to be moved by passion is not manly, but that mildness and gentleness, as they are more agreeable to human nature, so also are they more manly; and he who possesses these qualities possesses strength, nerves, and courage, and not the man who is subject to fits of passion and discontent. For in the same degree in which a man's mind is nearer to freedom from all passion, in the same degree also is it nearer to strength; and as the sense of pain is a characteristic of weakness, so also is anger. For he who yields to pain and he who yields to anger, both are wounded and both submit.

But if you will, receive also a tenth present from the leader of the Muses, Apollo, and it is this—that to expect bad men not to do wrong is madness, for he who expects this desires an impossibility. But to allow men to behave so to others, and to expect them not to do you any wrong, is irrational and tyrannical.

BOETHIUS, THE CONSOLATION OF PHILOSOPHY

Introduction

Coping with the swings and roundabouts of fortune is one of the fundamental challenges of being human. At best, even if we are fortunate enough to live lives that are long, full, happy, and go according to plan, illness and death will eventually catch up with us; in the more likely scenario, our lives will alternate between fortune and misfortune, as periods of success and joy are interrupted by spells of difficulty or trouble, some of which can be traced to decisions we have taken and some of which seem to descend upon us from out of the blue. This is why fortune has traditionally been depicted as wheel, tossing kings and princes downwards while thrusting rogues and clowns back up; less politely, perhaps, it is also why fortune has been depicted as a whore. As Solon, according to Herodotus, said, 'call no man happy until he is dead'.

The Consolation of Philosophy of Boethius—one of the most influential and popular works of the Middle Ages—is a sustained philosophical attempt to explore how best to deal with the changeability of our condition and the vicissitudes of fortune which each of us will inevitably have to endure.

Anicius Manlius Severinus Boethius was a Roman statesman and philosopher of the late fifth and early sixth century. Born around 477 AD into a patrician family in Rome at around the time that the last Roman emperor, Romulus Augustus, was deposed by the barbarian Odoacer, he lived most of his life under the Ostrogothic King Theoderic the Great. Boethius' parents died when he was young, and he was brought up instead by a Roman patrician, Symmachus, who from an early age instilled in him a love of literature and philosophy, and whose daughter, Rusticiana, he would go on to marry. While still a young man, Boethius entered the service of King Theoderic, and by 510 AD he had been made sole consul. The peak of his worldly success came in 522 AD when he was appointed to the office of *Magister Officiorum*, or head of the whole civil administration, and his two sons, Symmachus and Boethius, were created joint consuls. However, fortune turned against him when, having fallen out with others at court, he was accused of treason and imprisoned in Pavia. It was here that, awaiting execution, he wrote his masterpiece, *The Consolation of Philosophy*.

The Consolation of Philosophy presents an imagined dialogue between the prisoner Boethius and a lady who personifies Philosophy. Lady Philosophy begins by sharing some homespun wisdom as to the human condition. Part of the trouble, she explains, is our misapprehension of the nature of fortune: when we are doing well in life, she suggests, we neglect to consider what role fortune may be playing; it is only when life turns agains us that we complain, thinking that fortune has changed her ways towards us. In fact, fortune has always been with us, through good and through bad alike; mutability is in her very nature. But this same mutability should make her threats void of terror, for we ought to know that precisely that which she brings she is liable to take away, and that which she takes away she may (if it pleases her) bestow on us once again. What fortune has temporarily granted us to enjoy has never properly belonged to us: what right have we to complain, then, if what we appear to have lost was not our own in the first place? At most we can lose what we must sooner or later lose anyway, since the last day of life will be the death of all remaining fortune.

The life well lived cannot, therefore, be one that depends on the good graces of fortune, or indeed anything else that is external to man and therefore outside his control. Even when we are well favoured by fortune, that does not bring happiness: 'the more favoured a man is by fortune,' says Lady Philosophy, 'the more fastidiously sensitive is he; and, unless all things answer to his whim, he is overwhelmed by the most trifling misfortunes, because utterly unschooled in adversity.' Man can—by force of character—overcome these disturbances: nothing is wretched, Lady Philosophy adds, but thinking makes it so; conversely, every lot is happy if borne with equanimity. The blessings of fortune, however, are like the flowers of spring or the fruits of autumn—alien excellences that belong to no man and in respect of which no man can take credit.

The true 'good', explains Lady Philosophy, is that which when you have it you lack nothing further, since if anything is lacking then it cannot be the supreme good. It is self-evident that wealth cannot constitute this good, for we all know people living in affluence who are nevertheless unhappy with their lot; in fact, wealth not only does not get rid of wants, it also adds new wants of its own. Power, too, can never be a complete solution, for however far it can be extended, there will always be a limit to it. Fame and honour suffer similar limitations since there must always be people whom the fame of a single man cannot reach. Happiness, on the other hand, *can* be the 'good', for happiness is complete and an end in itself. God, if he is supreme in all things, must also be the 'good', otherwise there would be something more excellent than He. Happiness—being without lack—is, then, 'very Godship'.

We now have a formula for living well. The good and the bad alike seek after the 'good', but the good alone—by seeking it through the self-complete and natural action of the virtues—are able to attain it, whereas the bad—attempting to attain it through grasping at all manner of temptations—must fail. The bad, in this analysis, cease to have power, since (unlike the good) they are unable to attain their desires. More controversially, the bad, says Lady Philosophy, actually cease to be at all: for, she says, 'that only is which maintains its place and keeps its nature; whatever falls away from this forsakes the existence which is essential to its nature.' Providence nevertheless ensures that whatever evil exists is put to use, whether for trial of the good or for punishing or amending of the bad. To the extent that to us this is far from obvious, Boethius reminds us that all that is known can only be grasped in a manner comprehensible to the knower, and that human reason errs when it assumes the Divine Intelligence comprehends past and future only in the same limited way that we mortals can.

It is tempting today to see works of writers such as Boethius as having an exclusively, or predominantly, historical significance—as remnants of an age long gone and with little of practical value for the modern man. In the case of *The Consolation*, this is emphatically not the case. On the one hand, Boethius gives us homespun practical wisdom as to the fickleness of fortune and how to endure its reversals; on the other, he provides an elegant answer to one of the most intractable problems of philosophy—namely, theodicy and the 'problem of evil'. Above all, what Boethius manages to achieve is to bring together disparate strains of thought from classical philosophy and Christianity in a lucid and coherent work that centres upon a powerful and inspiring message: virtue, being self-sufficient, obtains to the 'good' that is both the only true happiness and a portion of the very Godship itself.

BOOK IV, PART VI

PHILOSOPHY DISCUSSES PROVIDENCE AND FATE

'True,' said I; 'but, since it is your office to unfold the hidden cause of things, and explain principles veiled in darkness, inform me, I pray you, of your own conclusions in this matter, since the marvel of it is what more than aught else disturbs my mind.'

A smile played one moment upon her lips as she replied: 'You call me to the greatest of all subjects of inquiry, a task for which the most exhaustive treatment barely suffices. Such is its nature that, as fast as one doubt is cut away, innumerable others spring up like Hydra's heads, nor could we set any limit to their renewal did we not apply the mind's living fire to suppress them. For there come within its scope the questions of the essential simplicity of providence, of the order of fate, of unforeseen chance, of the divine knowledge and predestination, and of the freedom of the will. How heavy is the weight of all this you can judge for thyself. But, inasmuch as to know these things also is part of the treatment of your malady, we will try to give them some consideration, despite the restrictions of the narrow limits of our time. Moreover, you must for a time dispense with the pleasures of music and song, if so be that you find any delight therein, whilst I weave together the connected train of reasons in proper order.'

'As you will,' said I.

Then, as if making a new beginning, she thus discoursed: 'The coming into being of all things, the whole course of development in things that change, every sort of thing that moves in any wise, receives its due cause, order, and form from the steadfastness of the divine mind. This mind, calm in the citadel of its own essential simplicity, has decreed that the method of its rule shall be manifold. Viewed in the very purity of the divine intelligence, this method is called providence; but viewed in regard to those things which it moves and disposes, it is what the ancients called fate. That these two are different will easily be clear to anyone who passes in review their respective efficacies. Providence is the divine reason itself, seated in the Supreme Being, which disposes all things; fate is the disposition inherent in all things which move, through which providence joins all things in their proper order. Providence embraces all things, however different, however infinite; fate sets in motion separately individual things, and assigns to them severally their position, form, and time.

'So the unfolding of this temporal order unified into the foreview of the divine mind is providence, while the same unity broken up and unfolded in time is fate. And although these are different, yet is there a dependence between them; for the order of destiny issues from the essential simplicity of providence. For as the artificer, forming in his mind beforehand the idea of the thing to be made, carries out his design, and develops from moment to moment what he had before seen in a single instant as a whole, so God in His providence ordains all things as parts of a single unchanging whole, but carries out these very ordinances by fate in a time of manifold unity. So whether fate is accomplished by divine spirits as the ministers of providence, or by a soul, or by the service of all nature—whether by the celestial motion of the stars, by the efficacy of angels, or by the many-sided cunning of demons—whether by all or by some of these the destined series is woven, this, at least, is manifest: that providence is the fixed and simple form of destined events, fate their shifting series in order of time, as by the disposal of the divine simplicity they are to take place. Whereby it is that all things which are under fate are subjected also to providence, on which fate itself is dependent; whereas certain things which are set under providence are above the chain of fate—viz., those things which by their nearness to the primal divinity are steadfastly fixed, and lie outside the order of fate's movements. For as the innermost of several circles revolving round the same centre approaches the simplicity of the midmost point, and is, as it were, a pivot round which the exterior circles turn, while the outermost, whirled in ampler orbit, takes in a wider and wider sweep of space in proportion to its departure from the indivisible unity of the centre—while, further, whatever joins and allies itself to the centre is narrowed to a like simplicity, and no longer expands vaguely into space—even so whatsoever departs widely from primal mind is involved more deeply in the meshes of fate, and things are free from fate in proportion as they seek to come nearer to that central pivot; while if aught cleaves close to supreme mind in its absolute fixity, this, too, being free from movement, rises above fate's necessity. Therefore, as is reasoning to pure intelligence, as that which is generated to that which is, time to eternity, a circle to its centre, so is the shifting series of fate to the steadfastness and simplicity of providence.

'It is this causal series which moves heaven and the stars, attempers the elements to mutual accord, and again in turn transforms them into new combinations; this which renews the series of all things that are born and die through like successions of germ and birth; it is its operation which binds the destinies of men by an indissoluble nexus of causality, and, since it issues in the beginning from unalterable providence, these destinies also must of necessity be immutable.

Accordingly, the world is ruled for the best if this unity abiding in the divine mind puts forth an inflexible order of causes. And this order, by its intrinsic immutability, restricts things mutable which otherwise would ebb and flow at random. And so it happens that, although to you, who are not altogether capable of understanding this order, all things seem confused and disordered, nevertheless there is everywhere an appointed limit which guides all things to good. Verily, nothing can be done for the sake of evil even by the wicked themselves; for, as we abundantly proved, they seek good, but are drawn out of the way by perverse error; far less can this order which sets out from the supreme centre of good turn aside anywhither from the way in which it began.

'"Yet what confusion," you will say, "can be more unrighteous than that prosperity and adversity should indifferently befall the good, what they like and what they loathe come alternately to the bad!" Yes; but have men in real life such soundness of mind that their judgments of righteousness and wickedness must necessarily correspond with facts? Why, on this very point their verdicts conflict, and those whom some deem worthy of reward, others deem worthy of punishment. Yet granted there were one who could rightly distinguish the good and bad, yet would he be able to look into the soul's inmost constitution, as it were, if we may borrow an expression used of the body? The marvel here is not unlike that which astonishes one who does not know why in health sweet things suit some constitutions, and bitter others, or why some sick men are best alleviated by mild remedies, others by severe. But the physician who distinguishes the precise conditions and characteristics of health and sickness does not marvel. Now, the health of the soul is nothing but righteousness, and vice is its sickness. God, the guide and physician of the mind, it is who preserves the good and banishes the bad. And He looks forth from the lofty watch-tower of His providence, perceives what is suited to each, and assigns what He knows to be suitable.

'This, then, is what that extraordinary mystery of the order of destiny comes to—that something is done by one who knows, whereat the ignorant are astonished. But let us consider a few instances whereby appears what is the competency of human reason to fathom the divine unsearchableness. Here is one whom you deem the perfection of justice and scrupulous integrity; to all-knowing Providence it seems far otherwise. We all know our Lucan's admonition that it was the winning cause that found favour with the gods, the beaten cause with Cato. So, should you see anything in this world happening differently from your expectation, doubt not but events are rightly ordered; it is in your judgment that there is perverse confusion.

'Grant, however, there be somewhere found one of so happy a character that God and man alike agree in their judgments about him; yet is he somewhat infirm in strength of mind. It may be, if he fall into adversity, he will cease to practise that innocency which has failed to secure his fortune. Therefore, God's wise dispensation spares him whom adversity might make worse, will not let him suffer who is ill fitted for endurance. Another there is perfect in all virtue, so holy and nigh to God that providence judges it unlawful that aught untoward should befall him; nay, doth not even permit him to be afflicted with bodily disease. As one more excellent than I has said:

The very body of the holy saint
Is built of purest ether.

Often it happens that the governance is given to the good that a restraint may be put upon superfluity of wickedness. To others providence assigns some mixed lot suited to their spiritual nature; some it will plague lest they grow rank through long prosperity; others it will suffer to be vexed with sore afflictions to confirm their virtues by the exercise and practice of patience. Some fear overmuch what they have strength to bear; others despise overmuch that to which their strength is unequal. All these it brings to the test of their true self through misfortune. Some also have bought a name revered to future ages at the price of a glorious death; some by invincible constancy under their sufferings have afforded an example to others that virtue cannot be overcome by calamity—all which things, without doubt, come to pass rightly and in due order, and to the benefit of those to whom they are seen to happen.

'As to the other side of the marvel, that the bad now meet with affliction, now get their hearts' desire, this, too, springs from the same causes. As to the afflictions, of course, no one marvels, because all hold the wicked to be ill deserving. The truth is, their punishments both frighten others from crime, and amend those on whom they are inflicted; while their prosperity is a powerful sermon to the good, what judgments they ought to pass on good fortune of this kind, which often attends the wicked so assiduously.

'There is another object which may, I believe, be attained in such cases: there is one, perhaps, whose nature is so reckless and violent that poverty would drive him more desperately into crime. His disorder providence relieves by allowing him to amass money. Such a one, in the uneasiness of a conscience stained with guilt, while he contrasts his character with his fortune, perchance grows alarmed lest he should come to mourn the loss of that whose possession is so pleasant to him. He will, then, reform his ways, and through the fear of losing his fortune he forsakes his iniquity. Some, through a prosperity unworthily borne, have been hurled headlong to ruin; to some the power of the sword has been committed, to the end that the good may be tried by discipline, and the bad punished. For while there can be no peace between the righteous and the wicked, neither can the wicked agree among themselves. How should they, when each is at variance with himself, because his vices rend his conscience, and ofttimes they do things which, when they are done, they judge ought not to have been done. Hence it is that this supreme providence brings to pass this notable marvel—that the bad make the bad good. For some, when they see the injustice which they themselves suffer at the hands of evil-doers, are inflamed with detestation of the offenders, and, in the endeavour to be unlike those whom they hate, return to the ways of virtue. It is the divine power alone to which things evil are also good, in that, by putting them to suitable use, it brings them in the end to some good issue. For order in some way or other embraces all things, so that even that which has departed from the appointed laws of the order, nevertheless falls within an order, though another order, that nothing in the realm of providence may be left to haphazard. But

Hard were the task, as a god, to recount all, nothing omitting.

Nor, truly, is it lawful for man to compass in thought all the mechanism of the divine work, or set it forth in speech. Let us be content to have apprehended this only—that God, the creator of universal nature, likewise disposes all things, and guides them to good; and while He studies to preserve in likeness to Himself all that He has created, He banishes all evil from the borders of His commonweal through the links of fatal necessity. Whereby it comes to pass that, if you look to disposing providence, you will nowhere find the evils which are believed so to abound on earth.

'But I see you have long been burdened with the weight of the subject, and fatigued with the prolixity of the argument, and now looks for some refreshment of sweet poesy. Listen, then, and may the draught so restore you that you will bend your mind more resolutely to what remains.'

BENEDICT DE SPINOZA, ETHICS

INTRODUCTION

Spinoza has been called 'the noblest and most lovable of all the great philosophers'.[1] Where he is noble, it is in his commitment to establishing the ethical basis for self-actualization and the expansion of man's powers of action. Where he is lovable, it is in appreciating the role that the emotions have to play in the matter. Spinoza's unique contribution to the evolution of virtue ethics is in humanising the idea of virtue and advocating for its cultivation in the context of the human being as a whole.

Baruch Spinoza, or 'Benedict de Spinoza' as he later called himself, was born in Amsterdam on 24 November 1632 into a prominent family in Amsterdam's Portuguese-Jewish community. Spinoza was from an early age made familiar with the Talmud and the writings of various representatives of Jewish medieval thought; later, in addition to that, he sought and obtained instruction in Latin, which opened up to him the world of modern philosophy and science that was represented most notably by Descartes. Perhaps as a result of his criticism

1. Bertrand Russell, *History of Western Philosophy* (London: Routledge, 2000), 552.

of established religion, Spinoza became estranged from Jewish orthodoxy, and in 1656 he was ultimately excommunicated from the faith: the members of the synagogue were prohibited from having any relationship with him, or from reading or listening to what he might have to say. Prompted by an attack on him as he was leaving a theatre, and probably looking for a quiet place to carry out his philosophical work, in 1661 Spinoza moved to the coastal town of Rijnsburg, where he worked on a study of Descartes, as well beginning work on his *Ethics*. Moving in the mid 1660s to The Hague, in 1670 Spinoza published his controversial *Tractatus Theologico-Politicus*, which argued that divine law was fixed and eternal (and could not be changed even by divine will) and that the scriptures were a historical rather than divine document. Spinoza lived an outwardly simple life and earned a modest living as an optical lens grinder. He died at the age of 44 in 1677 from a lung illness—the same year in which his greatest work, the *Ethics*, was published, a few months after his death.

To fully understand the *Ethics*, the reader must first engage with Spinoza's metaphysics and, in particular, with his notion of God. For Spinoza, the world—everything that exists—is divided into substance and modes. Substance is that which needs nothing else to exist: it is what we might more colloquially refer to as fundamental reality or essence. A mode, on the other hand, is something that needs a substance in order to exist: modes may be conceived of as local, individual instantiations of substance. There is only one substance that we can refer to as 'God' or 'Nature'. Cats, dogs, rocks, chairs, and all other individual things are just modes of this substance, which becomes cat- or dog-like at one place and time, and rock- or chair-like at another. God is therefore immanent within all things, but not as inert matters: rather, God is the fixed and unchangeable *order* of nature—its structuring laws and its chain of causes and effects.

The fact that God constitutes the same reality as the laws of nature means that there is no intelligent designer or 'grand watchmaker' standing outside creation and directing its affairs; God has no intellect or will, as such, being the sum of all causes and all laws, and his intellect the sum of all mind. Spinoza accepts that humans are predisposed to imagine the divinity in a human form, just as a triangle, he suggests, would say, if it could speak, that God is triangular, and a circle that He is circular. It is through projecting, anthropomorphically, our human will onto the deity that we take God to act for particular ends that are (or may be) comprehensive and agreeable to mankind. In fact, says Spinoza, God neither exists nor acts for an end. What we call 'final causes'—causes for which acts are done—are in reality nothing more than human desires projected onto the manifold nature of the world. The universe has no purpose; it simply exists because God is what God is.

'Good' and 'bad', then, are not absolutes or positive qualities regarded as things in themselves. There can be nothing imperfect or incomplete in God or Nature, since there is no end towards which it is striving and then falls short. To the extent to which anything seems to us ridiculous, absurd, or evil, it is because we have but partial knowledge of things, and because we want everything arranged according to the dictates of our own limited reason. Good and bad are, in fact, merely modes of thinking that are formed when we compare one thing with another. One and the same thing can be at the same time good, bad, or indifferent, observes Spinoza: music that is good for the melancholy may be bad for those who mourn, and for the deaf a matter of complete indifference.

Virtue, for Spinoza, is defined not by reference to an external system of values but as 'action in accordance with the laws of one's own nature', or—to put it in more modern terms—'the power of each individual to actualise its essence'.[2] Happiness, he says, is the goal of conduct, and happiness is considered to be the presence of pleasure and absence of pain. What distinguishes Spinoza's ethics from other philosophies of pleasure, however, lies in the details of what is meant by 'pleasure' and 'pain', for 'pleasure' signifies man's transition from a lesser state of perfection to a greater, and 'pain' his transition from a greater state of perfection to a lesser—the 'perfection' of a thing being its 'power of action'. We are at our most virtuous, then, and most happy, when we are in the process of expanding the power of preserving and realizing our own being. 'The more every man endeavours, and is able to seek what is useful to him—in other words, to preserve his own being—the more is he endowed with virtue; on the contrary, in proportion as a man neglects to seek what is useful to him, that is, to preserve his own being, he is wanting in power.'

There is tremendous complexity wrapped up within Spinoza's tense and concentrated prose. Nevertheless, let me suggest that there are several ways in which what he has to say remains of value for the modern man.

First, Spinoza provides a version of virtue ethics that is distinct in building upon, but also transcending, the philosophies of his Aristotelian and Stoic forebears. Spinoza agrees with his predecessors that virtue is self-mastery and control over one's emotions: when man is driven this way and that by his passions, he is rendered passive and his power of action reduced—less truly himself. But there is also a special, positive role for emotions in this philosophy, for according to Spinoza an emotion cannot be hindered or removed except by another, stronger emotion. There is no point in putting reason, which is anodyne and toothless, up against emotion; what we need to do is to deploy the emotions themselves—coordinated

---

2. Beth Lord, *Spinoza's Ethics: An Edinburgh Guide* (Edinburgh: Edinburgh University Press, 2010), 108

by our reasoning capacity—against the ungoverned passions. Self-knowledge leads not to the subjugation of emotion to reason, but to a substitution of passive emotions by active ones that contribute to a man's overall power of action.

Second, Spinoza provides in his ethics a touchstone by which the particular emotions can be judged. Mirth and cheerfulness are always good, because it they are a form of pleasure that heightens our power of activity. Love, which is pleasure accompanied by an external cause, may overcome all the rest of our emotions, and therefore impede our power; hatred, which reeks of powerlessness—since what we have power over we do not hate—can never be good. Hope and fear cannot be in themselves good, for fear is pain and hope cannot exist without fear, except insofar as they can be used to restrain excessive pleasure. Pity is bad and useless—which is not to say that we cannot take action, under the guidance of reason, to assist people who suffer. Humility is not a virtue as it is a pain arising from the contemplation of our own infirmities; nor is repentance, which is doubly noxious insofar as its presence indicates that we have allowed ourselves to be overcome first by evil desires, and secondarily by pain.

Above all, Spinoza sketches out for us a path towards human realisation and freedom both on a personal and a social level. Just as his 'God' and 'Nature' are self-sufficient in themselves, so man's proper virtue is the self-actualization which is the heightening and expansion of his own powers, and indeed it is precisely through the rational expansion of man's powers that society can be established and maintained. This is freedom not in the idle and sterile sense of liberty to do as one pleases; it is freedom in the sense of the holistic development of a man's inner self consistent with his rational mastery of self and world. The poet William Butler Yeats famously and presciently imagined, in his poem 'The Second Coming', an era of history to come in which 'The best lack all conviction, while the worst/ Are full of passionate intensity'. If there is an ethical path that might be opposed to this baleful trend, it is Spinoza's.

PART IV. OF HUMAN BONDAGE, OR THE STRENGTH OF THE EMOTIONS.

PREFACE

Human infirmity in moderating and checking the emotions I name bondage: for, when a man is a prey to his emotions, he is not his own master, but lies at the mercy of fortune: so much so, that he is often compelled, while seeing that which is better for him, to follow that which is worse. Why this is so, and what is good or evil in the emotions, I propose to show in this part of my treatise. But, before I begin, it would be well to make a few prefatory observations on perfection and imperfection, good and evil.

When a man has purposed to make a given thing, and has brought it to perfection, his work will be pronounced perfect, not only by himself, but by everyone who rightly knows, or thinks that he knows, the intention and aim of its author. For instance, suppose anyone sees a work (which I assume to be not yet completed), and knows that the aim of the author of that work is to build a house, he will call the work imperfect; he will, on the other hand, call it perfect, as soon as he sees that it is carried through to the end, which its author had purposed for it. But if a man sees a work, the like whereof he has never seen before, and if he knows not the intention of the artificer, he plainly cannot know whether that work be perfect or imperfect. Such seems to be the primary meaning of these terms.

But, after men began to form general ideas, to think out types of houses, buildings, towers, &c., and to prefer certain types to others, it came about that each man called perfect that which he saw agree with the general idea he had formed of the thing in question, and called imperfect that which he saw agree less with his own preconceived type, even though it had evidently been completed in accordance with the idea of its artificer. This seems to be the only reason for calling natural phenomena, which, indeed, are not made with human hands, perfect or imperfect: for men are wont to form general ideas of things natural, no less than of things artificial, and such ideas they hold as types, believing that Nature (who they think does nothing without an object) has them in view, and has set them as types before herself. Therefore, when they behold something in Nature, which does not wholly conform to the preconceived type which they have formed of the thing in question, they say that Nature has fallen short or has blundered, and has left her work incomplete. Thus we see that men are wont to style natural phenomena perfect or imperfect rather from their own prejudices, than from true knowledge of what they pronounce upon.

Now we showed in the Appendix to Part I, that Nature does not work with an end in view. For the eternal and infinite Being, which we call God or Nature, acts by the same necessity as that whereby it exists. For we have shown, that by the same necessity of its nature, whereby it exists, it likewise works (I. xvi.). The reason or cause why God or Nature exists, and the reason why he acts, are one and the same. Therefore, as he does not exist for the sake of an end, so neither does he act for the sake of an end; of his existence and of his action there is neither origin nor end. Wherefore, a cause which is called final is nothing else but human desire, in so far as it is considered as the origin or cause of anything. For example, when we say that to be inhabited is the final cause of this or that house, we mean nothing more than that a man, conceiving the conveniences of household life, had a desire to build a house. Wherefore, the being inhabited, in so far as it is regarded as a final cause, is nothing else but this particular desire, which is really the efficient cause; it is regarded as the primary cause, because men are generally ignorant of the causes of their desires. They are, as I have often said already, conscious of their own actions and appetites, but ignorant of the causes whereby they are determined to any particular desire. Therefore, the common saying that Nature sometimes falls short, or blunders, and produces things which are imperfect, I set down among the glosses treated of in the Appendix to Part I. Perfection and imperfection, then, are in reality merely modes of thinking, or notions which we form from a comparison among one another of individuals of the same species; hence I said above (II. Def. vi.) that by reality and perfection I mean the same thing. For we are wont to refer all the individual things in nature to one genus, which is called the highest genus, namely, to the category of Being, whereto absolutely all individuals in nature belong. Thus, in so far as we refer the individuals in nature to this category, and comparing them one with another, find that some possess more of being or reality than others, we, to this extent, say that some are more perfect than others. Again, in so far as we attribute to them anything implying negation—as term, end, infirmity, etc.—we, to this extent, call them imperfect, because they do not affect our mind so much as the things which we call perfect, not because they have any intrinsic deficiency, or because Nature has blundered. For nothing lies within the scope of a thing's nature, save that which follows from the necessity of the nature of its efficient cause, and whatsoever follows from the necessity of the nature of its efficient cause necessarily comes to pass.

As for the terms good and bad, they indicate no positive quality in things regarded in themselves, but are merely modes of thinking, or notions which we form from the comparison of things one with another. Thus one and the same thing can be at the same time good, bad, and indifferent. For instance, music is good for him that is melancholy, bad for him that mourns; for him that is deaf, it is neither good nor bad.

Nevertheless, though this be so, the terms should still be retained. For, inasmuch as we desire to form an idea of man as a type of human nature which we may hold in view, it will be useful for us to retain the terms in question, in the sense I have indicated.

In what follows, then, I shall mean by 'good' that which we certainly know to be a means of approaching more nearly to the type of human nature, which we have set before ourselves; by 'bad', that which we certainly know to be a hindrance to us in approaching the said type. Again, we shall say that men are more perfect, or more imperfect, in proportion as they approach more or less nearly to the said type. For it must be specially remarked that when I say that a man passes from a lesser to a greater perfection, or vice versa, I do not mean that he is changed from one essence or reality to another; for instance, a horse would be as completely destroyed by being changed into a man, as by being changed into an insect. What I mean is that we conceive the thing's power of action, in so far as this is understood by its nature, to be increased or diminished. Lastly, by perfection in general I shall, as I have said, mean reality—in other words, each thing's essence, in so far as it exists, and operates in a particular manner, and without paying any regard to its duration. For no given thing can be said to be more perfect because it has passed a longer time in existence. The duration of things cannot be determined by their essence, for the essence of things involves no fixed and definite period of existence; but everything, whether it be more perfect or less perfect, will always be able to persist in existence with the same force wherewith it began to exist; wherefore, in this respect, all things are equal.

Prop. XX. *The more every man endeavours, and is able to seek what is useful to him—in other words, to preserve his own being—the more is he endowed with virtue; on the contrary, in proportion as a man neglects to seek what is useful to him, that is, to preserve his own being, he is wanting in power.*

Proof.—Virtue is human power, which is defined solely by man's essence (IV. Def. viii.), that is, which is defined solely by the endeavour made by man to persist in his own being. Wherefore, the more a man endeavours, and is able to preserve his own being, the more is he endowed with virtue, and, consequently (III. iv. and vi.), in so far as a man neglects to preserve his own being, he is wanting in power. Q.E.D.

Note.—No one, therefore, neglects seeking his own good, or preserving his own being, unless he be overcome by causes external and foreign to his nature. No one, I say, from the necessity of his own nature, or otherwise than under compulsion from external causes, shrinks from food, or kills himself: which latter may be done in a variety of ways. A man, for instance, kills himself under the compulsion of another man, who twists round his right hand, wherewith he happened to have taken up a sword, and forces him to turn the blade against his own heart; or, again, he may be compelled, like Seneca, by a tyrant's command, to open his own veins—that is, to escape a greater evil by incurring a lesser; or, lastly, latent external causes may so disorder his imagination, and so affect his body, that it may assume a nature contrary to its former one, and whereof the idea cannot exist in the mind (III. x.). But that a man, from the necessity of his own nature, should endeavour to become non-existent, is as impossible as that something should be made out of nothing, as everyone will see for himself, after a little reflection.

Prop. XXIV. *To act absolutely in obedience to virtue is in us the same thing as to act, to live, or to preserve one's being (these three terms are identical in meaning) in accordance with the dictates of reason on the basis of seeking what is useful to one's self.*

Proof.—To act absolutely in obedience to virtue is nothing else but to act according to the laws of one's own nature. But we only act, in so far as we understand (III. iii.): therefore to act in obedience to virtue is in us nothing else but to act, to live, or to preserve one's being in obedience to reason, and that on the basis of seeking what is useful for us (IV. xxii. Coroll.). Q.E.D.

Prop. XXV. *No one wishes to preserve his being for the sake of anything else.*

Proof.—The endeavour, wherewith everything endeavours to persist in its being, is defined solely by the essence of the thing itself (III. vii.); from this alone, and not from the essence of anything else, it necessarily follows (III. vi.) that everyone endeavours to preserve his being. Moreover, this proposition is plain from IV. xxii. Coroll., for if a man should endeavour to preserve his being for the sake of anything else, the last-named thing would obviously be the basis of virtue, which, by the foregoing corollary, is absurd. Therefore no one, &c. Q.E.D.

Prop. XLI. *Pleasure in itself is not bad but good: contrariwise, pain in itself is bad.*

Proof.—Pleasure (III. xi. and note) is emotion, whereby the body's power of activity is increased or helped; pain is emotion, whereby the body's power of activity is diminished or checked; therefore (IV. xxxviii.) pleasure in itself is good, &c. Q.E.D.

Prop. XLII. *Mirth cannot be excessive, but is always good; contrariwise, Melancholy is always bad.*

Proof.—Mirth (see its Def. in III. xi. note) is pleasure, which, in so far as it is referred to the body, consists in all parts of the body being affected equally: that is (III. xi.), the body's power of activity is increased or aided in such a manner, that the several parts maintain their former proportion of motion and rest; therefore Mirth is always good (IV. xxxix.), and cannot be excessive. But Melancholy (see its Def. in the same note to III. xi.) is pain, which, in so far as it is referred to the body, consists in the absolute decrease or hindrance of the body's power of activity; therefore (IV. xxxviii.) it is always bad. Q.E.D.

Prop. XLIII. *Stimulation may be excessive and bad; on the other hand, grief may be good, in so far as stimulation or pleasure is bad.*
Proof.—Localized pleasure or stimulation (titillatio) is pleasure, which, in so far as it is referred to the body, consists in one or some of its parts being affected more than the rest (see its Definition, III. xi. note); the power of this emotion may be sufficient to overcome other actions of the body (IV. vi.), and may remain obstinately fixed therein, thus rendering it incapable of being affected in a variety of other ways: therefore (IV. xxxviii.) it may be bad. Again, grief, which is pain, cannot as such be good (IV. xli.). But, as its force and increase is defined by the power of an external cause compared with our own (IV. v.), we can conceive infinite degrees and modes of strength in this emotion (IV. iii.); we can, therefore, conceive it as capable of restraining stimulation, and preventing its becoming excessive, and hindering the body's capabilities; thus, to this extent, it will be good. Q.E.D.

Prop. XLIV. *Love and desire may be excessive.*
Proof.—Love is pleasure, accompanied by the idea of an external cause (Def. of Emotions, vi.); therefore stimulation

accompanied by the idea of an external cause is love (III. xi. note); hence love maybe excessive. Again, the strength of desire varies in proportion to the emotion from which it arises (III. xxxvii.). Now emotion may overcome all the rest of men's actions (IV. vi.); so, therefore, can desire, which arises from the same emotion, overcome all other desires, and become excessive, as we showed in the last proposition concerning stimulation.

Note.—Mirth, which I have stated to be good, can be conceived more easily than it can be observed. For the emotions, whereby we are daily assailed, are generally referred to some part of the body which is affected more than the rest; hence the emotions are generally excessive, and so fix the mind in the contemplation of one object, that it is unable to think of others; and although men, as a rule, are a prey to many emotions—and very few are found who are always assailed by one and the same—yet there are cases, where one and the same emotion remains obstinately fixed. We sometimes see men so absorbed in one object, that, although it be not present, they think they have it before them; when this is the case with a man who is not asleep, we say he is delirious or mad; nor are those persons who are inflamed with love, and who dream all night and all day about nothing but their mistress, or some woman, considered as less mad, for they are made objects of ridicule. But when a miser thinks of nothing but gain or money, or when an ambitious man thinks of nothing but glory, they are not reckoned to be mad, because they are generally harmful, and are thought worthy of being hated. But, in reality, Avarice, Ambition, Lust, &c., are species of madness, though they may not be reckoned among diseases.

Prop. XLV. *Hatred can never be good.*

Proof.—When we hate a man, we endeavour to destroy him (III. xxxix.), that is (IV. xxxvii.), we endeavour to do something that is bad. Therefore, &c. Q.E.D.

N.B. Here, and in what follows, I mean by hatred only hatred towards men.

Corollary I.—Envy, derision, contempt, anger, revenge, and other emotions attributable to hatred, or arising therefrom, are bad; this is evident from III. xxxix. and IV. xxxvii.

Corollary II.—Whatsoever we desire from motives of hatred is base, and in a State unjust. This also is evident from III. xxxix., and from the definitions of baseness and injustice in IV. xxxvii. note.

Note.—Between derision (which I have in Coroll. I. stated to be bad) and laughter I recognize a great difference. For laughter, as also jocularity, is merely pleasure; therefore, so long as it be not excessive, it is in itself good (IV. xli.). Assuredly nothing forbids man to enjoy himself, save grim and gloomy superstition. For why is it more lawful to satiate one's hunger and thirst than to drive away one's melancholy? I reason, and have convinced myself as follows: No deity, nor anyone else, save the envious, takes pleasure in my infirmity and discomfort, nor sets down to my virtue the tears, sobs, fear, and the like, which are signs of infirmity of spirit; on the contrary, the greater the pleasure wherewith we are affected, the greater the perfection whereto we pass; in other words, the more must we necessarily partake of the divine nature. Therefore, to make use of what comes in our way, and to enjoy it as much as possible (not to the point of satiety, for that would not be enjoyment) is the part of a wise man. I say it is the part of a wise man to refresh and recreate himself with moderate and pleasant food and drink, and also with perfumes, with the soft beauty of growing plants, with dress, with music, with many sports, with theatres, and the like, such as every man may make use of without injury to his neighbour. For the human body is composed of very numerous parts, of diverse nature, which continually stand in need of fresh and varied nourishment, so that the whole body may be equally capable of performing all the actions, which follow from the necessity of its own nature; and, consequently, so that the mind may also be equally capable of understanding many things simultaneously. This way of life, then, agrees best with our principles, and also with general practice; therefore, if there be any question of another plan, the plan we have mentioned is the best, and in every way to be commended. There is no need for me to set forth the matter more clearly or in more detail.

Prop. XLVII. *Emotions of hope and fear cannot be in themselves good.*
Proof.—Emotions of hope and fear cannot exist without pain. For fear is pain (Def. of the Emotions, xiii.), and hope (Def. of the Emotions, Explanation xii. and xiii.) cannot exist without fear; therefore (IV. xli.) these emotions cannot be good in themselves, but only in so far as they can restrain excessive pleasure (IV. xliii.). Q.E.D.

Note.—We may add that these emotions show defective knowledge and an absence of power in the mind; for the same reason confidence, despair, joy, and disappointment are signs of a want of mental power. For although confidence and joy are pleasurable emotions, they nevertheless imply a preceding pain, namely, hope and fear. Wherefore the more we endeavour to be guided by reason, the less do we depend on hope; we endeavour to free ourselves from fear, and, as far as we can, to dominate fortune, directing our actions by the sure counsels of wisdom.

Part V. Of the Power of the Understanding, or of Human Freedom.

Prop. X. *So long as we are not assailed by emotions contrary to our nature, we have the power of arranging and associating the modifications of our body according to the intellectual order.*

Proof.—The emotions, which are contrary to our nature, that is (IV. xxx.), which are bad, are bad in so far as they impede the mind from understanding (IV. xxvii.). So long, therefore, as we are not assailed by emotions contrary to our nature, the mind's power, whereby it endeavours to understand things (IV. xxvi.), is not impeded, and therefore it is able to form clear and distinct ideas and to deduce them one from another (II. xl. note. ii. and II. xlvii. note); consequently we have in such cases the power of arranging and associating the modifications of the body according to the intellectual order. Q.E.D.

Note.—By this power of rightly arranging and associating the bodily modifications we can guard ourselves from being easily affected by evil emotions. For (V. vii.) a greater force is needed for controlling the emotions, when they are arranged and associated according to the intellectual order, than when they, are uncertain and unsettled. The best we can do, therefore, so long as we do not possess a perfect knowledge of our emotions, is to frame a system of right conduct, or fixed practical precepts, to commit it to memory, and to apply it forthwith to the particular circumstances which now and again meet us in life, so that our imagination may become fully imbued therewith, and that it may be always ready to our hand. For instance, we have laid down among the rules of life (IV. xlvi. and note), that hatred should be overcome with love or high-mindedness, and not required with hatred in return. Now, that this precept of reason may be always ready to our hand in time of need, we should often think over and reflect upon the wrongs generally committed by men, and in what manner and way they may be best warded off by high-mindedness: we shall thus associate the idea of wrong with the idea of this precept, which accordingly will always be ready for use when a wrong is done to us (II. xviii.). If we keep also in readiness the notion of our true advantage, and of the good which follows from mutual friendships, and common fellowships; further, if we remember that complete acquiescence is the result of the right way of life (IV. lii.), and that men, no less than everything else, act by the necessity of their nature: in such case I say the wrong, or the hatred, which commonly arises therefrom, will engross a very small part of our imagination and will be easily overcome; or, if the anger which springs from a grievous wrong be not overcome easily, it will nevertheless be overcome, though not without a spiritual conflict, far sooner than if we had not thus reflected on the subject beforehand. As is indeed evident from V. vi. vii. viii. We should, in the same way, reflect on courage as a means of overcoming fear; the ordinary dangers of life should frequently be brought to mind and imagined, together with the means whereby through readiness of resource and strength of mind we can avoid and overcome them. But we must note, that in arranging our thoughts and conceptions we should always bear in mind that which is good in every individual thing (IV. lxiii. Coroll. and III. lix.), in order that we may always be determined to action by an emotion of pleasure. For instance, if a man sees that he is too keen in the pursuit of honour, let him think over its right use, the end for which it should be pursued, and the means whereby he may attain it. Let him not think of its misuse, and its emptiness, and the fickleness of mankind, and the like, whereof no man thinks except through a morbidness of disposition; with thoughts like these do the most ambitious most torment themselves, when they despair of gaining the distinctions they hanker after, and in thus giving vent to their anger would fain appear wise. Wherefore it is certain that those, who cry out the loudest against the misuse of honour and the vanity of the world, are those who most greedily covet it. This is not peculiar to the ambitious, but is common to all who are ill-used by fortune, and who are infirm in spirit. For a poor man also, who is miserly, will talk incessantly of the misuse of wealth and of the vices of the rich; whereby he merely torments himself, and shows the world that he is intolerant, not only of his own poverty, but also of other people's riches. So, again, those who have been ill received by a woman they love think of nothing but the inconstancy, treachery, and other stock faults of the fair sex; all of which they consign to oblivion, directly they are again taken into favour by their sweetheart. Thus he who would govern his emotions and appetite solely by the love of freedom strives, as far as he can, to gain a knowledge of the virtues and their causes, and to fill his spirit with the joy which arises from the true knowledge of them: he will in no wise desire to dwell on men's faults, or to carp at his fellows, or to revel in a false show of freedom. Whosoever will diligently observe and practise these precepts (which indeed are not difficult) will verily, in a short space of time, be able, for the most part, to direct his actions according to the commandments of reason.

DAVID HUME, A TREATISE ON HUMAN NATURE

Introduction

It is one of the great misconceptions that the ethical approach to life needs to pit a man against his society. Virtue ethics, as we have seen, conceives of the ethical life as a life lived in pursuit of personal excellence. This can take several forms. For Plato, it involved the cultivation of a well-regulated and harmonious inner state; for Aristotle, it meant making a habit of pursuing the 'golden mean' between corresponding vices; while for the Stoics, what was required was self-mastery and emotional detachment from the outcome of our actions. What is left out of these accounts is the social aspect of moral approbation or blame—the realisation that the conduct we call good and bad must, to some degree, be that which receives approval, or disapproval, from society as a whole. Of all the moral philosophers, it was David Hume who most clearly addressed this aspect of the matter. Virtue could never, he insisted, be attained by the self-regarding and the solipsistic.

Instead, the virtuous man must be socially aware and pleasing to others—convivial, urbane, and above all responsive to his fellow men.

David Hume (1711-1776) was one of the great philosophers of the Scottish enlightenment and perhaps one of the greatest skeptical philosophers of all time. Born in the early eighteenth century in Edinburgh, he was a precious boy in a precocious age, following his older brother to the University of Edinburgh at the age of only 11 or 12. As a result of his studious disposition and industriousness, his family hoped that he would pursue a career in the law, but he found in himself 'an unsurmountable aversion to every thing but the pursuits of philosophy and general learning'. Hume left university in 1729 without graduating, and dedicated the next several years to the solitary study of philosophy. Having only a slender fortune at his disposal, in 1734 he sought work in commerce at Bristol. Nevertheless, after working for a few months for a sugar merchant, he took off for France with a view to continuing his studies in a country retreat, resolving 'to make a very rigid frugality supply my deficiency of fortune, to maintain unimpaired my independency, and to regard every object as contemptible, except the improvement of my talents in literature.' It was there, at the age of only 23, that he began writing what would become his chief philosophical work, *A Treatise of Human Nature* (1738). After passing three years in France, he returned to England in 1737, and had published the *Treatise* by the end of 1738. It fell, so he records, 'dead-born from the press'. Soon recovering from the blow, he set to work on his essays, which several years later were published as *An Enquiry concerning Human Understanding* (1748) and *An Enquiry concerning the Principles of Morals* (1751), although none of this was enough to secure an academic career: he was turned down for a professorship at both Edinburgh University and then Glasgow University. Eventually, Hume secured a position as librarian to the Edinburgh Faculty of Advocates, which provided little in the way of remuneration but gave him the 'command of a large library'. He used it to write his *History of England* (1754-1762), which became a bestseller and gave Hume the financial independence he had always wanted. In 1763 he accepted a position as secretary to the British ambassador to France, and he stayed in Paris for two years, even acting for a short time as the British Embassy's *charge d'affaires*. By the time he returned to Edinburgh he was an affluent man, and he spent the final few years of his life revising his work. He died in 1776, but not before arranging for posthumous publication of his most controversial work, the *Dialogues concerning Natural Religion* (1779).

Hume's starting point is that everyone has it wrong in assuming there is some way of establishing moral imperatives from the observation of any factual state of affairs: that is to say, he observes that in every established moral system, there is always at some point a sudden shift in the reasoning from statements of fact, i.e. what 'is, and is not' (for example, the existence of God or some phenomenon of human nature), to statements of what 'ought' or 'ought not' to be, without there being a satisfactory logical connection between the two (the 'is-ought problem'). Hume prefers a naturalistic approach: consider what there is in any action considered to be virtuous or vicious, he says, and you will find nothing in it of the 'ought' or 'ought not'; you will only grasp the moral element when you turn your reflection inwards and find a sentiment of moral approval or blame, which arises in you, towards the action. Morals cannot, he adds, be purely a product of reason, for it is one thing to know virtue, and another to conform the will to it; morals go beyond reason because they excite passions and produce or prevent actions, and reason is 'utterly impotent' in this regard. Moral feelings arise instead through the working of a 'moral sense': virtue appears to us, through the functioning of this sense, in the form of an agreeable impression, whereas vice gives us uneasy one. An action or character is virtuous or vicious precisely because viewing it causes a pleasure or uneasiness of a particular kind.

The first broad category of moral rules that Hume identifies are those concerning 'justice and property'. He calls these the artificial virtues, because although he considers them to be obvious and absolutely necessary to the wellbeing of mankind, they do not arise spontaneously and immediately. Instead, each individual man has an interest in observing a convention whereby the rights and property of all are respected, despite the fact that respect for these rules might, on discrete occasions, work contrary to his particular interests. Every member of society is sensible of this interest: 'everyone expresses this sense to his fellows, along with the resolution he has taken of squaring his actions by it, on condition that others will do the same.' We never fail to recognise the prejudice we receive from the injustice of others, says Hume, and even when injustice is distant from us it displeases us, because it is prejudicial to human society and makes us feel uneasy. The same principle is true for the observance of promises as it is for the protection of property: we are willing to perform our obligations to others, without feeling any real kindness towards them, because we foresee that they will return the favour, in expectation of further service of the same kind—and alongside this interest there arises a moral 'sentiment' (or feeling) that those who observe these rules are 'good' and those who break them 'bad'.

The second category of moral rules are what Hume calls the 'natural virtues and vices' such as arise spontaneously and without any contrivance on our part. The good that arises from the natural virtues is one that arises in every particular case, rather than (as with the artificial virtues) merely 'on the whole': for example, the kind-hearted acts of a benevolent man are always beneficial and pleasing to society generally. Every quality of mind which gives pleasure, Hume suggests, is considered virtuous, and every quality of mind that produces pain is called vicious. This begs the question: which 'qualities of mind' cause pleasure and which cause pain? One type will be obvious: persons whose qualities dispose them to be useful to others will cause pleasure and hence be considered virtuous. We also approve of persons who are possessed of natural abilities which render them 'useful to themselves'—such as prudence and discretion, industry, perseverance, patience, good sense, and wisdom—as it is impossible without these to execute any design to success. Wit and eloquence are valued because they are agreeable to others; good humour, because it is agreeable to the person himself. In all cases, sympathy is the glue that holds together Hume's moral universe, for it is sympathy that arouses our moral feelings when we are not ourselves immediately affected by, or in the presence of, the characters whose qualities of mind are said to engage our moral sense. 'A violent cough in another gives us unease,' explains Hume, 'though in itself it does not in the least affect us.'

Underlying Hume's system of moral philosophy is his awareness of the importance and difficulty of preserving civil society in the face of man's lust for material gain. All the other passions, Hume says, are either easily restrained or not so harmful when indulged (e.g. vanity), or they operate only at intervals and are directed against particular persons considered as superiors and enemies (e.g. envy and revenge). The general hunger for property, however, is of a different scope and intensity altogether. 'This avidity alone, of acquiring goods and possessions for ourselves and our nearest friends, is insatiable, perpetual, universal, and directly destructive of society,' observes Hume. 'There scarce is any one, who is not actuated by it; and there is no one, who has not reason to fear from it, when it acts without any restraint, and gives way to its first and most natural movements.'

Hume's philosophy is not, however, simply that of the property owner; it is just as much the philosophy of the amiable good-natured man and the *bon viveur*. But Hume was no Epicurean—for making oneself happy is only part of the picture; nor was he a utilitarian *avant la lettre*—for there is a distinct place in Hume's philosophy for gaiety, sweetness and light, and other such unmeasurables. Ethics, for Hume, is rather the means by which a man adapts to the society of which he is a part, making himself useful and pleasing both to himself and to others. If ever there was an ethics for the 'man of the world'—a balanced ethics based upon what men in society actually call 'good' and 'bad' rather than dogmatic prescription—then this is it.

BOOK III: OF MORALS

PART III

OF THE OTHER VIRTUES AND VICES

SECTION I

OF THE ORIGIN OF THE NATURAL VIRTUES AND VICES

We come now to the examination of such virtues and vices as are entirely natural, and have no dependence on the artifice and contrivance of men. The examination of these will conclude this system of morals.

The chief spring or actuating principle of the human mind is pleasure or pain; and when these sensations are removed, both from our thought and feeling, we are, in a great measure, incapable of passion or action, of desire or volition. The most immediate effects of pleasure and pain are the propense and averse motions of the mind; which are diversified into volition, into desire and aversion, grief and joy, hope and fear, according as the pleasure or pain changes its situation, and becomes probable or improbable, certain or uncertain, or is considered as out of our power for the present moment. But when along with this, the objects that cause pleasure or pain acquire a relation to ourselves or others, they still continue to excite desire and aversion, grief and joy; but cause, at the same time, the indirect passions of pride or humility, love or hatred, which in this case have a double relation of impressions and ideas to the pain or pleasure.

We have already observed, that moral distinctions depend entirely on certain peculiar sentiments of pain and pleasure, and that whatever mental quality in ourselves or others gives us a satisfaction, by the survey or reflection, is of course virtuous; as everything of this nature that gives uneasiness is vicious. Now since every quality in ourselves or others, which gives pleasure, always causes pride or love, as every one that produces uneasiness excites humility or hatred, it follows, that these two particulars are to be considered as equivalent, with regard to our mental qualities, *virtue* and the power of producing love or pride, *vice* and the power of producing humility or hatred. In every case, therefore, we must judge of the one by the other, and may pronounce any *quality* of the mind virtuous, which causes love or pride, and any one vicious, which causes hatred or humility.

If any *action* be either virtuous or vicious, it is only as a sign of some quality or character. It must depend upon durable principles of the mind, which extend over the whole conduct, and enter into the personal character. Actions themselves, not proceeding from any constant principle, have no influence on love or hatred, pride or humility; and consequently are never considered in morality.

This refection is self-evident, and deserves to be attended

to, as being of the utmost importance in the present subject. We are never to consider any single action in our enquiries conceding the origin of morals, but only the quality or character from which the action proceeded. These alone are durable enough to affect our sentiments concerning the person. Actions are, indeed, better indications of a character than words, or even wishes and sentiments; but it is only so far as they are such indications, that they are attended with love or hatred, praise or blame.

To discover the true origin of morals, and of that love or hatred, which arises from mental qualities, we must take the matter pretty deep, and compare some principles which have been already examined and explained.

We may begin with considering anew the nature and force of *sympathy*. The minds of all men are similar in their feelings and operations nor can any one be actuated by any affection, of which all others are not, in some degree, susceptible. As in strings equally wound up, the motion of one communicates itself to the rest; so all the affections readily pass from one person to another, and beget correspondent movements in every human creature. When I see the *effects* of passion in the voice and gesture of any person, my mind immediately passes from these effects to their causes, and forms such a lively idea of the passion, as is presently converted into the passion itself. In like manner, when I perceive the *causes* of any emotion, my mind is conveyed to the effects, and is actuated with a like emotion. Were I present at any of the more terrible operations of surgery, it is certain, that even before it begun, the preparation of the instruments, the laying of the bandages in order, the heating of the irons, with all the signs of anxiety and concern in the patient and assistants, would have a great effect upon my mind, and excite the strongest sentiments of pity and terror. No passion of another discovers itself immediately to the mind. We are only sensible of its causes or effects. From *these* we infer the passion; and consequently *these* give rise to our sympathy.

Our sense of beauty depends very much on this principle; and where any object has a tendency to produce pleasure in its possessor, it is always regarded as beautiful; as every object that has a tendency to produce pain is disagreeable and deformed. Thus the convenience of a house, the fertility of a field, the strength of a horse, the capacity, security, and swift-sailing of a vessel, form the principal beauty of these several objects. Here the object, which is denominated beautiful, pleases only by its tendency to produce a certain effect. That effect is the pleasure or advantage of some other person. Now the pleasure of a stranger, for whom we have no friendship, pleases us only by sympathy. To this principle, therefore, is owing the beauty which we find in everything that is useful. How considerable a part this is of beauty will easily appear upon reflection. Wherever an object has a tendency to produce pleasure in the possessor, or, in other words, is the proper cause of pleasure, it is sure to please the spectator, by a delicate sympathy with the possessor. Most of the works of art are esteemed beautiful, in proportion to their fitness for the use of man; and even many of the productions of nature derive their beauty from that source. Handsome and beautiful, on most occasions, is not an absolute but a relative quality, and pleases us by nothing but its tendency to produce an end that is agreeable.

The same principle produces, in many instances, our sentiments of morals, as well as those of beauty. No virtue is more esteemed than justice, and no vice more detested than injustice; nor are there any qualities which go further to the fixing the character, either as amiable or odious. Now justice is a moral virtue, merely because it has that tendency to the good of mankind; and, indeed, is nothing but an artificial invention to that purpose. The same may be said of allegiance, of the laws of nations, of modesty, and of good manners. All these are mere human contrivances for the interest of society. And since there is a very strong sentiment of morals, which in all nations and all ages has attended them, we must allow that the reflecting on the tendency of characters and mental qualities is sufficient to give us the sentiments of approbation and blame. Now as the means to an end can only be agreeable where the end is agreeable, and as the good of society, where our own interest is not concerned, or that of our friends, pleases only by sympathy, it follows, that sympathy is the source of the esteem which we pay to all the artificial virtues.

Thus it appears that sympathy is a very powerful principle in human nature, that it has a great influence on our taste of beauty, and that it produces our sentiment of morals in all the artificial virtues. From thence we may presume that it also gives rise to many of the other virtues, and that qualities acquire our approbation because of their tendency to the good of mankind. This presumption must become a certainty when we find that most of those qualities which we *naturally* approve of have actually that tendency, and render a man a proper member of society; while the qualities which we *naturally* disapprove of have a contrary tendency, and render any intercourse with the person dangerous or disagreeable. For having found that such tendencies have force enough to produce the strongest sentiment of morals, we can never reasonably, in these cases, look for any other cause of approbation or blame; it being an inviolable maxim in philosophy that where any particular cause is sufficient for an effect, we ought to rest satisfied with it, and ought not to multiply causes without necessity. We have happily attained experiments in the artificial virtues where the tendency of qualities to the good of society is the sole cause of our approbation, without any suspicion of the concurrence of another principle. From thence we learn the force of that principle. And where that principle may take place, and the quality approved of is really beneficial to society, a true philosopher will never require any other principle to account for the strongest approbation and esteem.

That many of the natural virtues have this tendency to the good of society, no one can doubt of. Meekness, beneficence, charity, generosity, clemency, moderation, equity, bear the greatest figure among the moral qualities, and are commonly denominated the *social* virtues to mark their tendency to the good of society. This goes so far, that some philosophers have represented all moral distinctions as the effect of artifice and education, when skilful politicians endeavoured to retrain the turbulent passions of men, and make them operate to the public good, by the notions of honour and shame. This system, however, is not consistent with experience. For, *first*, there are other virtues and vices beside those which have this tendency to the public advantage and loss. *Secondly*, had not men a natural sentiment of approbation and blame, it could never be excited by politicians; nor would the words *laudable* and *praiseworthy, blameable* and *odious*, be any more intelligible than if they were a language perfectly unknown to us, as we have already observed. But though this system be erroneous, it may teach us that moral distinctions arise, in a great measure, from the tendency of qualities and characters to the interests of society, and that it is our concern for that interest which makes us approve or disapprove of them. Now we have no such extensive concern for society but from sympathy; and consequently it is that principle which takes us so far out of ourselves as to give us the same pleasure or uneasiness in the characters of others, as if they had a tendency to our own advantage or loss.

The only difference betwixt the natural virtues and justice lies in this, that the good which results from the former arises from every single act, and is the object of some natural passion; whereas a single act of justice, considered in itself, may often be contrary to the public good; and it is only the concurrence of mankind, in a general scheme or system of action, which is advantageous. When I relieve persons in distress, my natural humanity is my motive; and so far as my succour extends, so far have I promoted the happiness of my fellow-creatures. But if we examine all the questions that come before any tribunal of justice, we shall find that, considering each case apart, it would as often be an instance of humanity to decide contrary to the laws of justice as conformable to them. Judges take from a poor man to give to a rich; they bestow on the dissolute the labour of the industrious, and put into the hands of the vicious the means of harming both themselves and others. The whole scheme, however, of law and justice is advantageous to the society, and it was with a view to this advantage that men, by their voluntary conventions, established it. After it is once established by these conventions, it is naturally attended with a strong sentiment of morals, which can proceed from nothing but our sympathy with the interests of society. We need no other explication of that esteem, which attends such of the natural virtues, as have a tendency to the public good. ...

If we examine the panegyrics that are commonly made of great men, we shall find that most of the qualities which are attributed to them may be divided into two kinds, viz. such as make them perform their part in society, and such as render them serviceable to themselves and enable them to promote their own interest. Their *prudence, temperance, frugality, industry, assiduity, enterprise, dexterity*, are celebrated, as well as their *generosity* and *humanity*. If we ever give an indulgence to any quality that disables a man from making a figure in life, it is to that of *indolence*, which is not supposed to deprive one of his parts and capacity, but only suspends their exercise, and that without any inconvenience to the person himself, since it is, in some measure, from his own choice. Yet indolence is always allowed to be a fault, and a very great one, if extreme; nor do a man's friends ever acknowledge him to be subject to it, but in order to save his character in more material articles. He could make a figure, say they, if he pleased to give application: his understanding is sound, his conception quick, and his memory tenacious; but he hates business, and is indifferent about his fortune. And this a man sometimes may make even a subject of vanity, though with the air of confessing a fault, because he may think that this incapacity for business implies much more noble qualities, such as a philosophical spirit, a fine taste, a delicate wit, or a relish for pleasure and society. But take any other case: suppose a quality that, without being an indication of any other good qualities, incapacitates a man always for business, and is destructive to his interest, such as a blundering understanding, and a wrong judgment of everything in life, inconstancy and irresolution, or a want of address in the management of men and business. These are all allowed to be imperfections in a character, and many men would rather acknowledge the greatest crimes than have it suspected that they are, in any degree, subject to them.

It is very happy, in our philosophical researches, when we find the same phenomenon diversified by a variety of circumstances, and, by discovering what is common among them, can the better assure ourselves of the truth of any hypothesis we may make use of to explain it. Were nothing esteemed virtue but what were beneficial to society, I am persuaded that the foregoing explication of the moral sense ought still to be received, and that upon sufficient evidence; but this evidence must grow upon us when we find other kinds of virtue which will not admit of any explication except from that hypothesis. Here is a man, who is not remarkably defective in his social qualities; but what principally recommends him is his dexterity in business, by which he has extricated himself from the greatest difficulties, and conducted the most delicate affairs with a singular address and prudence. I find an esteem for him immediately to arise in me. His company is a satisfaction to me, and before I have any further acquaintance with him, I would rather do him a service than another, whose character is in every other respect equal, but is deficient in that particular. In this case, the qualities that please me are all considered as useful to the person, and as having a tendency to promote his interest and satisfaction. They are only regarded as means to an end, and please me in proportion to their fitness for that end. The end, therefore, must be agreeable to me. But what makes the end agreeable? The person is a stranger. I am no way interested in him, nor lie under any obligation to him. His happiness concerns not me, further than the happiness of every human, and indeed of every sensible creature; that is, it affects me only by sympathy. From that principle, whenever I discover his happiness and good, whether in its causes or effects, I enter so deeply into it, that it gives me a sensible emotion. The appearance of qualities that have a tendency to promote it have an agreeable effect upon my imagination, and command my love and esteem.

This theory may serve to explain why the same qualities, in all cases, produce both pride and love, humility and hatred, and the same man is always virtuous or vicious, accomplished or despicable to others, who is so to himself. A person in whom we discover any passion or habit, which originally is only incommodious to himself, becomes always disagreeable to us merely on its account; as, on the other hand, one whose character is only dangerous and disagreeable to others, can never be satisfied with himself, as long as he is sensible of that disadvantage. Nor is this observable only with regard to characters and manners, but may be remarked even in the most minute circumstances. A violent cough in another gives us uneasiness, though in itself it does not in the least affect us. A man will be mortified, if you tell him he has a stinking breath, though it is evidently no annoyance to himself. Our fancy easily changes its situation, and either surveying ourselves as we appear to others, or considering others as they feel themselves, we enter, by that means, into sentiments which no way belong to us, and in which nothing but sympathy is able to interest us. And this sympathy we sometimes carry so far, as even to be displeased with a quality commodious to us merely because it displeases others, and makes us disagreeable in their eyes, though perhaps we never can have any interest in rendering ourselves agreeable to them.

There have been many systems of morality advanced by philosophers in all ages, but if they are strictly examined they may be reduced to two, which alone merit our attention. Moral good and evil are certainly distinguished by our *sentiments*, not by *reason*; but these sentiments may arise either from the mere species or appearance of characters and passions, or from reflections on their tendency to the happiness of mankind, and of particular persons. My opinion is that both these causes are intermixed in our judgments of morals, after the same manner as they are in our decisions concerning most kinds of external beauty, though I am also of opinion that reflections on the tendencies of actions have by far the greatest influence, and determine all the great lines of our duty. There are, however, instances, in cases of less moment, wherein this immediate taste or sentiment produces our approbation. Wit, and a certain easy and disengaged behaviour, are qualities *immediately agreeable* to others, and command their love and esteem. Some of these qualities produce satisfaction in others by particular original principles of human nature which cannot be accounted for. Others may be resolved into principles which are more general. This will best appear upon a particular enquiry.

As some qualities acquire their merit from their being *immediately agreeable* to others, without any tendency to public interest, so some are denominated virtuous from their being *immediately agreeable* to the person himself who possesses them. Each of the passions and operations of the mind has a particular feeling which must be either agreeable or disagreeable. The first is virtuous, the second vicious. This particular feeling constitutes the very nature of the passion, and therefore needs not be accounted for.

But however directly the distinction of vice and virtue may seem to flow from the immediate pleasure or uneasiness which particular qualities cause to ourselves or others, it is easy to observe that it has also a considerable dependence on the principle of *sympathy* so often insisted on. We approve of a person, who is possessed of qualities *immediately agreeable* to those with whom he has any commerce, though perhaps we ourselves never reaped any pleasure from them. We also approve of one who is possessed of qualities that are *immediately agreeable* to himself, though they be of no service to any mortal. To account for this we must have recourse to the foregoing principles.

Thus, to take a general review of the present hypothesis: every quality of the mind is denominated virtuous which gives pleasure by the mere survey, as every quality which produces pain is called vicious. This pleasure and this pain may arise from four different sources. For we reap a pleasure from the view of a character which is naturally fitted to be useful to others, or to the person himself, or which is agreeable to others, or to the person himself. One may, perhaps, be surprised that amidst all these interests and pleasures we should forget our own, which touch us so nearly on every other occasion. But we shall easily satisfy ourselves on this head when we consider that, every particular person's pleasure and interest being different, it is impossible men could ever agree in their sentiments and judgments, unless they chose some common point of view from which they might survey their object, and which might cause it to appear the same to all of them. Now, in judging of characters, the only interest or pleasure which appears the same to every spectator is that of the person himself whose character is examined, or that of persons who have a connexion with him. And though such interests and pleasures touch us more faintly than our own, yet being more constant and universal, they counterbalance the latter even in practice, and are alone admitted in speculation as the standard of virtue and morality. They alone produce that particular feeling or sentiment on which moral distinctions depend.

As to the good or ill desert of virtue or vice, it is an evident consequence of the sentiments of pleasure or uneasiness. These sentiments produce love or hatred; and love or hatred, by the original constitution of human passion, is attended with benevolence or anger; that is, with a desire of making happy the person we love, and miserable the person we hate. We have treated of this more fully on another occasion.

IMMANUEL KANT, GROUNDWORK OF THE METAPHYSICS OF MORALS

Introduction

Immanuel Kant is, in many ways, the villain of our piece. That will no doubt come as a surprise to those for whom Kant is not only the enlightenment thinker *par excellence*, but also one of the most profoundly influential of moral thinkers that the Western tradition has known. What Kant did was to shift ethics away from its focus on the cultivation of virtuous character and towards an ethics of duty in the form of generalisable moral laws to which all men are said to be subject. His much-vaunted 'categorical imperative' was really a reworking of religious law in secular form: the Bible's 'do unto others as you would have them do unto you' reappears in Kant's 'act only on that maxim that you can at the same time will to become universal law'. From Kant onwards, ethics joined religion in formulating duties in the form of generally applicable commandments. Little by little, in the popular mind the 'good' gradually became identified with the observance of moral law, and the idea that ethics would provide for man's full realisation of his potential faded away like a forgotten dream.

Kant (1724-1804) was born in Königsberg—then the capital of East Prussia—into an artisan family of modest means. His parents were followers of the Pietist branch of Lutheranism which stressed both individual piety and our inner struggle with sin. At the age of 16, Kant enrolled at the University of Königsberg to study theology and classics, which he soon abandoned in favour of philosophy. After working as a private tutor for nine years, he began teaching at the university in 1755, where he remained for four decades. As an unsalaried lecturer, he was paid directly by students and needed to teach heavily to earn his keep, but he published widely and was a popular teacher. In 1770, he was promoted to the chair of logic and metaphysics at Königsberg: this began a period that would lead to the publication of his great works—the *Critique of Pure Reason* (1781) and *Critique of Practical Reason* (1788). He never married and, it is rumoured, never travelled more than ten miles from Königsberg; his life was so strict and disciplined that it is said that his neighbours would set their clocks by his daily walks.

At the heart of Kant's moral philosophy is what he calls the 'categorical imperative'. Moral action, according to Kant, must be underpinned by duties or directives (imperatives) that are absolute and unconditional (categorical) in nature. Such action is by its nature an end in itself rather than a means to an end, and is to be contrasted with various 'hypothetical' imperatives, i.e. conditional directives that provide for a means to an end. A categorical imperative is a straightforward injunction: 'do this'; 'don't do that'. A hypothetical imperative, on the other hand, stipulates the action required in order to achieve certain ends: 'you must do so-and-so if you wish to achieve such-and-such end'. Only acting from a sense of moral duty, for Kant, confers moral worth: it is not enough to do good for the sheer love of it; one must do good, it is suggested, because that is what is required by the moral law.

The first aspect of the categorical imperative is the directive to act only on that maxim (i.e. 'principle') that you can at the same time will to become universal law, or, in another formulation, to act as if the maxim of your action were to become through your will a general law. Kant gives the example of the borrower who knows he will not be able to repay, but wants to make the promise to do so anyway. Can he will his maxim ('When I think myself in want of money, I will borrow money and promise to repay it, although I know that I never can do so') to be become a universal law? Of course not: for if everyone in a difficulty should be able to promise whatever he pleases, with the purpose of not keeping his promise, then promises would have no value, and the promise itself become impossible. What about the man who wishes to keep great wealth for himself in the midst of general poverty and wretchedness—can he wish that his uncharitableness become a general law? Likewise, no: it is impossible to will that such a principle should have the universal validity of a law of nature, since if a man were to do so he would contradict himself, insofar as there are many cases in which he would likewise have need of the love and sympathy of others.

The second aspect of the categorical imperative is to act so as to treat humanity in every case as an end and never as means only. Kant establishes this second aspect of the categorical imperative based upon similar reasoning. Rational nature exists as an end in itself, he says, and every man necessarily conceives his own existence as being so; this is a subjective principle of human action. But every other man likewise regards himself as an end in himself, and on exactly the same basis. This 'ends not means' principle, then, is also an objective principle constituting what Kant calls a 'supreme practical law' from which 'all laws of the will must be capable of being deduced'. A man cannot break promises freely, for that would be treating those who are cheated as means to our own ends, since they could not possibly consent to this. A man should not, also, harm or kill other men, as this would be to treat them as means to ends; nor (perhaps more controversially) should he even commit suicide in order to obtain a more tolerable condition for himself, for to do so would be to treat his own life as a means to an end.

It was through the moral sense that man came, argued Kant, to God. The object of practical reason, the *summum bonum* or highest good, is the conjunction of virtue with happiness; but we can fulfil our duty of promoting the *summum bonum* only by believing it is possible. In other words, although men recognise that goodness and evil do not obtain their just rewards in this existence, man's moral sense expects that rewards and punishments must be effected somewhere. This implies a higher power who has the power to create an afterlife where virtue is rewarded by happiness. This is how Kant arrives at a faith in immortality and in God.

Kant's influence on subsequent moral thinking cannot be overstated. This is, perhaps, part of the trouble, for while there is much to be said in favour of the categorical imperative as a guide for the way in which we ought to treat others, it tells precious little as to how we ought to treat ourselves, and as such can never be a wholly satisfactory system of ethics. Kant's ethics is a deontological ethics rather than a virtue ethics: that is to say, it conceives of ethics as a system of abstract moral duties, rather than as guidance for cultivating virtuous character in aid of the 'good life'. Much, for Kant at least, hung upon this, for it was the awareness of moral right and wrong that founded his belief in an afterlife and in God. But much was also overlooked—not least, the best part of a philosophical tradition of two millennia that conceived of ethics as something directed towards the harmonious development of man and all his faculties, rather than subjection to a quasi-religious moral law.

Let me suggest, however, that there might be another way to read Kant—against the grain, so to speak, if not of Kant himself, than at least against the grain of the many writers who diligently trot out his categorical imperative whenever talk turns to matters of morality. The way to do this is to recognize that the categorical imperative does not impose duties only with regard to others—it also imposes duties with regard to ourselves. If we are to act as if the maxim of our action is to become a general law, then on what basis could we be entitled to neglect our own natural talents and gifts? For sure, Kant admits, a system could subsist in which men neglect their natural talents in favour of idleness, amusement, and propagation of their species—but he cannot possibly will that this should be the case, for 'as a rational being,' says Kant, 'he necessarily wills that his faculties be developed.' Similarly, to treat humanity in every case as an end (and never as means) also means to treat ourselves as ends (and not means). One aspect of these ends, says Kant, are the 'capacities of greater perfection' that nature has implanted in us. To neglect these capacities—in ourselves as much as anyone else—would simply not be consistent with the advancement of our ends. Viewed in this light, Kant need not be viewed merely as doctrinaire spokesman for the moral law. He can also—potentially—be seen as an advocate for the realisation of the full range of human faculties and gifts.

Second Section: Transition from Popular Moral Philosophy to the

METAPHYSIC OF MORALS

...There is therefore but one categorical imperative, namely, this: *Act only on that maxim whereby you can at the same time will that it should become a universal law.*

Now if all imperatives of duty can be deduced from this one imperative as from their principle, then, although it should remain undecided what is called duty is not merely a vain notion, yet at least we shall be able to show what we understand by it and what this notion means.

Since the universality of the law according to which effects are produced constitutes what is properly called nature in the most general sense (as to form), that is the existence of things so far as it is determined by general laws, the imperative of duty may be expressed thus: *Act as if the maxim of your action were to become by your will a universal law of nature.*

We will now enumerate a few duties, adopting the usual division of them into duties to ourselves and to others, and into perfect and imperfect duties

1. A man reduced to despair by a series of misfortunes feels wearied of life, but is still so far in possession of his reason that he can ask himself whether it would not be contrary to his duty to himself to take his own life. Now he inquires whether the maxim of his action could become a universal law of nature. His maxim is: 'From self-love I adopt it as a principle to shorten my life when its longer duration is likely to bring more evil than satisfaction.' It is asked then simply whether this principle founded on self-love can become a universal law of nature. Now we see at once that a system of nature of which it should be a law to destroy life by means of the very feeling whose special nature it is to impel to the improvement of life would contradict itself and, therefore, could not exist as a system of nature; hence that maxim cannot possibly exist as a universal

law of nature and, consequently, would be wholly inconsistent with the supreme principle of all duty.

2. Another finds himself forced by necessity to borrow money. He knows that he will not be able to repay it, but sees also that nothing will be lent to him unless he promises stoutly to repay it in a definite time. He desires to make this promise, but he has still so much conscience as to ask himself: 'Is it not unlawful and inconsistent with duty to get out of a difficulty in this way?' Suppose however that he resolves to do so: then the maxim of his action would be expressed thus: 'When I think myself in want of money, I will borrow money and promise to repay it, although I know that I never can do so.' Now this principle of self-love or of one's own advantage may perhaps be consistent with my whole future welfare; but the question now is, 'Is it right?' I change then the suggestion of self-love into a universal law, and state the question thus: 'How would it be if my maxim were a universal law?' Then I see at once that it could never hold as a universal law of nature, but would necessarily contradict itself. For supposing it to be a universal law that everyone when he thinks himself in a difficulty should be able to promise whatever he pleases, with the purpose of not keeping his promise, the promise itself would become impossible, as well as the end that one might have in view in it, since no one would consider that anything was promised to him, but would ridicule all such statements as vain pretences.

3. A third finds in himself a talent which with the help of some culture might make him a useful man in many respects. But he finds himself in comfortable circumstances and prefers to indulge in pleasure rather than to take pains in enlarging and improving his happy natural capacities. He asks, however, whether his maxim of neglect of his natural gifts, besides agreeing with his inclination to indulgence, agrees also with what is called duty. He sees then that a system of nature could indeed subsist with such a universal law although men (like the

South Sea islanders) should let their talents rest and resolve to devote their lives merely to idleness, amusement, and propagation of their species—in a word, to enjoyment; but he cannot possibly *will* that this should be a universal law of nature, or be implanted in us as such by a natural instinct. For, as a rational being, he necessarily wills that his faculties be developed, since they serve him and have been given him for all sorts of possible purposes.

4. A fourth, who is in prosperity, while he sees that others have to contend with great wretchedness and that he could help them, thinks: 'What concern is it of mine? Let everyone be as happy as Heaven pleases, or as he can make himself; I will take nothing from him nor even envy him, only I do not wish to contribute anything to his welfare or to his assistance in distress!' Now no doubt if such a mode of thinking were a universal law, the human race might very well subsist and doubtless even better than in a state in which everyone talks of sympathy and good-will, or even takes care occasionally to put it into practice, but, on the other side, also cheats when he can, betrays the rights of men, or otherwise violates them. But although it is possible that a universal law of nature might exist in accordance with that maxim, it is impossible to *will* that such a principle should have the universal validity of a law of nature. For a will which resolved this would contradict itself, inasmuch as many cases might occur in which one would have need of the love and sympathy of others, and in which, by such a law of nature, sprung from his own will, he would deprive himself of all hope of the aid he desires.

These are a few of the many actual duties, or at least what we regard as such, which obviously fall into two classes on the one principle that we have laid down. We must be *able to will* that a maxim of our action should be a universal law. This is the canon of the moral appreciation of the action generally. Some actions are of such a character that their maxim cannot without contradiction be even *conceived* as a universal law of nature, far from it being possible that we should *will* that it *should* be so. In others this intrinsic impossibility is not found, but still it is impossible to *will* that their maxim should be raised to the universality of a law of nature, since such a will would contradict itself. It is easily seen that the former violate strict or rigorous (inflexible) duty; the latter only laxer (meritorious) duty. Thus it has been completely shown how all duties depend as regards the nature of the obligation (not the object of the action) on the same principle.

If now we attend to ourselves on occasion of any transgression of duty, we shall find that we in fact do not will that our maxim should be a universal law, for that is impossible for us; on the contrary, we will that the opposite should remain a universal law, only we assume the liberty of making an *exception* in our own favour or (just for this time only) in favour of our inclination. Consequently if we considered all cases from one and the same point of view, namely, that of reason, we should find a contradiction in our own will, namely, that a certain principle should be objectively necessary as a universal law, and yet subjectively should not be universal, but admit of exceptions. As however we at one moment regard our action from the point of view of a will wholly conformed to reason, and then again look at the same action from the point of view of a will affected by inclination, there is not really any contradiction, but an antagonism of inclination to the precept of reason, whereby the universality of the principle is changed into a mere generality, so that the practical principle of reason shall meet the maxim half way. Now, although this cannot be justified in our own impartial judgement, yet it proves that we do really recognise the validity of the categorical imperative and (with all respect for it) only allow ourselves a few exceptions, which we think unimportant and forced from us.

...

Now I say: man and generally any rational being *exists* as an end in himself, *not merely as a means* to be arbitrarily used by this or that will, but in all his actions, whether they concern himself or other rational beings, must be always regarded at the same time as an end. All objects of the inclinations have only a conditional worth, for if the inclinations and the wants founded on them did not exist, then their object would be without value. But the inclinations, themselves being sources of want, are so far from having an absolute worth for which they should be desired that on the contrary it must be the universal wish of every rational being to be wholly free from them. Thus the worth of any object which is *to be acquired* by our action is always conditional. Beings whose existence depends not on our will but on nature's, have nevertheless, if they are irrational beings, only a relative value as means, and are therefore called *things*; rational beings, on the contrary, are called *persons*, because their very nature points them out as ends in themselves, that is as something which must not be used merely as means, and so far therefore restricts freedom of action (and is an object of respect). These, therefore, are not merely subjective ends whose existence has a worth *for us* as an effect of our action, but *objective ends*, that is, things whose existence is an end in itself; an end moreover for which no other can be substituted, which they should subserve *merely* as means, for otherwise nothing whatever would possess *absolute worth*; but if all worth were conditioned and therefore contingent, then there would be no supreme practical principle of reason whatever.

If then there is a supreme practical principle or, in respect of the human will, a categorical imperative, it must be one which, being drawn from the conception of that which is necessarily an end for everyone because it is *an end in itself*, constitutes an *objective* principle of will, and can therefore serve as a universal practical law. The foundation of this principle is: *rational nature exists as an end in itself.* Man necessarily conceives his own existence as being so; so far then this is a *subjective* principle of human actions. But every other rational being regards its existence similarly, just on the same rational principle that holds for me: so that it is at the same time an objective principle, from which as a supreme practical law all laws of the will must be capable of being deduced. Accordingly the practical imperative will be as follows: *So act as to treat humanity, whether in your own person or in that of any other, in every case as an end withal, never as means only.* We will now inquire whether this can be practically carried out.

To abide by the previous examples:

Firstly, under the head of necessary duty to oneself: he who contemplates suicide should ask himself whether his action can be consistent with the idea of humanity *as an end in itself*. If he destroys himself in order to escape from painful circumstances, he uses a person merely as *a mean* to maintain a tolerable condition up to the end of life. But a man is not a thing, that is to say, something which can be used merely as means, but must in all his actions be always considered as an end in himself. I cannot, therefore, dispose in any way of a man in my own person so as to mutilate him, to damage or kill him. (It belongs to ethics proper to define this principle more precisely, so as to avoid all misunderstanding, e.g., as to the amputation of the limbs in order to preserve myself, as to exposing my life to danger with a view to preserve it, etc. This question is therefore omitted here.)

Secondly, as regards necessary duties, or those of strict obligation, towards others: he who is thinking of making a lying promise to others will see at once that he would be using another man *merely as a mean*, without the latter containing at the same time the end in himself. For he whom I propose by such a promise to use for my own purposes cannot possibly assent to my mode of acting towards him and, therefore, cannot himself contain the end of this action. This violation of the principle of humanity in other men is more obvious if we take in examples of attacks on the freedom and property of others. For then it is clear that he who transgresses the rights of men intends to use the person of others merely as a means, without considering that as rational beings they ought always to be esteemed also as ends, that is, as beings who must be capable of containing in themselves the end of the very same action.

Thirdly, as regards contingent (meritorious) duties to oneself: it is not enough that the action does not violate humanity in our own person as an end in itself, it must also *harmonize with* it. Now there are in humanity capacities of greater perfection, which belong to the end that nature has in view in regard to humanity in ourselves as the subject: to neglect these might perhaps be consistent with the *maintenance* of humanity as an end in itself, but not with the *advancement* of this end.

Fourthly, as regards meritorious duties towards others: the natural end which all men have is their own happiness. Now humanity might indeed subsist, although no one should contribute anything to the happiness of others, provided he did not intentionally withdraw anything from it; but after all this would only harmonize negatively not positively with *humanity as an end in itself*, if every one does not also endeavour, as far as in him lies, to forward the ends of others. For the ends of any subject which is an end in himself ought as far as possible to be *my* ends also, if that conception is to have its *full effect* with me. ...

8

FRIEDRICH SCHILLER, ON GRACE AND DIGNITY

INTRODUCTION

The proposition that the ethical life can—and should—be lived in a way that is aesthetically attractive is not often made. Whatever influence the tradition of virtue ethics has had among the classically educated, for the great majority of people moral observance is considered to be something of a gloomy affair—the province of pious old men or crabby schoolmarms whose rigidities walk hand-in-hand with joylessness, censoriousness, and other morbidities. Ethics has never needed to be this way. As Schiller explains in his long essay *On Grace and Dignity* (1793), popular morality has made a false dichotomy between duty and inclination: in fact, ethics is the province of the healthy, well-balanced man, and gracefulness the very hallmark of ethical accomplishment.

Friedrich Schiller (1759-1805) was one of Germany's leading dramatists, poets, historians, and philosophers. Born in Marbach, Württemberg, he was recruited by Duke Carl Eugen at the age of thirteen to attend the Military Academy (the *Karlsschule*), where he studied first law and then medicine, becoming an army doctor in 1780. His first play, *The Robbers* (*Die Räuber*) was a great success, but on hearing that Schiller had gone to Mannheim to be present on the first night, the Duke had him arrested and forbade him from writing any more plays. In response, Schiller fled from Stuttgart by night back to Mannheim, where he was eventually offered a job as a resident playwright at the Mannheim theatre. He was later appointed professor of history at the University of Jena, having been recommended by Goethe for the job, where Schiller lectured in both history and aesthetics. Although in around 1792 Schiller's health gave way as a result of the strain of overwork, he obtained a pension that allowed him to work not only on his poems and his plays, but also on letters and essays exploring the relationship between ethics and aesthetics.

At the heart of Schiller's ethics is the proposition that the destiny of man is not to accomplish isolated moral acts but rather to be a moral being. Schiller's ideal is that of the 'noble soul'—the perfection of the inner man that is reached when there has been established a true harmony between his inclination and his duty. There is an accord, in the noble soul, between reason and sense, and between reason and instinct, such that moral actions come effortlessly and without the least hesitation or discomfort. For the noble soul, Schiller explains, it is not the individual actions that are properly to be considered moral—it is his character as a whole. The noble soul accomplishes the most heroic actions and carries out the most painful duties of humanity not against its own inclinations or instincts but as easily and naturally as if those actions were prompted by the instinct itself. Virtue is an 'inclination for duty'.

The noble soul is to be contrasted with what Schiller calls 'the moralist formed by the school and the rule'. Schiller expressly points here to the moral philosophy of Kant—particularly, it appears, to the moral law established by the categorical imperative, as well as the presupposition that only acts carried out through a sense of duty can qualify as moral acts. In Kant's ethics, says Schiller, the idea of duty is proposed 'with a harshness enough to ruffle the Graces', and one that could tempt a 'feeble mind' into monastic or ascetic paths. As a corrective to the materialistic and other tendencies of the age in which he lived, Kant's rigorism may have been understandable, but by opposing to each other two principles which act upon the human will—inclination and duty—it sent philosophy on a wrong path.

The simple fact is that nature has made man a being at once reasonable and sensuous. It is neither helpful nor possible to sacrifice the sensuous in favour of the rational being, says Schiller, however much the latter may partake of the divine; nor ought we to found the triumph of rationality on the suppression or alienation of our sensual being. In practical morals, it is more important that we are able to bring our sentiments into conformity with duty than to insist upon the correctness of a fixed rules, for the will is in a more immediate relation with the faculty of feeling than it is with the cognitive faculties. In fact, a man's moral condition can only be secure when ethical conduct has become a kind of second nature. What kind of assurance can we have in he who must always check whether his actions conform to some dry and abstract moral law?

'Grace' is the name Schiller gives to this harmony between reason and sense, and between duty and inclination, in the sensuous world. Grace is not synonymous with beauty ('architectonic beauty', as Schiller calls it) as such, which is a pure product of nature; instead, it is beauty of movement through which a man's soul speaks in his smallest gestures. A noble soul, having established the inner harmony which gives effect to its full humanity, conveys as its basic expression the quality of *ease*. There is no constraint: all its movements are easy, sweet, and animated—the 'eye beams with a serenity as with liberty, and with the brightness of sentiment', the 'voice becomes music', and 'there is no effort in the varied play of the physiognomy'. When a man's inner self is gifted with such vivacity, it acquires influence over all the movements of the body, upon which—through frequent repetition—it leaves durable traces. Over the course of the years, the faces of such men become infinitely expressive, says Schiller, in the final triumph of grace—'all soul'.

Schiller's work is striking in presenting an 'aesthetic ethic' which holds out the prospect of an ethical path that at the same time renders a man's life more pleasing to himself and more attractive to others. He lets us see that the contradiction between what feel we *ought* to do, and what we *want* to do, is an unnecessary one: not only is it possible to cultivate an 'inclination for duty', but, in fact, any practical ethical system must be able to do so. This has implications for the way we view ourselves: no longer, Schiller suggests, should we strive to impose abstract moral laws against our own natures, for that is both impractical and the root cause of our uglification. It also has implications for the way we view others: if the noble soul is forged from an inner harmony of the rational and the sensual parts of man—and if this inner nobility is unconstrainedly expressed with ease, naturalness, and unselfconscious grace—should we not look askance at those who would preach their moral codes before us with such loud, aggressive, and unbalanced postures? Above all, it has implications for the way we view ethics itself: the cultivation and perfection of man, after Schiller, can never again be conceived as an enterprise in which the establishment of a harmonious inner state, manifesting in a graceful and dignified outer state, can be neglected.

'On Grace and Dignity'

...We can conceive three sorts of relation of man with himself: I mean the sensuous part of man with the reasonable part. From these three relations we have to seek which is that one which best suits him in the sensuous world, and the expression of which constitutes the beautiful. Either man enforces silence upon the exigencies of his sensuous nature, to govern himself conformably with the superior exigencies of his reasonable nature; or else, on the contrary, he subjects the reasonable portion of his being to the sensuous part, reducing himself thus to obey only the impulses which the necessity of nature imprints upon him, as well as upon the other phenomena; or lastly, harmony is established between the impulsions of the one and the laws of the other, and man is in perfect accord with himself.

If he has the consciousness of his spiritual person, of his pure autonomy, man rejects all that is sensuous, and it is only when thus isolated from matter that he feels to the full his moral liberty. But for that, as his sensuous nature opposes an obstinate and vigorous resistance to him, he must, on his side, exercise upon it a notable pressure and a strong effort, without which he could neither put aside the appetites nor reduce to silence the energetic voice of instinct. A mind of this quality makes the physical nature which depends on him feel that it has a master in him, whether it fulfils the orders of the will or endeavors to anticipate them. Under its stern discipline sensuousness appears then repressed, and interior resistance will betray itself exteriorly by the constraint. This moral state cannot, then, be favorable to beauty, because nature cannot produce the beautiful but as far as it is free, and consequently that which betrays to us the struggles of moral liberty against matter cannot either be grace.

If, on the contrary, subdued by its wants, man allows himself to be governed without reserve by the instinct of nature, it is his interior autonomy that vanishes, and with it all trace of this autonomy is exteriorly effaced. The animal nature is alone visible upon his visage; the eye is watery and languishing, the mouth rapaciously open, the voice trembling and muffled, the breathing short and rapid, the limbs trembling with nervous agitation: the whole body by its languor betrays its moral degradation. Moral force has renounced all resistance, and physical nature, with such a man, is placed in full liberty. But precisely this complete abandonment of moral independence, which occurs ordinarily at the moment of sensuous desire, and more still at the moment of enjoyment, sets suddenly brute matter at liberty which until then had been kept in equilibrium by the active and passive forces. The inert forces of nature commence from thence to gain the upper hand over the living forces of the organism; the form is oppressed by matter, humanity by common nature. The eye, in which the soul shone forth, becomes dull, or it protrudes from its socket with I know not what glassy haggardness; the delicate pink of the cheeks thickens, and spreads as a coarse pigment in uniform layers. The mouth is no longer anything but a simple opening, because its form no longer depends upon the action of forces, but on their non-resistance; the gasping voice and breathing are no more than an effort to ease the laborious and oppressed lungs, and which show a simple mechanical want, with nothing that reveals a soul. In a word, in that state of liberty which physical nature arrogates to itself from its chief, we must not think of beauty. Under the empire of the moral agent, the liberty of form was only restrained, here it is crushed by brutal matter, which gains as much ground as is abstracted from the will. Man in this state not only revolts the moral sense, which incessantly claims of the face an expression of human dignity, but the aesthetic sense, which is not content with simple matter, and which finds in the form an unfettered pleasure—the aesthetic sense will turn away with disgust from such a spectacle, where concupiscence could alone find its gratification.

Of these two relations between the moral nature of man and his physical nature, the first makes us think of a monarchy, where strict surveillance of the prince holds in hand all free movement; the second is an ochlocracy,[1] where the citizen, in refusing to obey his legitimate sovereign, finds he has liberty quite as little as the human face has beauty when the moral autonomy is oppressed; nay, on the contrary, just as the citizens are given over to the brutal despotism of the lowest classes, so the form is given over here to the despotism of matter. Just as liberty finds itself between the two extremes of legal oppression and anarchy, so also we shall find the beautiful between two extremes, between the expression of dignity which bears witness to the domination exercised by the mind, and the voluptuous expression which reveals the domination exercised by instinct.

In other terms, if the beauty of expression is incompatible with the absolute government of reason over sensuous nature, and with the government of sensuous nature over the reason, it follows that the third state (for one could not conceive a fourth)—that in which the reason and the senses, duty and inclination, are in harmony—will be that in which the beauty of play is produced. In order that obedience to reason may become an object of inclination, it must represent for us the principle of pleasure; for pleasure and pain are the only springs which set the instincts in motion. It is true that in life it is the reverse that takes place, and pleasure is ordinarily the motive for which we act according to reason. If morality itself has at last ceased to hold this language, it is to the immortal author[2] of the 'Critique' to whom we must offer our thanks; it is to him

---

1. Government by the mob.
2. Immanuel Kant.

to whom the glory is due of having restored the healthy reason in separating it from all systems. But in the manner in which the principles of this philosopher are ordinarily expressed by himself and also by others, it appears that the inclination can never be for the moral sense otherwise than a very suspicious companion, and pleasure a dangerous auxiliary for moral determinations. In admitting that the instinct of happiness does not exercise a blind domination over man, it does not the less desire to interfere in the moral actions which depend on free arbitration, and by that it changes the pure action of the will, which ought always to obey the law alone, never the instinct. Thus, to be altogether sure that the inclination has not interfered with the demonstrations of the will, we prefer to see it in opposition rather than in accord with the law of reason; because it may happen too easily, when the inclination speaks in favor of duty, that duty draws from the recommendation all its credit over the will. And in fact, as in practical morals, it is not the conformity of the acts with the law, but only the conformity of the sentiments with duty, which is important. We do not attach, and with reason, any value to this consideration, that it is ordinarily more favorable to the conformity of acts with the law that inclination is on the side of duty. As a consequence, this much appears evident: that the assent of sense, if it does not render suspicious the conformity of the will with duty, at least does not guarantee it. Thus the sensuous expression of this assent, expression that grace offers to us, could never bear a sufficient available witness to the morality of the act in which it is met; and it is not from that which an action or a sentiment manifests to the eyes by graceful expression that we must judge of the moral merit of that sentiment or of that action.

Up to the present time I believe I have been in perfect accord with the rigorists in morals. I shall not become, I hope, a relaxed moralist in endeavoring to maintain in the world of phenomena and in the real fulfilment of the law of duty those rights of sensuous nature which, upon the ground of pure reason and in the jurisdiction of the moral law, are completely set aside and excluded.

I will explain. Convinced as I am, and precisely because I am convinced, that the inclination in associating itself to an act of the will offers no witness to the pure conformity of this act with the duty, I believe that we are able to infer from this that the moral perfection of man cannot shine forth except from this very association of his inclination with his moral conduct. In fact, the destiny of man is not to accomplish isolated moral acts, but to be a moral being. That which is prescribed to him does not consist of virtues, but of virtue, and virtue is not anything else 'than an inclination for duty'. Whatever, then, in the objective sense, may be the opposition which separates the acts suggested by the inclination from those which duty determines, we cannot say it is the same in the subjective sense; and not only is it permitted to man to accord duty with pleasure, but he ought to establish between them this accord, he ought to obey his reason with a sentiment of joy. It is not to throw it off as a burden, nor to cast it off as a too coarse skin. No, it is to unite it, by a union the most intimate, with his ego, with the most noble part of his being, that a sensuous nature has been associated in him to his purely spiritual nature. By the fact that nature has made of him a being both at once reasonable and sensuous, that is to say, a man, it has prescribed to him the obligation not to separate that which she has united; not to sacrifice in him the sensuous being, were it in the most pure manifestations of the divine part; and never to found the triumph of one over the oppression and the ruin of the other. It is only when he gathers, so to speak, his entire humanity together, and his way of thinking in morals becomes the result of the united action of the two principles, when morality has become to him a second nature, it is then only that it is secure;

for, as far as the mind and the duty are obliged to employ violence, it is necessary that the instinct shall have force to resist them. The enemy which only is overturned can rise up again, but the enemy reconciled is truly vanquished. In the moral philosophy of Kant the idea of duty is proposed with a harshness enough to ruffle the Graces, and one which could easily tempt a feeble mind to seek for moral perfection in the sombre paths of an ascetic and monastic life. Whatever precautions the great philosopher has been able to take in order to shelter himself against this false interpretation, which must be repugnant more than all else to the serenity of the free mind, he has lent it a strong impulse, it seems to me, in opposing to each other by a harsh contrast the two principles which act upon the human will. Perhaps it was hardly possible, from the point of view in which he was placed, to avoid this mistake; but he has exposed himself seriously to it. Upon the basis of the question there is no longer, after the demonstration he has given, any discussion possible, at least for the heads which think and which are quite willing to be persuaded; and I am not at all sure if it would not be better to renounce at once all the attributes of the human being than to be willing to reach on this point, by reason, a different result. But although he began to work without any prejudice when he searched for the truth, and though all is here explained by purely objective reasons, it appears that when he put forward the truth once found he had been guided by a more subjective maxim, which is not difficult, I believe, to be accounted for by the time and circumstances.

What, in fact, was the moral of his time, either in theory or in its application? On one side, a gross materialism, of which the shameless maxims would revolt his soul; impure resting-places offered to the bastard characters of a century by the unworthy complacency of philosophers; on the other side, a pretended system of perfectibility, not less suspicious, which, to realize the chimera of a general perfection common to the whole universe, would not be embarrassed for a choice of means. This is what would meet his attention. So he carried there, where the most pressing danger lay and reform was the most urgent, the strongest forces of his principles, and made it a law to pursue sensualism without pity, whether it walks with a bold face, impudently insulting morality, or dissimulates under the imposing veil of a moral, praiseworthy end, under which a certain fanatical kind of order know how to disguise it. He had not to disguise ignorance, but to reform perversion; for such a cure a violent blow, and not persuasion or flattery, was necessary; and the more the contrast would be violent between the true principles and the dominant maxims, the more he would hope to provoke reflection upon this point. He was the Draco of his time, because his time seemed to him as yet unworthy to possess a Solon, neither capable of receiving him. From the sanctuary of pure reason he drew forth the moral law, unknown then, and yet, in another way, so known; he made it appear in all its saintliness before a degraded century, and troubled himself little to know whether there were eyes too enfeebled to bear the brightness.

But what had the children of the house done for him to have occupied himself only with the valets? Because strongly impure inclinations often usurp the name of virtue, was it a reason for disinterested inclinations in the noblest heart to be also rendered suspicious? Because the moral epicurean had willingly relaxed the law of reason, in order to fit it as a plaything to his customs, was it a reason to thus exaggerate harshness, and to make the fulfilment of duty, which is the most powerful manifestation of moral freedom, another kind of decorated servitude of a more specious name? And, in fact, between the esteem and the contempt of himself has the truly moral man a more free choice than the slave of sense between pleasure and pain? Is there less of constraint there for a pure will than here for a depraved will? Must one, by this imperative form given to the moral law, accuse man and humble him, and make of this law, which is the most sublime witness of our grandeur, the most crushing argument for our fragility? Was it possible with this imperative force to avoid that a prescription which man imposes on himself, as a reasonable being, and which is obligatory only for him on that account, and which is conciliatory with the sentiment of his liberty only—that this prescription, say I, took the appearance of a foreign law, a positive law, an appearance which could hardly lessen the radical tendency which we impute to man to react against the law?

It is certainly not an advantage for moral truth to have against itself sentiments which man can avow without shame. Thus, how can the sentiment of the beautiful, the sentiment of liberty, accord with the austere mind of a legislation which governs man rather through fear than trust, which tends constantly to separate that which nature has united, and which is reduced to hold us in defiance against a part of our being, to assure its empire over the rest? Human nature forms a whole more united in reality than it is permitted to the philosopher, who can only analyze, to allow it to appear. The reason can never reject as unworthy of it the affections which the heart recognizes with joy; and there, where man would be morally fallen, he can hardly rise in his own esteem. If in the moral order the sensuous nature were only the oppressed party and not an ally, how could it associate with all the ardour of its sentiments in a triumph which would be celebrated only over itself? How could it be so keen a participator in the satisfaction of a pure spirit having consciousness of itself, if in the end it could not attach itself to the pure spirit with such closeness that it is not possible even to intellectual analysis to separate it without violence.

The will, besides, is in more immediate relation with the

faculty of feeling than with the cognitive faculties, and it would be regrettable in many circumstances if it were obliged, in order to guide itself, to take advice of pure reason. I prejudge nothing good of a man who dares so little trust to the voice of instinct that he is obliged each time to make it appear first before the moral law; he is much more estimable who abandons himself with a certain security to inclination, without having to fear being led astray by her. That proves in fact that with him the two principles are already in harmony—in that harmony which places a seat upon the perfection of the human being, and which constitutes that which we understand by a noble soul.

It is said of a man that he has a great soul when the moral sense has finished assuring itself of all the affections, to the extent of abandoning without fear the direction of the senses to the will, and never incurring the risk of finding himself in discord with its decisions. It follows that in a noble soul it is not this or that particular action, it is the entire character which is moral. Thus we can make a merit of none of its actions because the satisfaction of an instinct could not be meritorious. A noble soul has no other merit than to be a noble soul. With as great a facility as if the instinct alone were acting, it accomplishes the most painful duties of humanity, and the most heroic sacrifice that she obtains over the instinct of nature seems the effect of the free action of the instinct itself. Also, it has no idea of the beauty of its act, and it never occurs to it that any other way of acting could be possible; on the contrary, the moralist formed by the school and by rule is always ready at the first question of the master to give an account, with the most rigorous precision, of the conformity of its acts with the moral law. The life of this one is like a drawing where the pencil has indicated by harsh and stiff lines all that the rule demands, and which could, if necessary, serve for a student to learn the elements of art. The life of a noble soul, on the contrary, is like a painting of Titian; all the harsh outlines are effaced, which does not prevent the whole face being more true, lifelike and harmonious. ...

SØREN KIERKEGAARD, FEAR AND TREMBLING

Introduction

'Philosophy is perfectly right in saying that life must be understood backwards,' wrote Kierkegaard in his journal in 1843. 'But then one forgets the other clause—that it must be lived forwards.'[1] Probably none of Kierkegaard's insights communicate his vision quite like this one. It expresses a deep and haunting truth: namely, that by the time we can conceive of the meaning of our life as a whole, that life has already been lived. In addition, this truth is one that is fundamentally absurd in nature—for what could be more inane and unfathomable than the predicament of having a grasp of one's life only when it is already too late to change it? Above all, it manifests the characteristic Kierkegaardian engagement with life—not as a problem to be solved, but as a reality to be experienced.

Søren Kierkegaard (1813-1855) is widely considered to have

---

1. Søren Kierkegaard, *Journals* IV.A.164 (1843).

been the 'father of existentialism'. Born and educated in Copenhagen, he entered the University there to study theology, only to find himself drawn towards literature and philosophy instead. In 1837, he met the love of his life, Regine Olsen, and by 1840 he had proposed to her, but in 1841 he broke the relationship off, apparently on the basis that his melancholy made him unsuitable for marriage. The experience marked him profoundly and triggered a period of great literary productivity: in the few years after this event, he published the masterpieces *Either/Or: A Fragment of Life* (1843), *Fear and Trembling* (1843), *The Concept of Anxiety* (1844), and *Stages on Life's Way* (1845). Troubled to the end by his disappointment at what passed for Christianity in the modern era and the need 'again to introduce Christianity into Christendom', Kierkegaard's later years were taken up with a sustained attack on the contemporary church. He collapsed in a Copenhagen street in late 1855, and died in hospital a month and a half later, at the age of just 42.

Central to Kierkegaard's ethical philosophy are the three basic stages or modes of existence: the aesthetic, the ethical, and the religious. Although he refers to them as 'stages in life's way', for Kierkegaard they are not developmental stages as much as they are states of being, each manifesting a different degree or intensity of engagement with life. In the aesthetic stage, we are caught up in a restless seeking out of pleasures—both sensual and the artistic—and the avoidance of pain; however, this is ultimately unrewarding, for with the attainment of desire comes a loosening of interest, and an endlessly unsatisfying concatenation of once-thrilling events results only in long drawn-out *ennui*. During the ethical stage, we come to accept responsibility towards others, which takes shape as a kind of productive subordination of ourselves to the demands of the social order and customary expectations—but this stage, too, is ultimately unsatisfactory, as it does little to nurture man's spiritual self and his need for self-exploration. The final stage is the religious stage which, for those who reach it, offers a deepening and intensification of our relationship with of existence, made by way of a leap of faith, that comes through embracing what Kierkegaard calls 'the absurd'.

Kierkegaard elaborates upon the religious stage by reference to the biblical story of Abraham and Isaac. In this story, Abraham is commanded by God to sacrifice his own son, Isaac, on Mount Moriah. Obedient to the last, Abraham is in the process of carrying out the frightful task when—at the final moment—a messenger from God interrupts him, stops the sacrifice, and provides a ram for him to sacrifice instead. The story is often made the subject of sermons as an example of unshakeable religious faith, but Kierkegaard excoriates the inauthentic way in which this is usually done: in fact, says Kierkegaard, should anyone proceed to imitate Abraham, and sacrifice his own son as an expression of faith, he would be viewed by society as a madman and a murderer. In fact, Kierkegaard wants us to acknowledge the true horror of the scene as it would have been lived from Abraham's perspective: Isaac is that which Abraham loves most in all the world, and yet on God's instruction he has to ride for three and a half days, taking the time to collect the firewood, to bind Isaac, and to whet his knife—three and a half days that subjectively would have felt 'infinitely longer than the few thousand years that separate me [Kierkegaard] from Abraham'. How can one obtain the faith, asks Kierkegaard, to overcome the terrors of such a trial?

Kierkegaard tackles the issue by asking us to imagine the hypothetical case of a young swain falling in love with a princess in circumstances such that it is impossible he can ever marry her. There are many people who would, in such a case, simply say: 'Such a love is folly, the rich brewer's wife is quite as good and solid a match.' This is the viewpoint taken by the un-idealistic, the mercenary, the conventional ones. For them, there is no reason to do anything other than simply 'get on'. They are 'slaves of paltriness', says Kierkegaard—'frogs in the sloughs of life'.

The first step on the path towards faith, suggests Kierkegaard, is to make a movement away from this 'sordid view of life' by becoming what he calls a 'knight of resignation'. The young swain in the example shows us how it is done: he does not surrender his love as advised by the 'slaves' and the 'frogs' of the mundane order; no—while he is no fool, and not one to waste himself on mere intoxication, he lets his love 'insinuate itself into his most secret and his most remote thoughts' and 'wind itself around every fibre of his consciousness'. He is willing to reduce his thought to a single wish, a single act of consciousness, that is dedicated to the one he loves; and yet at the same time he is willing to give himself over to 'infinite resignation'—not in order to forget himself, but so that he may become reconciled with existence. If he has correctly made this movement, then he will no longer be interested in what the princess actually does; nothing that she does can disturb him, for it is only 'lower natures' whose actions are determined by the conduct of other people. His mode of being will have completely changed—but he is still not yet, as we shall see, in the final stage of development, for he has not yet made the final movement towards faith.

To become a 'knight of faith' takes, then, one more movement. This movement is, says Kierkegaard, 'strange beyond comparison', for what the swain must do—after having resigned his love and reconciled himself to pain—is to say: 'And still I believe that I shall marry her by virtue of the absurd, by virtue of the act that to God nothing is impossible'. All the while, the 'knight of faith' knows that his intellect has been right: his love was, and is, an impossibility—in the world of finalities in which reason holds sway. But faith goes beyond this: it holds in suspension the fact of the impossibility of consummation alongside the unflinching faith that such consummation is a foregone conclusion. This is the acknowledgment of the 'absurd'—that phenomenon of existence by which what is most illogical and ridiculous is at the same tine the very source of our hope, our faith, and our salvation.

For the rare man who can make this final movement—what then? Kierkegaard imagines this 'knight of faith' as being vigorous, steady-footed, and practical; he takes pleasure in all things and exhibits a zest characteristic of one who dedicates himself to the affairs of this world. As he walks home, this knight might wonder whether his wife has some special little dish waiting for him (a 'roasted lamb's head garnished with greens'), and he firmly believes that she has it ready for him—but if she has not prepared it, he remains altogether untroubled by the fact; or, as he talks with a man about putting up a building, although he has not four shillings to spare, he is taken with the thought that if it came to it he would unquestionably have the means at his disposal. There is not the slightest air of superiority about him; and yet—with as much unconcern as any happy-go-lucky fellow—he has resigned everything absolutely, and then seized it all again on the strength of the absurd.

While Kierkegaard must describe the phenomenon to us in language, it is not a mere idea or even a doctrine; it is a mode of facing existence that can only be established through the absurdity of winning the world by letting go of it. Anybody can make the movement of absolute resignation, says Kierkegaard, but not everyone can take the final step towards faith. Kierkegaard admits that he himself has been unable to do it.

Kierkegaard's philosophy provides for the modern man an ethics that is rooted in the texture of lived human experience.

Here are no abstract and arid Sunday-school rules that speak only to the head and not the heart. Instead, Kierkegaard insists on us facing our existential and ethical dilemmas without claiming that they can be easily dealt with or reconciled; he acknowledges that life does not make things so simple. It may be that the moral fabric of our lived experience simply cannot be straightened out by the human intellect. So be it: a man can still live on, and live well, for is our ability to hold fast to our faith—in a world that admits of nothing that is not doubtful—that makes us most powerfully alive.

Preliminary Expectoration

...An old saying, derived from the world of experience, has it that 'he who will not work shall not eat. But, strange to say, this does not hold true in the world where it is thought applicable; for in the world of matter the law of imperfection prevails, and we see, again and again, that he also who will not work has bread to eat—indeed, that he who sleeps has a greater abundance of it than he who works. In the world of matter everything belongs to whosoever happens to possess it; it is thrall to the law of indifference, and he who happens to possess the Ring also has the Spirit of the Ring at his beck and call, whether now he be Noureddin or Aladdin, and he who controls the treasures of this world, controls them, howsoever he managed to do so. It is different in the world of spirit. There, an eternal and divine order obtains, there the rain does not fall on the just and the unjust alike, nor does the sun shine on the good and the evil alike; but there the saying does hold true that he who will not work shall not eat, and only he who was troubled shall find rest, and only he who descends into the nether world shall rescue his beloved, and only he who unsheathes his knife shall be given Isaac again. There, he who will not work shall not eat, but shall be deceived, as the gods deceived Orpheus with an immaterial figure instead of his beloved Euridice, deceived him because he was love-sick and not courageous, deceived him because he was a player on the cithara rather than a man. There, it avails not to have an Abraham for one's father, or to have seventeen ancestors. But in that world the saying about Israel's maidens will hold true of him who will not work: he shall bring forth wind; but he who will work shall give birth to his own father.

There is a kind of learning which would presumptuously introduce into the world of spirit the same law of indifference under which the world of matter groans. It is thought that to know about great men and great deeds is quite sufficient, and that other exertion is not necessary. And therefore this learning shall not eat, but shall perish of hunger while seeing all things transformed into gold by its touch. And what, forsooth, does this learning really know? There were many thousands of contemporaries, and countless men in after times, who knew all about the triumphs of Miltiades; but there was only one whom they rendered sleepless. There have existed countless generations that knew by heart, word for word, the story of Abraham; but how many has it rendered sleepless?

Now the story of Abraham has the remarkable property of always being glorious, in however limited a sense it is understood; still, here also the point is whether one means to labour and exert one's self. Now people do not care to labour and exert themselves, but wish nevertheless to understand the story. They extol Abraham, but how? By expressing the matter in the most general terms and saying: 'the great thing about him was that he loved God so ardently that he was willing to sacrifice to Him his most precious possession.' That is very true; but 'the most precious possession' is an indefinite expression. As one's thoughts, and one's mouth, run on one assumes, in a very easy fashion, the identity of Isaac and 'the most precious possession'—and meanwhile he who is meditating may smoke his pipe, and his audience comfortably stretch out their legs. If the rich youth whom Christ met on his way had sold all his possessions and given all to the poor, we would extol him as we extol all which is great—aye, would not understand even him without labour; and yet would he never have become an Abraham, notwithstanding his sacrificing the most precious possessions he had. That which people generally forget in the story of Abraham is his fear and anxiety; for as regards money, one is not ethically responsible for it, whereas for his son a father has the highest and most sacred responsibility. However, fear is a dreadful thing for timorous spirits, so they omit it. And yet they wish to speak of Abraham.

So they keep on speaking, and in the course of their speech the two terms Isaac and 'the most precious thing' are used alternately, and everything is in the best order. But now suppose that among the audience there was a man who suffered with sleeplessness—and then the most terrible and profound, the most tragic, and at the same time the most comic misunderstanding is within the range of possibility. That is, suppose this man goes home and wishes to do as did Abraham; for his son is his most precious possession. If a certain preacher learned of this he would, perhaps, go to him, he would gather up all his spiritual dignity and exclaim: 'Thou abominable creature, thou scum of humanity, what devil possessed thee to wish to murder thy son?' And this preacher, who had not felt any particular warmth, nor perspired while speaking about Abraham, this preacher would be astonished himself at the earnest wrath with which he poured forth his thunders against that poor wretch; indeed, he would rejoice over himself, for never had he spoken with such power and unction, and he would have said to his wife: 'I am an orator, the only thing I have lacked so far was the occasion. Last Sunday, when speaking about Abraham, I did not feel thrilled in the least.' Now, if this same orator had just a bit of sense to spare, I believe he would lose it if the sinner would reply, in a quiet and dignified manner: 'Why, it was on this very same matter you preached, last Sunday!' But however could the preacher have entertained such thoughts? Still, such was the case, and the preacher's mistake was merely not knowing what he was talking about. Ah, would that some poet might see his way clear to prefer such a situation to the stuff and nonsense of which novels and comedies are full! For the comic and the tragic here run parallel to infinity. The sermon probably was ridiculous enough in itself, but it became infinitely ridiculous through the very natural consequence it had. Or, suppose now the sinner was converted by this lecture without daring to raise any objection, and this zealous divine now went home elated, glad in the consciousness of being effective, not only in the pulpit, but chiefly, and with irresistible power, as a spiritual guide, inspiring his congregation on Sunday, whilst on Monday he would place himself like a cherub with flaming sword before the man who by his actions tried to give the lie to the old saying that 'the course of the world follows not the priest's word'.

If, on the other hand, the sinner were not convinced of his error his position would become tragic. He would probably be executed, or else sent to the lunatic asylum—at any rate, he would become a sufferer in this world; but in another sense I should think that Abraham rendered him happy; for he who labours, he shall not perish. Now how shall we explain the contradiction contained in that sermon? Is it due to Abraham's having the reputation of being a great man—so that whatever he does is great, but if another should undertake to do the same it is a sin, a heinous sin? If this be the case I prefer not to participate in such thoughtless laudations. If faith cannot make it a sacred thing to wish to sacrifice one's son, then let the same judgment be visited on Abraham as on any other man. And if we perchance lack the courage to drive our thoughts to the logical conclusion and to say that Abraham was a murderer, then it were better to acquire that courage, rather than to waste one's time on undeserved encomiums. The fact is, the ethical expression for what Abraham did is that he wanted to murder Isaac; the religious, that he wanted to sacrifice him. But precisely in this contradiction is contained the fear which may well rob one of one's sleep. And yet Abraham were not Abraham without this fear. Or, again, supposing Abraham did not do what is attributed to him, if his action was an entirely different one, based on conditions of those times, then let us forget him; for what is the use of calling to mind that past which can no longer become a present reality? Or, the speaker had perhaps forgotten the essential fact that Isaac was the son. For if faith is eliminated, having been reduced to a mere nothing, then only the brutal fact remains that Abraham wanted to murder Isaac—which is easy for everybody to imitate who has not the faith—the faith, that is, which renders it most difficult for him. ...

Love has its priests in the poets, and one hears at times a poet's voice which worthily extols it. But not a word does one hear of faith. Who is there to speak in honour of that passion? Philosophy 'goes right on'. Theology sits at the window with a painted visage and sues for philosophy's favor, offering it her charms. It is said to be difficult to understand the philosophy of Hegel; but to understand Abraham, why, that is an easy matter! To proceed further than Hegel is a wonderful feat, but to proceed further than Abraham, why, nothing is easier! Personally, I have devoted a considerable amount of time to a study of Hegelian philosophy and believe I understand it fairly well; in fact, I am rash enough to say that when, notwithstanding an effort, I am not able to understand him in some passages, it is because he is not entirely clear about the matter himself. All this intellectual effort I perform easily and naturally, and it does not cause my head to ache. On the other hand, whenever I attempt to think about Abraham I am, as it were, overwhelmed. At every moment I am aware of the enormous paradox which forms the content of Abraham's life, at every moment I am repulsed, and my thought, notwithstanding its passionate attempts, cannot penetrate into it, cannot forge on the breadth of a hair. I strain every muscle in order to envisage the problem—and become a paralytic in the same moment.

I am by no means unacquainted with what has been admired as great and noble, my soul feels kinship with it, being satisfied, in all humility, that it was also my cause the hero espoused; and when contemplating his deed I say to myself: '*jam tua causa agitur*'. I am able to identify myself with the hero; but I cannot do so with Abraham, for whenever I have reached his height I fall down again, since he confronts me as the paradox. It is by no means my intention to maintain that faith is something inferior, but, on the contrary, that it is the highest of all things; also that it is dishonest in philosophy to offer something else instead, and to pour scorn on faith; but it ought to understand its own nature in order to know what it can offer. It should take away nothing; least of all, fool people out of something as if it were of no value. I am not unacquainted with the sufferings and dangers of life, but I do not fear them, and cheerfully go forth to meet them. ... But my courage is not, for all that, the courage of faith, and is as nothing compared with it. I cannot carry out the movement of faith: I cannot close my eyes and confidently plunge into the absurd—it is impossible for me; but neither do I boast of it. ... Now I wonder if every one of my contemporaries is really able to perform the movements of faith. Unless I am much mistaken they are, rather, inclined to be proud of making what they perhaps think me unable to do, viz., the imperfect movement. It is repugnant to my soul to do what is so often done, to speak inhumanly about great deeds, as if a few thousands of years were an immense space of time. I prefer to speak about them in a human way and as though they had been done but yesterday, to let the great deed itself be the distance which either inspires or condemns me. Now if I, in the capacity of tragic hero—for a higher flight I am unable to take—if I had been summoned to such an extraordinary royal progress as was the one to Mount Moriah, I know very well what I would have done. I would not have been craven enough to remain at home; neither would I have dawdled on the way; nor would I have forgot my knife—just to draw out the end a bit. But I am rather sure that I would have been promptly on the spot, with everything in order—in fact, would probably have been there before the appointed time, so as to have the business soon over with. But I know also what I would have done besides. In the moment I mounted my horse I would have said to myself: 'Now all is lost, God demands Isaac, I shall sacrific him, and with him all my joy—but for all that, God is love and will remain so for me; for in this world God and I cannot speak together, we have no language in common.'

Possibly, one or the other of my contemporaries will be stupid enough, and jealous enough of great deeds, to wish to persuade himself and me that if I had acted thus I should have done something even greater than what Abraham did; for my sublime resignation was (he thinks) by far more ideal and poetic than Abraham's literal-minded action. And yet this is absolutely not so, for my sublime resignation was only a substitute for faith. I could not have made more than the infinite movement (of resignation) to find myself and again repose in myself. Nor would I have loved Isaac as Abraham loved him. The fact that I was resolute enough to resign is sufficient to prove my courage in a human sense, and the fact that I loved him with my whole heart is the very presupposition without which my action would be a crime; but still I did not love as did Abraham, for else I would have hesitated even in the last minute, without, for that matter, arriving too late on Mount Moriah. Also, I would have spoiled the whole business by my behaviour; for if I had had Isaac restored to me I would have been embarrassed. That which was an easy matter for Abraham would have been difficult for me, I mean, to rejoice again in Isaac; for he who with all the energy of his soul *propio motu et propriis auspiciis* has made the infinite movement of resignation and can do no more, he will retain possession of Isaac only in his sorrow.

But what did Abraham? He arrived neither too early nor too late. He mounted his ass and rode slowly on his way. And all the while he had faith, believing that God would not demand Isaac of him, though ready all the while to sacrifice him, should it be demanded of him. He believed this on the strength of the absurd; for there was no question of human calculation any longer. And the absurdity consisted in God's, who yet made this demand of him, recalling his demand the very next moment. Abraham ascended the mountain and whilst the knife already gleamed in his hand he believed—that God would not demand Isaac of him. He was, to be sure, surprised at the outcome; but by a double movement he had returned at his first state of mind and therefore received Isaac back more gladly than the first time. ...

On this height, then, stands Abraham. The last stage he loses sight of is that of infinite resignation. He does really proceed further, he arrives at faith. For all these caricatures of faith, wretched lukewarm sloth, which thinks: 'Oh, there is no hurry, it is not necessary to worry before the time comes'; and miserable hopefulness, which says: 'One cannot know what will happen, there might perhaps—,' all these caricatures belong to the sordid view of life and have already fallen under the infinite scorn of infinite resignation. Abraham, I am not able to understand; and in a certain sense I can learn nothing from him without being struck with wonder. They who flatter themselves that by merely considering the outcome of Abraham's story they will necessarily arrive at faith, only deceive themselves and wish to cheat God out of the first movement of faith—it were tantamount to deriving worldly wisdom from the paradox. But who knows, one or the other of them may succeed in doing this; for our times are not satisfied with faith, and not even with the miracle of changing water into wine—they 'go right on' changing wine into water.

Is it not preferable to remain satisfied with faith, and is it not outrageous that every one wishes to 'go right on'? If people in our times decline to be satisfied with love, as is proclaimed from various sides, where will we finally land? In worldly shrewdness, in mean calculation, in paltriness and baseness, in all that which renders man's divine origin doubtful. Were it not better to stand fast in the faith, and better that he that standeth take heed lest he fall; for the movement of faith must ever be made by virtue of the absurd, but, note well, in such wise that one does not lose the things of this world but wholly and entirely regains them.

As far as I am concerned, I am able to describe most excellently the movements of faith; but I cannot make them myself. When a person wishes to learn how to swim he has himself suspended in a swimming-belt and then goes through the motions; but that does not mean that he can swim. In the same fashion I too can go through the motions of faith; but when I am thrown into the water I swim; to be sure (for I am not a wader in the shallows), but I go through a different set of movements, to-wit, those of infinity; whereas faith does the opposite, to-wit, makes the movements to regain the finite after having made those of infinite resignation. Blessed is he who can make these movements, for he performs a marvellous feat, and I shall never weary of admiring him, whether now it be Abraham himself or the slave in Abraham's house, whether it be a professor of philosophy or a poor servant-girl: it is all the same to me, for I have regard only to the movements. But these movements I watch closely, and I will not be deceived, whether by myself or by any one else. The knights of infinite resignation are easily recognized, for their gait is dancing and bold. But they who possess the jewel of faith frequently deceive one because their bearing is curiously like that of a class of people heartily despised by infinite resignation as well as by faith—the philistines.

Let me admit frankly that I have not in my experience encountered any certain specimen of this type; but I do not refuse to admit that, as far as I know, every other person may be such a specimen. At the same time I will say that I have searched vainly for years. It is the custom of scientists to travel around the globe to see rivers and mountains, new stars, gay-coloured birds, misshapen fish, ridiculous races of men. They abandon themselves to a bovine stupor which gapes at existence and believe they have seen something worthwhile. All this does not interest me; but if I knew where there lived such a knight of faith I would journey to him on foot, for that marvel occupies my thoughts exclusively. Not a moment would I leave him out of sight, but would watch how he makes the movements, and I would consider myself provided for life, and would divide my time between watching him and myself practicing the movements, and would thus use all my time in admiring him.

As I said, I have not met with such a one; but I can easily imagine him. Here he is. I make his acquaintance and am introduced to him. The first moment I lay my eyes on him I push him back, leaping back myself, I hold up my hands in amazement and say to myself: 'Good Lord! That person? Is it really he—why, he looks like a parish-beadle!' But it is really he. I become more closely acquainted with him, watching his every movement to see whether some trifling incongruous movement of his has escaped me, some trace, perchance, of a signalling from the infinite, a glance, a look, a gesture, a melancholy air, or a smile, which might betray the presence of infinite resignation contrasting with the finite. But no! I examine his figure from top to toe to discover whether there be anywhere a chink through which the infinite might be seen to peer forth. But no! He is of a piece, all through. And how about his footing? Vigorous, altogether that of finiteness, no citizen dressed in his very best, prepared to spend his Sunday afternoon in the park, treads the ground more firmly. He belongs altogether to this world, no philistine more so. There is no trace of the somewhat exclusive and haughty demeanor which marks off the knight of infinite resignation. He takes pleasure in all things, is interested in everything, and perseveres in whatever he does with the zest characteristic of persons wholly given to worldly things. He attends to his business, and when one sees him one might think he was a clerk who had lost his soul in doing double bookkeeping, he is so exact. He takes a day off on Sundays. He goes to church. But no hint of anything supernatural or any other sign of the incommensurable betrays him, and if one did not know him it would be impossible to distinguish him in the congregation, for his brisk and manly singing proves only that he has a pair of good lungs.

In the afternoon he walks out to the forest. He takes delight in all he sees, in the crowds of men and women, the new omnibusses, the Sound—if one met him on the promenade one might think he was some shopkeeper who was having a good time, so simple is his joy; for he is not a poet, and in vain have I tried to lure him into betraying some sign of the poet's detachment. Toward evening he walks home again, with a gait as steady as that of a mail-carrier. On his way he happens to wonder whether his wife will have some little special warm dish ready for him when he comes home—as she surely has—as, for instance, a roasted lamb's head garnished with greens. And if he met one minded like him he is very likely to continue talking about this dish with him till they reach the East Gate, and to talk about it with a zest befitting a chef. As it happens, he has not four shillings to spare, and yet he firmly believes that his wife surely has that dish ready for him. If she has, it would be an enviable sight for distinguished people, and an inspiring one for common folks, to see him eat, for he has an appetite greater than Esau's. His wife has not prepared it—strange, he remains altogether the same.

Again, on his way he passes a building lot and there meets another man. They fall to talking, and in a trice he erects a building, freely disposing of everything necessary. And the stranger will leave him with the impression that he has been talking with a capitalist—the fact being that the knight of my admiration is busy with the thought that if it really came to the point he would unquestionably have the means wherewithal at his disposal.

Now he is lying on his elbows in the window and looking over the square on which he lives. All that happens there, if it be only a rat creeping into a gutter-hole, or children playing together—everything engages his attention, and yet his mind is at rest as though it were the mind of a girl of sixteen. He smokes his pipe in the evening, and to look at him you would swear it was the greengrocer from across the street who is lounging at the window in the evening twilight. Thus he shows as much unconcern as any worthless happy-go-lucky fellow; and yet, every moment he lives he purchases his leisure at the highest price, for he makes not the least movement except by virtue of the absurd; and yet, yet—indeed, I might become furious with anger, if for no other reason than that of envy—and yet, this man has performed, and is performing every moment, the movement of infinity... He has resigned everything absolutely, and then again seized hold of it all on the strength of the absurd...

But this miracle may so easily deceive one that it will be best if I describe the movements in a given case which may illustrate their aspect in contact with reality; and that is the important point. Suppose, then, a young swain falls in love with a princess, and all his life is bound up in this love. But circumstances are such that it is out of the question to think of marrying her, an impossibility to translate his dreams into reality. The slaves of paltriness, the frogs in the sloughs of life, they will shout, of course: 'Such a love is folly, the rich brewer's widow is quite as good and solid a match.' Let them but croak. The knight of infinite resignation does not follow their advice, he does not surrender his love, not for all the riches in the world. He is no fool, he first makes sure that this love really is the contents of his life, for his soul is too sound and too proud to waste itself on a mere intoxication. He is no coward, he is not afraid to let his love insinuate itself into his most secret and most remote thoughts, to let it wind itself in innumerable coils about every fibre of his consciousness—if he is disappointed in his love he will never be able to extricate himself again. He feels a delicious pleasure in letting love thrill his every nerve, and yet his soul is solemn as is that of him who has drained a cup of poison and who now feels the virus mingle with every drop of his blood, poised in that moment between life and death.

Having thus imbibed love, and being wholly absorbed in it, he does not lack the courage to try and dare all. He surveys the whole situation, he calls together his swift thoughts which like tame pigeons obey his every beck, he gives the signal, and they dart in all directions. But when they return, every one bearing a message of sorrow, and explain to him that it is impossible, then he becomes silent, he dismisses them, he remains alone; and then he makes the movement. Now if what I say here is to have any significance, it is of prime importance that the movement be made in a normal fashion. The knight of resignation is supposed to have sufficient energy to concentrate the entire contents of his life and the realization of existing conditions into one single wish. But if one lacks this concentration, this devotion to a single thought; if his soul from the very beginning is scattered on a number of objects, he will never be able to make the movement—he will be as worldly-wise in the conduct of his life as the financier who invests his capital in a number of securities to win on the one if he should lose on the other; that is, he is no knight. Furthermore, the knight is supposed to possess sufficient energy to concentrate all his thought into a single act of consciousness. If he lacks this concentration he will only run errands in life and will never be able to assume the attitude of infinite resignation; for the very minute he approaches it he will suddenly discover that he forgot something so that he must remain behind. The next minute, thinks he, it will be attainable again, and so it is; but such inhibitions will never allow him to make the movement but will, rather, tend to let him sink ever deeper into the mire.

Our knight, then, performs the movement—which movement? Is he intent on forgetting the whole affair, which, too, would presuppose much concentration? No, for the knight does not contradict himself, and it is a contradiction to forget the main contents of one's life and still remain the same person. And he has no desire to become another person; neither does he consider such a desire to smack of greatness. Only lower natures forget themselves and become something different. Thus the butterfly has forgotten that it once was a caterpillar—who knows but it may forget altogether that it once was a butterfly, and turn into a fish! Deeper natures never forget themselves and never change their essential qualities. So the knight remembers all; but precisely this remembrance is painful. Nevertheless, in his infinite resignation he has become reconciled with existence. His love for the princess has become for him the expression of an eternal love, has assumed a religious character, has been transfigured into a love for the eternal being which, to be sure, denied him the fulfilment of his love, yet reconciled him again by presenting him with the abiding consciousness of his love's being preserved in an everlasting form of which no reality can rob him....

Now, he is no longer interested in what the princess may do, and precisely this proves that he has made the movement of infinite resignation correctly. In fact, this is a good criterion for detecting whether a person's movement is sincere or just make-believe. Take a person who believes that he too has resigned, but lo! time passed, the princess did something on her part, for example, married a prince, and then his soul lost the elasticity of its resignation. This ought to show him that he did not make the movement correctly, for he who has resigned absolutely is sufficient unto himself. The knight does not cancel his resignation, but preserves his love as fresh and young as it was at the first moment, he never lets go of it just because his resignation is absolute. Whatever the princess does, cannot disturb him, for it is only the lower natures who have the law for their actions in some other person, i.e. have the premises of their actions outside of themselves....

Infinite resignation is the last stage which goes before faith, so that everyone who has not made the movement of infinite resignation cannot have faith; for only through absolute resignation do I become conscious of my eternal worth, and only then can there arise the problem of again grasping hold of this world by virtue of faith.

We will now suppose the knight of faith in the same case. He does precisely as the other knight, he absolutely resigns the love which is the contents of his life, he is reconciled to the pain; but then the miraculous happens, he makes one more movement, strange beyond comparison, saying: 'And still I believe that I shall marry her—marry her by virtue of the absurd, by virtue of the act that to God nothing is impossible.'

Now the absurd is not one of the categories which belong to the understanding proper. It is not identical with the improbable, the unforeseen, the unexpected. The very moment our knight resigned himself he made sure of the absolute impossibility, in any human sense, of his love. This was the result reached by his reflections, and he had sufficient energy to make them. In a transcendent sense, however, by his very resignation, the attainment of his end is not impossible; but this very act of again taking possession of his love is at the same time a relinquishment of it. Nevertheless this kind of possession is by no means an absurdity to the intellect; for the intellect all the while continues to be right, as it is aware that in the world of finalities, in which reason rules, his love was and is, an impossibility. The knight of faith realizes this fully as well. Hence the only thing which can save him is recourse to the absurd, and this recourse he has through his faith. That is, he clearly recognizes the impossibility, and in the same moment he believes the absurd; for if he imagined he had faith, without at the same time recognizing, with all the passion his soul is capable of, that his love is impossible, he would be merely deceiving himself, and his testimony would be of no value, since he had not arrived even at the stage of absolute resignation....

This last movement, the paradoxical movement of faith, I cannot make, whether or no it be my duty, although I desire nothing more ardently than to be able to make it. It must be left to a person's discretion whether he cares to make this confession; and at any rate, it is a matter between him and the Eternal Being, who is the object of his faith, whether an amicable adjustment can be affected. But what every person can do is to make the movement of absolute resignation, and I for my part would not hesitate to declare him a coward who imagines he cannot perform it. It is a different matter with faith. But what no person has a right to, is to delude others into the belief that faith is something of no great significance, or that it is an easy matter, whereas it is the greatest and most difficult of all things.

But the story of Abraham is generally interpreted in a different way. God's mercy is praised which restored Isaac to him—it was but a trial! A trial. This word may mean much or little, and yet the whole of it passes off as quickly as the story is told: one mounts a winged horse, in the same instant one arrives on Mount Moriah, and *presto* one sees the ram. It is not remembered that Abraham only rode on an ass which travels but slowly, that it was a three days' journey for him, and that he required some additional time to collect the firewood, to bind Isaac, and to whet his knife.

And yet one extols Abraham. He who is to preach the sermon may sleep comfortably until a quarter of an hour before he is to preach it, and the listener may comfortably sleep during the sermon, for everything is made easy enough, without much exertion either to preacher or listener. But now suppose a man was present who suffered with sleeplessness and who went home and sat in a corner and reflected as follows: 'The whole lasted but a minute, you need only wait a little while, and then the ram will be shown and the trial will be over.' Now if the preacher should find him in this frame of mind, I believe he would confront him in all his dignity and say to him: 'Wretch that thou art, to let thy soul lapse into such folly; miracles do not happen, all life is a trial.' And as he proceeded he would grow more and more passionate, and would become ever more satisfied with himself; and whereas he had not noticed any congestion in his head whilst preaching about Abraham, he now feels the veins on his forehead swell. Yet who knows but he would stand aghast if the sinner should answer him in a quiet and dignified manner that it was precisely this about which he preached the Sunday before.

Let us then either waive the whole story of Abraham, or

else learn to stand in awe of the enormous paradox which constitutes his significance for us, so that we may learn to understand that our age, like every age, may rejoice if it has faith. If the story of Abraham is not a mere nothing, an illusion, or if it is just used for show and as a pastime, the mistake cannot by any means be in the sinner's wishing to do likewise; but it is necessary to find out how great was the deed which Abraham performed, in order that the man may judge for himself whether he has the courage and the mission to do likewise. The comical contradiction in the procedure of the preacher was his reduction of the story of Abraham to insignificance whereas he rebuked the other man for doing the very same thing.

But should we then cease to speak about Abraham? I certainly think not. But if I were to speak about him I would first of all describe the terrors of his trial. To that end leechlike I would suck all the suffering and distress out of the anguish of a father, in order to be able to describe what Abraham suffered whilst yet preserving his faith. I would remind the hearer that the journey lasted three days and a goodly part of the fourth—in fact, these three and a half days ought to become infinitely longer than the few thousand years which separate me from Abraham. I would remind him, as I think right, that every person is still permitted to turn about before trying his strength on this formidable task; in fact, that he may return every instant in repentance. Provided this is done, I fear for nothing. Nor do I fear to awaken great desire among people to attempt to emulate Abraham. But to get out a cheap edition of Abraham and yet forbid everyone to do as he did, that I call ridiculous.

ARTHUR SCHOPENHAUER, ON HUMAN NATURE

Introduction

Schopenhauer is the philosopher the academic establishment doesn't much want you to read. The reason for this is simple: Schopenhauer was never able to keep his opinions within the bounds of polite and socially acceptable discourse. University philosophy, he said, was 'mere juggling', for governments will 'not pay people to contradict directly, or even only indirectly, what it has had promulgated from all the pulpits', with the result that professors have 'nothing left but to look for new turns of phrase and forms of speech' for the orthodox way of thinking.[1] If Schopenhauer's derisory views of the academic establishment were not provocative enough, his views on women went still further beyond the pale: he thought that 'women remain children all their lives, for they always see only what is near at hand, cling to the present, take the appearance

---

1. Arthur Schopenhauer, "On Philosophy at the Universities," in *Parerga and Paralipomena*, trans. E. F. J. Payne (New York: Oxford University Press, 1974), 1:139-140.

of a thing for reality, and prefer trifling matters to the most important'; it was in woman's nature, he added, 'to look upon everything only as a means for winning man, and her interest in anything else is always a simulated one, a mere roundabout way to gain her ends, consisting of coquetry and pretence'.[2] Schopenhauer's most penetrating criticism, though, was targeted at the naive optimism characteristic of conventional society and its eagerness to turn away from the fundamental truths of existence. 'If, finally, we should bring clearly to a man's sight the terrible sufferings and miseries to which his life is constantly exposed,' insisted Schopenhauer, 'he would be seized with horror: and if we were to conduct the confirmed optimist through the hospitals, infirmaries, and surgical operating-rooms, through the prisons, torture chambers, and slave kennels, over battle-fields and places of execution; if we were to open to him all the dark abodes of misery, where it hides itself from the glance of cold curiosity, and finally allow him to glance into Ugolino's dungeon of starvation—he too would understand at last the nature of this "best of possible worlds".'[3]

Arthur Schopenhauer (1788-1860) was born in Danzig (now Gdańsk, Poland) into a family of successful merchants and shipowners. After Prussia annexed the city in 1793, the Schopenhauers moved to the Free and Hanseatic City of Hamburg, although during this period they also travelled widely in France and England. Schopenhauer's father died when he was just seventeen, possibly through suicide, and although Schopenhauer honoured his father's wishes by continuing his Hamburg business apprenticeship for two years, he found that the life of a merchant was unsuitable for his

---

2. Arthur Schopenhauer, "On Women," in *Essays*, trans. T. Bailey Saunders (New York: A.L. Burt, 1902), 340, 344.
3. Arthur Schopenhauer, *The World as Will and Idea*, trans. Richard Burdon Haldane and John Kemp (London: Trübner & Co., 1886), 1:419.

scholarly disposition. While his mother, Johanna, established a literary salon of her own in Weimar, then, the young Schopenhauer commenced studies at the Universities of Göttingen and later Berlin, before submitting his doctoral dissertation at the University of Jena. His great work, *The World as Will and as Representation* (1818), came shortly thereafter: it conceives of humanity as driven by a blind and restless 'Will-to-Life' that makes us cling to existence and thrust ourselves ever forwards. Taking an academic position at the University of Berlin, Schopenhauer famously scheduled his class at the same time as the popular lectures of the celebrated GWF Hegel, whom Schopenhauer considered a 'clumsy and nauseating charlatan' whose 'artful trick' it was to produce such gibberish that the reader 'must think he is in the wrong if he does not understand it'.[4] Hegel, however, won the day, and only five students turned up to listen to Schopenhauer; later attempts at an academic career would also be unsuccessful. Fleeing Berlin in 1831 from the cholera epidemic that finished off his rival, Schopenhauer settled ultimately in Frankfurt, where he remained for the final 27 years of his life, enjoying a leisurely daily routine that consisted of study in the mornings, quiet walks with his poodles in the afternoons, and a concert or reading from the Hindu classics in the evenings.

Schopenhauer's philosophy centres on the idea of the 'Will'. The Will is the 'thing in itself': it is the raw stuff of existence that pulsates through all living beings and things as a ceaseless impulse to survive and expand. In man, Will manifests itself in the constant striving for food, mates, power, property, and children. It even shapes the very structures of the body, so that teeth, throat and bowels, for example, can properly be considered a form of 'objectified hunger'. Will is present in plants and animals, as well as in the forces that determine the

---

4. Arthur Schopenhauer, "On Philosophy at the Universities," in *Parerga and Paralipomena*, trans. EFJ Payne (New York: Oxford University Press, 1974), 1:162.

structure of the physical universe, such as gravity, magnetism, and electricity. Despite man's pretensions, the Will reigns supreme over the intellect, which waits upon it as a handmaiden waits upon her master: reason is designed to know things only insofar as knowing would assist the Will to realise its objectives; it is not reason's function to comprehend reality in itself.

The ethics of Schopenhauer can only be understood in the context of the Will. Every one of us is, he suggests, merely a particular embodiment of this universal craving: born of the same stuff and afflicted by the same drives, while we live we are—each of us—marked by the same basic sins of our nature. The individual, it is true, remains significant in Schopenhauer's doctrine. To the extent, however, that the individual is differentiated from the universal Will, his destiny is determined by his character rather than the particular actions which are but a particular manifestation of such character. Man's freedom is all metaphysical: his individual character is to be regarded as a free act—he is such and such a man, because once and for all it is his will to be that man—but his actions are not free.

We may also free, having recognised the Will, to adjust our relationship towards it. Schopenhauer's philosophy leads directly towards a type of asceticism not dissimilar from that found in Eastern traditions such as Buddhism. The Will, says Schopenhauer, is that which endlessly torments us, for we either obtain that which it impels us towards, and meet with disappointment, boredom, and *ennui*, or we fail and are frustrated. The only solace available to us arises in those moments when the constant agitated striving of the Will is put to rest, giving a brief respite for intellect and heart to shine forth in tranquil repose. All else is folly.

At the heart of Schopenhauer's ethics is the recognition that each and every one of us is an aspect of the universal Will. The thing to grasp is that our antagonists in this life bear, as much as we, the sufferings of this world, and that we, as much as they, are culpable for its sins: tormentor and tormented are part of the same fabric of reality and the same humanity looks out from each. Compassion releases us from the endless striving for individual existence and the endless oscillation between pain and ennui that characterises this; it awakens in us a hoary wisdom that we share a common fate and common destiny from which none can escape but from which all can hope for relief.

Schopenhauer's philosophy requires us to look with some scepticism on morality as it is commonly understood—for moral doctrines are themselves created, adopted, and deployed by men and women acting not in the light of abstract intelligence but rather under the unacknowledged urgings of the Will. Nevertheless, there is also a positive dimension to Schopenhauer's ethics. We do have freedom of a sort, he suggests, although our moral freedom lies not in our individual acts—these are determined by our character—but in willing, on the metaphysical place, the kind of person that we will be. Furthermore, while the Will cannot be permanently triumphed over, it can through asceticism, as well as through contemplation of ideas and beauty, be put to sleep. There is much that is pessimistic and gloomy in Schopenhauer, and much too that is darkly humorous, but in this respect, at least, he offers to modern man a realistic and practical guide to faring well in the tragicomedy of our common condition.

FREE WILL AND FATALISM

No thoughtful man can have any doubt, after the conclusions reached in my prize-essay on *Moral Freedom*, that such freedom is to be sought, not anywhere in nature, but outside of it. The only freedom that exists is of a metaphysical character. In the physical world freedom is an impossibility. Accordingly, while our several actions are in no wise free, every man's individual character is to be regarded as a free act. He is such and such a man, because once for all it is his will to be that man. For the will itself, and in itself, and also in so far as it is manifest in an individual, and accordingly constitutes the original and fundamental desires of that individual, is independent of all knowledge, because it is antecedent to such knowledge. All that it receives from knowledge is the series of motives by which it successively develops its nature and makes itself cognisable or visible; but the will itself, as something that lies beyond time, and so long as it exists at all, never changes. Therefore every man, being what he is and placed in the circumstances which for the moment obtain, but which on their part also arise by strict necessity, can absolutely never do anything else than just what at that moment he does do. Accordingly, the whole course of a man's life, in all its incidents great and small, is as necessarily predetermined as the course of a clock.

The main reason of this is that the kind of metaphysical free act which I have described tends to become a knowing consciousness—a perceptive intuition, which is subject to the forms of space and time. By means of those forms the unity and indivisibility of the act are represented as drawn asunder into a series of states and events, which are subject to the Principle of Sufficient Reason in its four forms—and it is this that is meant by *necessity*. But the result of it all assumes a moral complexion. It amounts to this, that by what we do we know what we are, and by what we suffer we know what we deserve.

Further, it follows from this that a man's *individuality* does not rest upon the principle of individuation alone, and therefore is not altogether phenomenal in its nature. On the contrary, it has its roots in the thing-in-itself, in the will which is the essence of each individual. The character of this individual is itself individual. But how deep the roots of individuality extend is one of the questions which I do not undertake to answer.

In this connection it deserves to be mentioned that even Plato, in his own way, represented the individuality of a man as a free act.[5] He represented him as coming into the world with a given tendency, which was the result of the feelings and character already attaching to him in accordance with the doctrine of metempsychosis. The Brahmin philosophers also express the unalterable fixity of innate character in a mystical fashion. They say that Brahma, when a man is produced, engraves his doings and sufferings in written characters on his skull, and that his life must take shape in accordance therewith. They point to the jagged edges in the sutures of the skull-bones as evidence of this writing; and the purport of it, they say, depends on his previous life and actions. The same view appears to underlie the Christian, or rather, the Pauline, dogma of Predestination.

But this truth, which is universally confirmed by experience, is attended with another result. All genuine merit, moral as well as intellectual, is not merely physical or empirical in its origin, but metaphysical; that is to say, it is given *a priori* and not *a posteriori*; in other words, it lies innate and is not acquired, and therefore its source is not a mere phenomenon, but the thing-in-itself. Hence it is that every man achieves only that which is irrevocably established in his nature, or is born with him. Intellectual capacity needs, it is true, to be developed just as many natural products need to be cultivated in order that we may enjoy or use them; but just as in the case of a natural product no cultivation can take the place of original material, neither can it do so in the case of intellect. That is the reason

---

5. *Phaedrus* and *Laws*, bk. x.

why qualities which are merely acquired, or learned, or enforced—that is, qualities *a posteriori*, whether moral or intellectual—are not real or genuine, but superficial only, and possessed of no value. This is a conclusion of true metaphysics, and experience teaches the same lesson to all who can look below the surface. Nay, it is proved by the great importance which we all attach to such innate characteristics as physiognomy and external appearance, in the case of a man who is at all distinguished; and that is why we are so curious to see him. Superficial people, to be sure—and, for very good reasons, commonplace people too—will be of the opposite opinion; for if anything fails them they will thus be enabled to console themselves by thinking that it is still to come.

The world, then, is not merely a battlefield where victory and defeat receive their due recompense in a future state. No! The world is itself the Last Judgment on it. Every man carries with him the reward and the disgrace that he deserves; and this is no other than the doctrine of the Brahmins and Buddhists as it is taught in the theory of metempsychosis.

The question has been raised, what two men would do, who lived a solitary life in the wilds and met each other for the first time. Hobbes, Pufendorf, and Rousseau have given different answers. Pufendorf believed that they would approach each other as friends; Hobbes, on the contrary, as enemies; Rousseau, that they would pass each other by in silence. All three are both right and wrong. This is just a case in which *the incalculable difference that there is in innate moral disposition between one individual and another* would make its appearance. The difference is so strong that the question here raised might be regarded as the standard and measure of it. For there are men in whom the sight of another man at once rouses a feeling of enmity, since their inmost nature exclaims at once: *That is not me!* There are, others in whom the sight awakens immediate sympathy; their inmost nature says: *That is me over again!* Between the two there are countless degrees. That in this most important matter we are so totally different is a great problem, nay, a mystery.

In regard to this *a priori* nature of moral character there is matter for varied reflection in a work by Bastholm, a Danish writer, entitled *Historical Contributions to the Knowledge of Man in the Savage State*. He is struck by the fact that intellectual culture and moral excellence are shown to be entirely independent of each other, inasmuch as one is often found without the other. The reason of this, as we shall find, is simply that moral excellence in no wise springs from reflection, which is developed by intellectual culture, but from the will itself, the constitution of which is innate and not susceptible in itself of any improvement by means of education. Bastholm represents most nations as very vicious and immoral; and on the other hand he reports that excellent traits of character are found amongst some savage peoples; as, for instance, amongst the Orotchyses, the inhabitants of the island Savu, the Tunguses, and the Pelew islanders. He thus attempts to solve the problem, how it is that some tribes are so remarkably good, when their neighbours are all bad,

It seems to me that the difficulty may be explained as follows: moral qualities, as we know, are heritable, and an isolated tribe, such as is described, might take its rise in some one family, and ultimately in a single ancestor who happened to be a good man, and then maintain its purity. Is it not the case, for instance, that on many unpleasant occasions, such as repudiation of public debts, filibustering raids and so on, the English have often reminded the North Americans of their descent from English penal colonists? It is a reproach, however, which can apply only to a small part of the population.

It is marvellous how *every man's individuality* (that is to say, the union of a definite character with a definite intellect) accurately determines all his actions and thoughts down to the most unimportant details, as though it were a dye which pervaded them; and how, in consequence, one man's whole course of life, in other words, his inner and outer history, turns out so absolutely different from another's. As a botanist knows a plant in its entirety from a single leaf; as Cuvier from a single bone constructed the whole animal, so an accurate knowledge of a man's whole character may be attained from a single characteristic act; that is to say, he himself may to some extent be constructed from it, even though the act in question is of very trifling consequence. Nay, that is the most perfect test of all, for in a matter of importance people are on their guard; in trifles they follow their natural bent without much reflection. That is why Seneca's remark, that even the smallest things may be taken as evidence of character, is so true: *argumenta morum ex minimis quoque licet capere*.[6] If a man shows by his absolutely unscrupulous and selfish behaviour in small things that a sentiment of justice is foreign to his disposition, he should not be trusted with a penny unless on due security. For who will believe that the man who every day shows that he is unjust in all matters other than those which concern property, and whose boundless selfishness everywhere protrudes through the small affairs of ordinary life which are subject to no scrutiny, like a dirty shirt through the holes of a ragged jacket—who, I ask, will believe that such a man will act honourably in matters of *meum* and *tuum* without any other incentive but that of justice? The man who has no conscience in small things will be a scoundrel in big things. If we neglect small traits of character, we have only ourselves to blame if we afterwards learn to our disadvantage what this character is in the great affairs of life. On the same principle, we ought to break with so-called friends even in matters of trifling moment, if they show a character that is malicious or bad or vulgar,

6. *Ep.*, 52.

so that we may avoid the bad turn which only waits for an opportunity of being done us. The same thing applies to servants. Let it always be our maxim: Better alone than amongst traitors.

Of a truth the first and foremost step in all knowledge of mankind is the conviction that a man's conduct, taken as a whole, and in all its essential particulars, is not governed by his reason or by any of the resolutions which he may make in virtue of it. No man becomes this or that by wishing to be it, however earnestly. His acts proceed from his innate and unalterable character, and they are more immediately and particularly determined by motives. A man's conduct, therefore, is the necessary product of both character and motive. It may be illustrated by the course of a planet, which is the result of the combined effect of the tangential energy with which it is endowed, and the centripetal energy which operates from the sun. In this simile the former energy represents character, and the latter the influence of motive. It is almost more than a mere simile. The tangential energy which properly speaking is the source of the planet's motion, whilst on the other hand the motion is kept in check by gravitation, is, from a metaphysical point of view, the will manifesting itself in that body.

To grasp this fact is to see that we really never form anything more than a conjecture of what we shall do under circumstances which are still to happen; although we often take our conjecture for a resolve. When, for instance, in pursuance of a proposal, a man with the greatest sincerity, and even eagerness, accepts an engagement to do this or that on the occurrence of a certain future event, it is by no means certain that he will fulfil the engagement; unless he is so constituted that the promise which he gives, in itself and as such, is always and everywhere a motive sufficient for him, by acting upon him, through considerations of honour, like some external compulsion.

But above and beyond this, what he will do on the occurrence of that event may be foretold from true and accurate knowledge of his character and the external circumstances under the influence of which he will fall; and it may with complete certainty be foretold from this alone. Nay, it is a very easy prophecy if he has been already seen in a like position; for he will inevitably do the same thing a second time, provided that on the first occasion he had a true and complete knowledge of the facts of the case. For, as I have often remarked, a final cause does not impel a man by being real, but by being known; *causa finalis non movet secundum suum esse reale, sed secundum esse cognitum.*[7] Whatever he failed to recognise or understand the first time could have no influence upon his will; just as an electric current stops when some isolating body hinders the action of the conductor. This unalterable nature of character, and the consequent necessity of our actions, are made very clear to a man who has not, on any given occasion, behaved as he ought to have done, by showing a lack either of resolution or endurance or courage, or some other quality demanded at the moment. Afterwards he recognises what it is that he ought to have done; and, sincerely repenting of his incorrect behaviour, he thinks to himself, *If the opportunity were offered to me again, I should act differently*. It is offered once more; the same occasion recurs; and to his great astonishment he does precisely the same thing over again.[8]

The best examples of the truth in question are in every way furnished by Shakespeare's plays. It is a truth with which he was thoroughly imbued, and his intuitive wisdom expressed it in a concrete shape on every page. I shall here, however, give an instance of it in a case in which he makes it remarkably clear,

---

7. Suarez, *Disp. Metaph.*, xxiii.; §§7 and 8.
8. Cf. *World as Will*, ii., pp. 251 ff. .sqq.. (third edition).

without exhibiting any design or affectation in the matter; for he was a real artist and never set out from general ideas. His method was obviously to work up to the psychological truth which he grasped directly and intuitively, regardless of the fact that few would notice or understand it, and without the smallest idea that some dull and shallow fellows in Germany would one day proclaim far and wide that he wrote his works to illustrate moral commonplaces. I allude to the character of the Earl of Northumberland, whom we find in three plays in succession, although he does not take a leading part in any one of them; nay, he appears only in a few scenes distributed over fifteen acts. Consequently, if the reader is not very attentive, a character exhibited at such great intervals, and its moral identity, may easily escape his notice, even though it has by no means escaped the poet's. He makes the Earl appear everywhere with a noble and knightly grace, and talk in language suitable to it; nay, he sometimes puts very beautiful and even elevated passages, into his mouth. At the same time he is very far from writing after the manner of Schiller, who was fond of painting the devil black, and whose moral approval or disapproval of the characters which he presented could be heard in their own words. With Shakespeare, and also with Goethe, every character, as long as he is on the stage and speaking, seems to be absolutely in the right, even though it were the devil himself. In this respect let the reader compare Duke Alba as he appears in Goethe with the same character in Schiller.

We make the acquaintance of the Earl of Northumberland in the play of *Richard II*, where he is the first to hatch a plot against the King in favour of Bolingbroke, afterwards Henry IV, to whom he even offers some personal flattery (Act II, Sc. 3). In the following act he suffers a reprimand because, in speaking of the King he talks of him as 'Richard', without more ado, but protests that he did it only for brevity's sake. A little later his insidious words induce the King to surrender. In the following act, when the King renounces the crown, Northumberland treats him with such harshness and contempt that the unlucky monarch is quite broken, and losing all patience once more exclaims to him: *Fiend, thou torment'st me ere I come to hell!* At the close, Northumberland announces to the new King that he has sent the heads of the former King's adherents to London.

In the following tragedy, *Henry IV*, he hatches a plot against the new King in just the same way. In the fourth act we see the rebels united, making preparations for the decisive battle on the morrow, and only waiting impatiently for Northumberland and his division. At last there arrives a letter from him, saying that he is ill, and that he cannot entrust his force to anyone else; but that nevertheless the others should go forward with courage and make a brave fight. They do so, but, greatly weakened by his absence, they are completely defeated; most of their leaders are captured, and his own son, the valorous Hotspur, falls by the hand of the Prince of Wales.

Again, in the following play, the *Second Part of Henry IV*, we see him reduced to a state of the fiercest wrath by the death of his son, and maddened by the thirst for revenge. Accordingly he kindles another rebellion, and the heads of it assemble once more. In the fourth act, just as they are about to give battle, and are only waiting for him to join them, there comes a letter saying that he cannot collect a proper force, and will therefore seek safety for the present in Scotland; that, nevertheless, he heartily wishes their heroic undertaking the best success. Thereupon they surrender to the King under a treaty which is not kept, and so perish.

So far is character from being the work of reasoned choice and consideration that in any action the intellect has nothing to do but to present motives to the will. Thereafter it looks on as a mere spectator and witness at the course which life takes, in accordance with the influence of motive on the given character. All the incidents of life occur, strictly speaking, with the same necessity as the movement of a clock. On this point let me refer to my prize-essay on *The Freedom of the Will*. I have there explained the true meaning and origin of the persistent illusion that the will is entirely free in every single action; and I have indicated the cause to which it is due. I will only add here the following teleological explanation of this natural illusion.

Since every single action of a man's life seems to possess the freedom and originality which in truth only belong to his character as he apprehends it, and the mere apprehension of it by his intellect is what constitutes his career; and since what is original in every single action seems to the empirical consciousness to be always being performed anew, a man thus receives in the course of his career the strongest possible moral lesson. Then, and not before, he becomes thoroughly conscious of all the bad sides of his character. Conscience accompanies every act with the comment: *You should act differently*, although its true sense is: *You could be other than you are*. As the result of this immutability of character on the one hand, and, on the other, of the strict necessity which attends all the circumstances in which character is successively placed, every man's course of life is precisely determined from Alpha right through to Omega. But, nevertheless, one man's course of life turns out immeasurably happier, nobler and more worthy than another's, whether it be regarded from a subjective or an objective point of view, and unless we are to exclude all ideas of justice, we are led to the doctrine which is well accepted in Brahmanism and Buddhism, that the subjective conditions in which, as well as the objective conditions under which, every man is born, are the moral consequences of a previous existence.

Macchiavelli, who seems to have taken no interest whatever in philosophical speculations, is drawn by the keen subtlety of his very unique understanding into the following observation, which possesses a really deep meaning. It shows that he had an intuitive knowledge of the entire necessity with which, characters and motives being given, all actions take place. He makes it at the beginning of the prologue to his comedy *Clitia*. *If*, he says, *the same men were to recur in the world in the way that the same circumstances recur, a hundred years would never elapse without our finding ourselves together once more, and doing the same things as we are doing now—Se nel mondo tornassino i medesimi uomini, como tornano i medesimi casi, non passarebbono mai cento anni che noi non ci trovassimo un altra volta insieme, a fare le medesime cose che hora.* He seems however to have been drawn into the remark by a reminiscence of what Augustine says in his *De Civitate Dei*, bk. xii., ch. xiii.

Again, Fate, or the *eimarmenae* of the ancients, is nothing but the conscious certainty that all that happens is fast bound by a chain of causes, and therefore takes place with a strict necessity; that the future is already ordained with absolute certainty and can undergo as little alteration as the past. In the fatalistic myths of the ancients all that can be regarded as fabulous is the prediction of the future; that is, if we refuse to consider the possibility of magnetic clairvoyance and second sight. Instead of trying to explain away the fundamental truth of Fatalism by superficial twaddle and foolish evasion, a man should attempt to get a clear knowledge and comprehension of it; for it is demonstrably true, and it helps us in a very important way to an understanding of the mysterious riddle of our life. Predestination and Fatalism do not differ in the main. They differ only in this, that with Predestination the given character and external determination of human action proceed from a rational Being, and with Fatalism from an irrational one. But in either case the result is the same: that happens which must happen.

On the other hand the conception of *Moral Freedom* is inseparable from that of *Originality*. A man may be said, but he cannot be conceived, to be the work of another, and at the same time be free in respect of his desires and acts. He who called him into existence out of nothing in the same process created and determined his nature—in other words, the whole of his qualities. For no one can create without creating a something, that is to say, a being determined throughout and in all its qualities. But all that a man says and does necessarily proceeds from the qualities so determined; for it is only the qualities themselves set in motion. It is only some external impulse that they require to make their appearance. As a man is, so must he act; and praise or blame attaches, not to his separate acts, but to his nature and being.

That is the reason why Theism and the moral responsibility of man are incompatible; because responsibility always reverts to the creator of man and it is there that it has its centre. Vain attempts have been made to make a bridge from one of these incompatibles to the other by means of the conception of moral freedom; but it always breaks down again. What is *free* must also be *original*. If our will is *free*, our will is also *the original element*, and conversely. Pre-Kantian dogmatism tried to separate these two predicaments. It was thereby compelled to assume two kinds of freedom, one cosmological, of the first cause, and the other moral and theological, of human will. These are represented in Kant by the third as well as the fourth antimony of freedom.

On the other hand, in my philosophy the plain recognition of the strictly necessary character of all action is in accordance with the doctrine that what manifests itself even in the organic and irrational world is *will*. If this were not so, the necessity under which irrational beings obviously act would place their action in conflict with will; if, I mean, there were really such a thing as the freedom of individual action, and this were not as strictly necessitated as every other kind of action. But, as I have just shown, it is this same doctrine of the necessary character of all acts of will which makes it needful to regard a man's existence and being as itself the work of his freedom, and consequently of his will. The will, therefore, must be self-existent; it must possess so-called *a-se-ity*. Under the opposite supposition all responsibility, as I have shown, would be at an end, and the moral like the physical world would be a mere machine, set in motion for the amusement of its manufacturer placed somewhere outside of it. So it is that truths hang together, and mutually advance and complete one another; whereas error gets jostled at every corner.

What kind of influence it is that *moral instruction* may exercise on conduct, and what are the limits of that influence, are questions which I have sufficiently examined in the twentieth section of my treatise on the *Foundation of Morality*. In all essential particulars an analogous influence is exercised by *example*, which, however, has a more powerful effect than doctrine, and therefore it deserves a brief analysis.

In the main, example works either by restraining a man or by encouraging him. It has the former effect when it determines him to leave undone what he wanted to do. He sees, I mean, that other people do not do it; and from this he judges, in general, that it is not expedient; that it may endanger his person, or his property, or his honour. He rests content, and gladly finds himself relieved from examining into the matter for himself. Or he may see that another man, who has not refrained, has incurred evil consequences from doing it; this is example of the deterrent kind. The example which encourages a man works in a twofold manner. It either induces him to do what he would be glad to leave undone, if he were not afraid lest the omission might in some way endanger him, or injure him in others' opinion; or else it encourages him to do what he is glad to do, but has hitherto refrained from doing from fear of danger or shame; this is example of the seductive kind. Finally, example may bring a man to do what he would have otherwise never thought of doing. It is obvious that in this last case example works in the main only on the intellect; its effect on the will is secondary, and if it has any such effect, it is by the interposition of the man's own judgment, or by reliance on the person who presented the example.

The whole influence of example—and it is very strong—rests on the fact that a man has, as a rule, too little judgment of his own, and often too little knowledge, to explore his own way for himself, and that he is glad, therefore, to tread in the footsteps of some one else. Accordingly, the more deficient he is in either of these qualities, the more is he open to the influence of example; and we find, in fact, that most men's guiding star is the example of others; that their whole course of life, in great things and in small, comes in the end to be mere imitation; and that not even in the pettiest matters do they act according to their own judgment. Imitation and custom are the spring of almost all human action. The cause of it is that men fight shy of all and any sort of reflection, and very properly mistrust their own discernment. At the same time this remarkably strong imitative instinct in man is a proof of his kinship with apes.

But the kind of effect which example exercises depends upon a man's character, and thus it is that the same example may possibly seduce one man and deter another. An easy opportunity of observing this is afforded in the case of certain social impertinences which come into vogue and gradually spread. The first time that a man notices anything of the kind, he may say to himself: *For shame! How can he do it! How selfish and inconsiderate of him! Really, I shall take care never to do anything like that*. But twenty others will think: *Aha! If he does that, I may do it too*.

As regards morality, example, like doctrine, may, it is true, promote civil or legal amelioration, but not that inward amendment which is, strictly speaking, the only kind of moral amelioration. For example always works as a personal motive alone, and assumes, therefore, that a man is susceptible to this sort of motive. But it is just the predominating sensitiveness of a character to this or that sort of motive that determines whether its morality is true and real; though, of whatever kind it is, it is always innate. In general it may be said that example operates as a means of promoting the good and the bad qualities of a character, but it does not create them; and so it is that Seneca's maxim, *velle non discitur—will cannot be learned*—also holds good here. But the innateness of all truly moral qualities, of the good as of the bad, is a doctrine that consorts better with the metempsychosis of the Brahmins and Buddhists, according to which a man's good and bad deeds follow him from one existence to another like his shadow, than with Judaism. For Judaism requires a man to come into the world as a moral blank, so that, in virtue of an inconceivable free will, directed to objects which are neither to be sought nor avoided—*liberum arbitrium indifferentiae*—and consequently as the result of reasoned consideration, he may choose whether he is to be an angel or a devil, or anything else that may lie between the two. Though I am well aware what the Jewish scheme is, I pay no attention to it; for my standard is truth. I am no professor of philosophy, and therefore I do not find my vocation in establishing the fundamental ideas of Judaism at any cost, even though they for ever bar the way to all and every kind of philosophical knowledge. *Liberum arbitrium indifferentiae* under the name of *moral freedom* is a charming doll for professors of philosophy to dandle; and we must leave it to those intelligent, honourable and upright gentlemen.

11

FRIEDRICH NIETZSCHE, BEYOND GOOD AND EVIL & THE GENEALOGY OF MORALS

Introduction

Friedrich Nietzsche was one of the most profoundly influential, if widely misunderstood, of the modern philosophers. On the one hand, he was an arch-reactionary: he was an unashamed proponent of the doctrine of the *ubermensch* ('overman'), herald of the 'will to power' as ultimate motivating factor in human affairs, and obstreperous critic of 'the dwarfing and levelling of European man'. At the same time, he was a true radical—a bold and provocative critic of conservative values who excoriated the stiff bourgeois morality of his day, famously announcing the 'death of God'. Whether as a darling of the right-wing or the left, Nietzsche's most significant contribution was to lay stress upon the relativity of ethical and moral values—and to teach that the task of the truly great man is to forge his own.

Friedrich Nietzsche (1844–1900) was born in Röcken, near Leipzig, in the Prussian Province of Saxony. Although his father, a Lutheran minister, died in 1849 when he was only four years old, Nietzsche had a brilliant school and university career, and was appointed to a professorship in classical philology at Basel in 1869 at the age of just twenty-four. His health, however, began to get the better of him, and he was forced to take leave from Basel in 1876-77, and ultimately, in 1879, resign his professorship altogether. As an independent author freed from conventional professional responsibility, Nietzsche published a book almost every year, and in the effusive and rambunctious idiosyncratic style that suited him best: *Daybreak* (1881), *The Gay Science* (1882), *Thus Spoke Zarathustra* (1883–5), *Beyond Good and Evil* (1886), *The Genealogy of Morals* (1887), *Twilight of the Idols* (1888) and *The Wagner Case* (1888), along with *The Antichrist* and his intellectual biography, *Ecce Homo*, which were published only later. During this period, mindful of his health, Nietzsche increasingly spent his summers in Sils Maria (near St Moritz in Switzerland) and winters in the Mediterranean (the Italian cities of Genoa, Rapallo, and Turin, and the French city of Nice), but on 3 January 1889 he suffered a breakdown in Turin, it being said that upon witnessing the flogging of a horse, he ran to the horse and threw his arms around to protect it, then collapsed to the ground. Treatment in Basel and Jena was unsuccessful, although he lived in until 1900, when he died of a stroke complicated by pneumonia.

Nietzsche's great insight is that all moral values have a history. In *The Genealogy of Morals* (1887)—a work in which he lays out the groundwork that underpins the rest of his thinking—he traces the evolution of moral concepts and prejudices in the Western world. He describes how at the dawn of European history it was 'the aristocratic, the powerful, the high-stationed, the high-minded' who felt that they themselves were good, and since at that time they were in a position to do so, they 'arrogated the right to create values for their own profit'. This analysis is supported by Nietzsche's account of the etymological development of the word 'good' in the various languages from the root idea of 'aristocratic' or 'noble'. Good, Nietzsche concluded, was at its origin the self-appellation of the aristocratic class: there was, in this context and milieux, what he calls a simple 'aristocratic equation' along the lines of 'good = aristocratic = beautiful = happy = loved by the gods'. This notion of 'good' stood in opposition to 'the low, the low-minded, the vulgar, and the plebeian'—all of which were at that time identified with the 'bad'. 'The pathos of nobility and distance,' explains Nietzsche, 'the chronic and despotic *esprit de corps* and fundamental instinct of a higher dominant race coming into association with a meaner race, an "under race", this is the origin of the antithesis of good and bad.'

Against this aristocratic mode of valuation there arose, says Nietzsche, that of the 'priestly caste'—most triumphantly represented by the moral values of the Jewish nation. It was the Jews, alleges Nietzsche—'that priestly nation'—who eventually realised that one devastatingly effective method of effecting revenge on their enemies was by means of 'a radical transvaluation of values'. In opposition to the 'aristocratic equation', they dared to suggest the contrary equation, namely: 'the wretched are alone the good; the poor, the weak, the lowly, are alone the good; the suffering, the needy, the sick, the loathsome, are the only ones who are pious, the only ones who are blessed, for them alone is salvation.' Lest we misunderstand the full context of Nietzsche's critique, it is important to stress that it was not Judaism, but Christianity, that reaped the benefit of the transvaluation. The 'revolt of the slaves', as Nietzsche characterises it, now 'has behind it a history of two millennia'; it has only become invisible, he suggests, because it has already achieved victory.

What, then, is so objectionable about this 'transvaluation of values'?

First, the nature, quality, and tenor of the aristocratic morality differs from that of the slave or herd morality, and not always to the latter's advantage. The aristocratic morality, says Nietzsche, 'springs from a triumphant affirmation of its own demands': its fundamental conception is the positive one ('we aristocrats, we good ones, we beautiful ones, we happy ones'), it acts and grows spontaneously, and it is saturated with life and passion; aristocratic hatreds, where they occur, fulfil and exhaust themselves in an immediate reaction and without venom. 'In point of fact,' adds Nietzsche, 'there is in contempt too strong an admixture of nonchalance, of casualness, of boredom, of impatience, even of personal exultation, for it to be capable of distorting its victim into a real caricature or a real monstrosity.' The slave morality, on the other hand, is born of a fundamental negation: it 'says "no" from the very outset to what is "outside itself", "different from itself", and "not itself": and this "no" is its creative deed.' The resentful man—the advocate and bearer *par excellence* of the slave morality—being unable to find the source of 'good' within himself, instead conceives of his enemies as 'evil', and it is in contrast to this 'evil' that he is able to consider himself, finally, as a representative of the 'good'.

Second, the herd morality proceeds on an unwarranted—or at any rate exaggerated—distinction between our nature and our actions, or (to put it differently) between our character and our conduct. The idea that there must be a separable subject self that determines and conditions our every action is a fallacy arising from language: there is, Nietzsche suggests, no 'being' behind doing, working, or becoming; the 'doer' is the mere appendage to the action; the action, he says, is everything. The weak exploit this confusion by presenting their own weakness as if it were a moral choice, and likewise that 'the strong has the option of being weak, and the bird of prey of being a lamb'. As Nietzsche explains: 'The subject (or, to use popular language, the soul) has perhaps proved itself the best dogma in the world, simply because it rendered possible to the horde of mortal, weak, and oppressed individuals of every kind, that most sublime specimen of self-deception, the interpretation of weakness as freedom, of being this, or being that, as merit.'

Third, the overwhelming dominance of the herd morality over all other possible moralities is leading us, says Nietzsche, towards the final degradation of our very humanity. What we desperately need, he argues, is a 'glimpse of a man that justifies the existence of man'. Instead, all around we find men like worms pullulating in the foreground; but the worm-like man of modernity is not in the least modest, and instead considers himself to be the product if historic principle and a 'higher man'. In this dwarfing and levelling of the European man, says Nietzsche, lurks the greatest peril—for, by presenting history as a process that tends ineluctably backwards towards mediocrity and indifference, it demoralises and fatigues us all.

How is one to live positively in the world that Nietzsche has sketched out? The answer lies to a considerable degree in his much misunderstood concept of the *ubermensch* ('overman'). The *ubermensch* is the ideal man of the future, for—in a world in which the herd morality has had almost total victory—he alone will have the wisdom and the strength to forge his own new system of values. These values may be inspired in part by the old aristocratic morality but without seeking to reinstitute this bygone system: specifically, the *ubermensch* will embody the raising up of man in his true potentiality and fullness of being, free of the shackles of a wearying and anti-life morality. It goes without saying that the *ubermensch* will, without doubt, be opposed to the herd morality and its degrading influence on mankind; he will have no truck with resentment and incapacity masquerading as moral virtue.

Nietzsche's significance for the modern man is profound and far-reaching. His insights can help us to inquire more critically into the motivations that lie behind the positions we take on moral or ethical issues: are we (or our fellows) truly acting in a spirit of altruism or self-sacrifice when we seek to demonstrate our moral credentials in some way or other—or are we instead acting from a position of weakness, resentment, and a desire to paint others as 'evil' so that we can feel ourselves to be 'good'? From here, it is but a short step to ask similar questions of our societies more broadly: is it really the case, for example, that in pursuing moral values through political means, we are acting in the interests of social justice—or are we merely expressing our own 'will to power' by restraining those whose greater strength would otherwise overwhelm or embarrass us? Ultimately, Nietzsche holds out for us two potential futures: the future that is likely to come to pass if we continue on our current path of celebrating that which is cretinous and weak, and resenting that which is strong and beautiful; or, on the other hand, the future that can be if we apply our wills to boldly assert new values that are better adapted to man's full range of needs and potentialities. The choice is, Nietzsche insists, ours.

Beyond Good and Evil

Fifth Chapter

The Natural History of Morals

199. Inasmuch as in all ages, as long as mankind has existed, there have also been human herds (family alliances,

communities, tribes, peoples, states, churches), and always a great number who obey in proportion to the small number who command—in view, therefore, of the fact that obedience has been most practised and fostered among mankind hitherto, one may reasonably suppose that, generally speaking, the need thereof is now innate in everyone, as a kind of *formal conscience* which gives the command 'Thou shalt unconditionally do something, unconditionally refrain from something', in short, 'Thou shalt'. This need tries to satisfy itself and to fill its form with a content, according to its strength, impatience, and eagerness, it at once seizes as an omnivorous appetite with little selection, and accepts whatever is shouted into its ear by all sorts of commanders—parents, teachers, laws, class prejudices, or public opinion. The extraordinary limitation of human development, the hesitation, protractedness, frequent retrogression, and turning thereof, is attributable to the fact that the herd-instinct of obedience is transmitted best, and at the cost of the art of command. If one imagine this instinct increasing to its greatest extent, commanders and independent individuals will finally be lacking altogether, or they will suffer inwardly from a bad conscience, and will have to impose a deception on themselves in the first place in order to be able to command just as if they also were only obeying. This condition of things actually exists in Europe at present—I call it the moral hypocrisy of the commanding class. They know no other way of protecting themselves from their bad conscience than by playing the role of executors of older and higher orders (of predecessors, of the constitution, of justice, of the law, or of God himself), or they even justify themselves by maxims from the current opinions of the herd, as 'first servants of their people', or 'instruments of the public weal'. On the other hand, the gregarious European man nowadays assumes an air as if he were the only kind of man that is allowable, he glorifies his qualities, such as public spirit, kindness, deference, industry, temperance, modesty, indulgence, sympathy, by virtue of which he is gentle, endurable, and useful to the herd, as the peculiarly human virtues. In cases, however, where it is believed that the leader and bell-wether cannot be dispensed with, attempt after attempt is made nowadays to replace commanders by the summing together of clever gregarious men: all representative constitutions, for example, are of this origin. In spite of all, what a blessing, what a deliverance from a weight becoming unendurable, is the appearance of an absolute ruler for these gregarious Europeans—of this fact the effect of the appearance of Napoleon was the last great proof: the history of the influence of Napoleon is almost the history of the higher happiness to which the entire century has attained in its worthiest individuals and periods. ...

201. As long as the utility which determines moral estimates is only gregarious utility, as long as the preservation of the community is only kept in view, and the immoral is sought precisely and exclusively in what seems dangerous to the maintenance of the community, there can be no 'morality of love to one's neighbour'. Granted even that there is already a little constant exercise of consideration, sympathy, fairness, gentleness, and mutual assistance, granted that even in this condition of society all those instincts are already active which are latterly distinguished by honourable names as 'virtues', and eventually almost coincide with the conception 'morality': in that period they do not as yet belong to the domain of moral valuations—they are still *ultra-motal*. A sympathetic action, for instance, is neither called good nor bad, moral nor immoral, in the best period of the Romans; and should it be praised, a sort of resentful disdain is compatible with this praise, even at the best, directly the sympathetic action is compared with one which contributes to the welfare of the whole, to the *res publica*. After all, 'love to our neighbour' is always a secondary matter, partly conventional and arbitrarily manifested in relation to

our *fear of our neighbour*. After the fabric of society seems on the whole established and secured against external dangers, it is this fear of our neighbour which again creates new perspectives of moral valuation. Certain strong and dangerous instincts, such as the love of enterprise, foolhardiness, revengefulness, astuteness, rapacity, and love of power, which up till then had not only to be honoured from the point of view of general utility—under other names, of course, than those here given—but had to be fostered and cultivated (because they were perpetually required in the common danger against the common enemies), are now felt in their dangerousness to be doubly strong—when the outlets for them are lacking—and are gradually branded as immoral and given over to calumny. The contrary instincts and inclinations now attain to moral honour, the gregarious instinct gradually draws its conclusions. How much or how little dangerousness to the community or to equality is contained in an opinion, a condition, an emotion, a disposition, or an endowment—that is now the moral perspective, here again fear is the mother of morals. It is by the loftiest and strongest instincts, when they break out passionately and carry the individual far above and beyond the average, and the low level of the gregarious conscience, that the self-reliance of the community is destroyed, its belief in itself, its backbone, as it were, breaks, consequently these very instincts will be most branded and defamed. The lofty independent spirituality, the will to stand alone, and even the cogent reason, are felt to be dangers, everything that elevates the individual above the herd, and is a source of fear to the neighbour, is henceforth called *evil*, the tolerant, unassuming, self-adapting, self-equalizing disposition, the *mediocrity* of desires, attains to moral distinction and honour. Finally, under very peaceful circumstances, there is always less opportunity and necessity for training the feelings to severity and rigour, and now every form of severity, even in justice, begins to disturb the conscience, a lofty and rigorous nobleness and self-responsibility almost offends, and awakens distrust, 'the lamb', and still more 'the sheep', wins respect. There is a point of diseased mellowness and effeminacy in the history of society, at which society itself takes the part of him who injures it, the part of the *criminal*, and does so, in fact, seriously and honestly. To punish, appears to it to be somehow unfair—it is certain that the idea of 'punishment' and 'the obligation to punish' are then painful and alarming to people. 'Is it not sufficient if the criminal be rendered *harmless*? Why should we still punish? Punishment itself is terrible!'—with these questions gregarious morality, the morality of fear, draws its ultimate conclusion. If one could at all do away with danger, the cause of fear, one would have done away with this morality at the same time, it would no longer be necessary, it *would not consider itself* any longer necessary!—Whoever examines the conscience of the present-day European, will always elicit the same imperative from its thousand moral folds and hidden recesses, the imperative of the timidity of the herd: 'we wish that some time or other there may be *nothing more to fear!*' Some time or other—the will and the way *thereto* is nowadays called 'progress' all over Europe.

202. Let us at once say again what we have already said a hundred times, for people's ears nowadays are unwilling to hear such truths—*our* truths. We know well enough how offensive it sounds when anyone plainly, and without metaphor, counts man among the animals, but it will be accounted to us almost a *crime*, that it is precisely in respect to men of 'modern ideas' that we have constantly applied the terms 'herd', 'herd-instincts', and such like expressions. What avail is it? We cannot do otherwise, for it is precisely here that our new insight is. We have found that in all the principal moral judgments, Europe has become unanimous, including likewise the countries where European influence prevails: in

Europe people evidently *know* what Socrates thought he did not know, and what the famous serpent of old once promised to teach—they 'know' today what is good and evil. It must then sound hard and be distasteful to the ear, when we always insist that that which here thinks it knows, that which here glorifies itself with praise and blame, and calls itself good, is the instinct of the herding human animal, the instinct which has come and is ever coming more and more to the front, to preponderance and supremacy over other instincts, according to the increasing physiological approximation and resemblance of which it is the symptom. *Morality in Europe at present is herding-animal morality*, and therefore, as we understand the matter, only one kind of human morality, beside which, before which, and after which many other moralities, and above all *higher* moralities, are or should be possible. Against such a 'possibility', against such a 'should be', however, this morality defends itself with all its strength, it says obstinately and inexorably 'I am morality itself and nothing else is morality!' Indeed, with the help of a religion which has humoured and flattered the sublimest desires of the herding-animal, things have reached such a point that we always find a more visible expression of this morality even in political and social arrangements: the *democratic* movement is the inheritance of the Christian movement. That its *tempo*, however, is much too slow and sleepy for the more impatient ones, for those who are sick and distracted by the herding-instinct, is indicated by the increasingly furious howling, and always less disguised teeth-gnashing of the anarchist dogs, who are now roving through the highways of European culture. Apparently in opposition to the peacefully industrious democrats and Revolution-ideologues, and still more so to the awkward philosophasters and fraternity-visionaries who call themselves Socialists and want a 'free society', those are really at one with them all in their thorough and instinctive hostility to every form of society other than that of the *autonomous* herd (to the extent even of repudiating the notions 'master' and 'servant'—*ni dieu ni maître*, says a socialist formula); at one in their tenacious opposition to every special claim, every special right and privilege (this means ultimately opposition to *every* right, for when all are equal, no one needs 'rights' any longer); at one in their distrust of punitive justice (as though it were a violation of the weak, unfair to the *necessary* consequences of all former society); but equally at one in their religion of sympathy, in their compassion for all that feels, lives, and suffers (down to the very animals, up even to 'God'—the extravagance of 'sympathy for God' belongs to a democratic age); altogether at one in the cry and impatience of their sympathy, in their deadly hatred of suffering generally, in their almost feminine incapacity for witnessing it or *allowing* it; at one in their involuntary beglooming and heart-softening, under the spell of which Europe seems to be threatened with a new Buddhism; at one in their belief in the morality of *mutual* sympathy, as though it were morality in itself, the climax, the *attained* climax of mankind, the sole hope of the future, the consolation of the present, the great discharge from all the obligations of the past; altogether at one in their belief in the community as the *deliverer*, in the herd, and therefore in 'themselves'.

203. We, who hold a different belief—we, who regard the democratic movement, not only as a degenerating form of political organization, but as equivalent to a degenerating, a waning type of man, as involving his mediocrising and depreciation: where have *we* to fix our hopes? In *new philosophers*—there is no other alternative: in minds strong and original enough to initiate opposite estimates of value, to transvalue and invert 'eternal valuations'; in forerunners, in men of the future, who in the present shall fix the constraints and fasten the knots which will compel millenniums to take *new* paths. To teach man the future of humanity as his *will*, as

depending on human will, and to make preparation for vast hazardous enterprises and collective attempts in rearing and educating, in order thereby to put an end to the frightful rule of folly and chance which has hitherto gone by the name of 'history' (the folly of the 'greatest number' is only its last form)—for that purpose a new type of philosopher and commander will some time or other be needed, at the very idea of which everything that has existed in the way of occult, terrible, and benevolent beings might look pale and dwarfed. The image of such leaders hovers before *our* eyes:—is it lawful for me to say it aloud, ye free spirits? The conditions which one would partly have to create and partly utilize for their genesis; the presumptive methods and tests by virtue of which a soul should grow up to such an elevation and power as to feel a *constraint* to these tasks; a transvaluation of values, under the new pressure and hammer of which a conscience should be steeled and a heart transformed into brass, so as to bear the weight of such responsibility; and on the other hand the necessity for such leaders, the dreadful danger that they might be lacking, or miscarry and degenerate:—these are *our* real anxieties and glooms, ye know it well, ye free spirits! These are the heavy distant thoughts and storms which sweep across the heaven of *our* life. There are few pains so grievous as to have seen, divined, or experienced how an exceptional man has missed his way and deteriorated; but he who has the rare eye for the universal danger of 'man' himself *deteriorating*, he who like us has recognized the extraordinary fortuitousness which has hitherto played its game in respect to the future of mankind—a game in which neither the hand, nor even a 'finger of God' has participated!—he who divines the fate that is hidden under the idiotic unwariness and blind confidence of 'modern ideas', and still more under the whole of Christo-European morality—suffers from an anguish with which no other is to be compared. He sees at a glance all that could still *be made out of man* through a favourable accumulation and augmentation of human powers and arrangements; he knows with all the knowledge of his conviction how unexhausted man still is for the greatest possibilities, and how often in the past the type man has stood in presence of mysterious decisions and new paths:—he knows still better from his painfulest recollections on what wretched obstacles promising developments of the highest rank have hitherto usually gone to pieces, broken down, sunk, and become contemptible. The *universal degeneracy of man* to the level of the 'man of the future'—as idealized by the socialistic fools and shallow-pates—this degeneracy and dwarfing of man to an absolutely gregarious animal (or as they call it, to a man of 'free society'), this brutalizing of man into a pigmy with equal rights and claims, is undoubtedly *possible!* He who has thought out this possibility to its ultimate conclusion knows *another* loathing unknown to the rest of mankind—and perhaps also a new *mission!*

THE GENEALOGY OF MORALS

FIRST ESSAY

'GOOD AND EVIL', 'GOOD AND BAD'

10. The revolt of the slaves in morals begins in the very principle of *resentment* becoming creative and giving birth to values—a resentment experienced by creatures who, deprived as they are of the proper outlet of action, are forced to find their compensation in an imaginary revenge. While every aristocratic morality springs from a triumphant affirmation of its own demands, the slave morality says 'no' from the very

outset to what is 'outside itself', 'different from itself', and 'not itself': and this 'no' is its creative deed. This volte-face of the valuing standpoint—this *inevitable* gravitation to the objective instead of back to the subjective—is typical of resentment: the slave-morality requires as the condition of its existence an external and objective world, to employ physiological terminology, it requires objective stimuli to be capable of action at all—its action is fundamentally a reaction. The contrary is the case when we come to the aristocrat's system of values: it acts and grows spontaneously, it merely seeks its antithesis in order to pronounce a more grateful and exultant 'yes' to its own self; its negative conception, 'low', 'vulgar', 'bad', is merely a pale late-born foil in comparison with its positive and fundamental conception (saturated as it is with life and passion), of 'we aristocrats, we good ones, we beautiful ones, we happy ones.'

When the aristocratic morality goes astray and commits sacrilege on reality, this is limited to that particular sphere with which it is not sufficiently acquainted—a sphere, in fact, from the real knowledge of which it disdainfully defends itself. It misjudges, in some cases, the sphere which it despises, the sphere of the common vulgar man and the low people: on the other hand, due weight should be given to the consideration that in any case the mood of contempt, of disdain, of superciliousness, even on the supposition that it *falsely* portrays the object of its contempt, will always be far removed from that degree of falsity which will always characterise the attacks—in effigy, of course—of the vindictive hatred and revengefulness of the weak in onslaughts on their enemies. In point of fact, there is in contempt too strong an admixture of nonchalance, of casualness, of boredom, of impatience, even of personal exultation, for it to be capable of distorting its victim into a real caricature or a real monstrosity. Attention again should be paid to the almost benevolent *nuances* which, for instance, the Greek nobility imports into all the words by which it distinguishes the common people from itself; note how continuously a kind of pity, care, and consideration imparts its honeyed *flavour*, until at last almost all the words which are applied to the vulgar man survive finally as expressions for 'unhappy', 'worthy of pity' (compare δειλός, δείλαιος, πονηρός, μοχθηρός; the latter two names really denoting the vulgar man as labour-slave and beast of burden)—and how, conversely, 'bad', 'low', 'unhappy' have never ceased to ring in the Greek ear with a tone in which 'unhappy' is the predominant note: this is a heritage of the old noble aristocratic morality, which remains true to itself even in contempt (let philologists remember the sense in which ὀϊζυρός, ἄνολβος, τλήμων, δυστυχεῖν, ξυμφορά used to be employed). The 'well-born' simply felt themselves the 'happy'; they did not have to manufacture their happiness artificially through looking at their enemies, or in cases to talk and lie themselves into happiness (as is the custom with all resentful men); and similarly, complete men as they were, exuberant with strength, and consequently necessarily energetic, they were too wise to dissociate happiness from action—activity becomes in their minds *necessarily* counted as happiness (that is the etymology of εὖ πράττειν)—all in sharp contrast to the 'happiness' of the weak and the oppressed, with their festering venom and malignity, among whom happiness appears essentially as a narcotic, a deadening, a quietude, a peace, a 'Sabbath', an enervation of the mind and relaxation of the limbs—in short, a purely passive phenomenon. While the aristocratic man lived in confidence and openness with himself (γενναῖος, 'noble-born', emphasises the nuance 'sincere', and perhaps also 'naïf'), the resentful man, on the other hand, is neither sincere nor naïf, nor honest and candid with himself. His soul *squints*; his mind loves hidden crannies, tortuous paths and back-doors, everything secret appeals to him as *his* world, *his* safety, *his* balm; he is past master in silence, in not forgetting, in waiting, in provisional self-depreciation and self-abasement. A race of such *resentful* men will of necessity eventually prove more *prudent* than any aristocratic race, it will honour prudence on quite a distinct scale, as, in fact, a paramount condition of existence, while prudence among aristocratic men is apt to be tinged with a delicate flavour of luxury and refinement; so among them it plays nothing like so integral a part as that complete certainty of function of the governing *unconscious* instincts, or as indeed a certain lack of prudence, such as a vehement and valiant charge, whether against danger or the enemy, or as those ecstatic bursts of rage, love, reverence, gratitude, by which at all times noble souls have recognised each other. When the resentment of the aristocratic man manifests itself, it fulfils and exhausts itself in an immediate reaction, and consequently instills no *venom*: on the other hand, it never manifests itself at all in countless instances, when in the case of the feeble and weak it would be inevitable. An inability to take seriously for any length of time their enemies, their disasters, their *misdeeds*—that is the sign of the full strong natures who possess a superfluity of moulding plastic force, that heals completely and produces forgetfulness: a good example of this in the modern world is Mirabeau, who had no memory for any insults and meannesses which were practised on him, and who was only incapable of forgiving because he forgot. Such a man indeed shakes off with a shrug many a worm which would have buried itself in another; it is only in characters like these that we see the possibility (supposing, of course, that there is such a possibility in the world) of the real '*love* of one's enemies'. What respect for his enemies is found, forsooth, in an aristocratic man—and such a reverence is already a bridge to love! He insists on having his enemy to himself as his distinction. He tolerates no other enemy but a man in whose character there is nothing to despise and *much* to honour! On the other hand, imagine the 'enemy' as the resentful man conceives him—and it is here exactly that we see his work, his creativeness; he has conceived 'the evil enemy', the 'evil one', and indeed that is the root idea from which he now evolves as a contrasting and corresponding figure a 'good one', himself—his very self!

JOHN STUART MILL, ON LIBERTY & UTILITARIANISM

INTRODUCTION

Utilitarianism is a much talked about but often imperfectly understood ethical system. It is based on the proposition that right actions are those that increase the overall happiness in the community—a doctrine which is often mistakenly thought to envisage happiness as reducible to a mere surplus of pleasure over pain. We owe it, in a great part, to John Stuart Mill to have drawn our attention to its deeper and more profound significance. For Mill, utilitarianism was directed towards happiness, but happiness that comprised only physical pleasure would, he maintained, be beastly; the happiness that is proper to man must extend far beyond that to the pleasures of the intellect, the feelings, the imagination, and the moral sentiments—and even, in certain cases, to the enjoyment of virtue itself. Above all, the free development of man's individuality and the full realisation of his faculties are the fundamentals upon which the good life must be built. What

Mill advocated was not some new morality based upon mechanistic social engineering. It was, own the contrary, a reimagination of the grand tradition of Greek virtue ethics in a world that had forgotten that the advantage of society as a whole must always depend on the wellbeing of the unique and variegated individuals who comprise it.

John Stuart Mill (1806-1783) was born and brought up in London by his father, James Mill. His was no ordinary childhood, however, for the elder Mill was intent upon cultivating in his son the intellect required to carry forward the cause of utilitarianism into the next generation. The younger man thus became the subject of an educational experiment: encouraged to ask questions about everything he read, while being shielded from association with children his own age other than siblings, it was thought that he could be taught far more than other parents and schools even attempted to teach. When his father became a senior administrator with the East India Company, the younger Mill followed him into the company's employment. In 1826, however, Mill was hit by a mental crisis when he realised that even the creation of a just society, his life's goal, would not make him happy. Mill concluded from this that education must cultivate the emotions as well as the intellect, and that there were important values existing outside the scope of the utilitarian philosophy, such as autonomy and dignity. Of the two works for which he is best known today, *On Liberty* (1859)—that paean to individual flourishing—came first. The principal text of the utilitarian philosophy Mill published next as three articles—later collected and reprinted in a single book, *Utilitarianism* (1863)—which set out and expanded upon his core ethical principle: namely, that actions are right in proportion as they tend to promote happiness, and wrong as they tend to produce the reverse of happiness (the 'greatest happiness principle').

In his later years, Mill was Liberal MP for the City of Westminster. He died in Avignon, France.

Freedom, for Mill, means optimal cultivation of individuality: a man should be free not only to think and speak as he pleases, but also to act as he pleases, subject only to the condition that he cause no harm to others. Individuality is the basis for improvement of society: it is through people expressing their full range of individuality that society becomes aware of new and better practices. Individuality is, just as importantly, the basis for the growth of each human being according to his own particular needs. The end of man is not to act as a cog in a societal machine; the end of man is 'the highest and most harmonious development of his powers'. Nevertheless, viewed correctly, there is no contradiction between the flourishing of the individual and the flourishing of society. We strengthen 'the tie which binds every individual to the race,' says Mill, 'by making the race infinitely better worth belonging to.'

This is a philosophy to which most of us, at least in broad terms, would subscribe. There remain aspects of Mill's thinking, however, that remain under-appreciated in the popular mind to this day.

First, liberalism is not progressivism. The spirit of liberty is not the same thing as the spirit of progress or improvement, as progressivism may aim at forcing improvements on people without their consent. In particular, liberty stands to obstruct what the moral and social reformers consider 'in their own judgment' would be the best for mankind. The spirit of liberty may therefore ally itself with the opponents of progressivism. Mill, indeed, is emphatic about one thing: the only reliable and permanent source of improvement is not progressivism but liberty.

Second, we need to be alert to the particular dangers confronting Western civilisation. When in the East conformity to custom took the upper hand, the result was to bring development to a standstill. That is not the way that it will play out in the West, suggests Mill. The 'despotism of custom' that we face in the West will not be stationariness but *singularity*. 'It is not progress we object to,' explained Mill, 'on the contrary, we flatter ourselves that we are the most progressive people who ever lived. It is individuality that we war against: we should think we had done wonders if we had made ourselves all alike.'

Finally, 'On Liberty' advocates boldly for diversity. 'Diversity' here means the cultivating of all that is individual in mankind so that 'human beings become a noble and beautiful object of contemplation' and that life becomes 'rich, diversified, and animating, furnishing more abundant aliment to high thoughts and elevated feelings'. Diversity, Mill makes clear, should include difference of thought and feeling; it is not difference for the sake of difference, but the cultivation of variety for the sake of fostering what is best in man.

This is a comprehensive philosophy of human wellbeing. Mill advocates for an expansive ethos of freedom that encompasses, at the positive end, the full flowering of human potentiality in its variegated forms, and at the negative pole, resistance not just to political oppression but also—and more fundamentally—to the tyranny of public opinion and the despotism of custom.

Pressures to conform are stronger in our era than ever before: governments and the owners of global media channels have taken it upon themselves to assert their own notion of truth and their own notion of proper conduct, at the same time that technological innovation facilitates the spreading of conventionally 'correct' thought and behaviour across social classes and into the remotest corners of the globe. To resist these forces a man needs a coherent philosophy to ground, justify, and give shape to his resistance. 'On Liberty' offers him precisely that.

Utilitarianism

Chapter 2

What Utilitarianism Is

A passing remark is all that needs be given to the ignorant blunder of supposing that those who stand up for utility as the test of right and wrong, use the term in that restricted and merely colloquial sense in which utility is opposed to pleasure. An apology is due to the philosophical opponents of utilitarianism, for even the momentary appearance of confounding them with anyone capable of so absurd a misconception; which is the more extraordinary, inasmuch as the contrary accusation, of referring everything to pleasure, and that too in its grossest form, is another of the common charges against utilitarianism: and, as has been pointedly remarked by an able writer, the same sort of persons, and often the very same persons, denounce the theory as impracticably dry when the word utility precedes the word pleasure, and as too practicably voluptuous when the word pleasure precedes the word utility. Those who know anything about the matter are aware that every writer, from Epicurus to Bentham, who maintained the theory of utility, meant by it, not something to be contradistinguished from pleasure, but pleasure itself, together with exemption from pain; and instead of opposing the useful to the agreeable or the ornamental, have always declared that the useful means these, among other things. Yet the common herd, including the herd of writers, not only in newspapers and periodicals, but in books of weight and pretension, are perpetually falling into this shallow mistake. Having caught up the word utilitarian, while knowing nothing whatever about it but its sound, they habitually express by it the rejection, or the neglect, of pleasure in some of its forms; of beauty, of ornament, or of amusement. Nor is the term thus ignorantly misapplied solely in disparagement, but occasionally in compliment; as though it implied superiority to frivolity and the mere pleasures of the moment. And this perverted use is the only one in which the word is popularly known, and the one from which the new generation are acquiring their sole notion of its meaning. Those who introduced the word, but who had for many years discontinued it as a distinctive appellation, may well feel themselves called upon to resume it, if by doing so they can hope to contribute anything towards rescuing it from this utter degradation.[1]

The creed which accepts as the foundation of morals, Utility, or the Greatest Happiness Principle, holds that actions are right in proportion as they tend to promote happiness, wrong as they tend to produce the reverse of happiness. By happiness is intended pleasure, and the absence of pain; by unhappiness, pain, and the privation of pleasure. To give a clear view of the moral standard set up by the theory, much more requires to be said; in particular, what things it includes in the ideas of pain and pleasure; and to what extent this is left an open question. But these supplementary explanations do not affect the theory of life on which this theory of morality is grounded—namely, that pleasure, and freedom from pain, are the only things

---

1. The author of this essay has reason for believing himself to be the first person who brought the word utilitarian into use. He did not invent it, but adopted it from a passing expression in Mr. Galt's *Annals of the Parish*. After using it as a designation for several years, he and others abandoned it from a growing dislike to anything resembling a badge or watchword of sectarian distinction. But as a name for one single opinion, not a set of opinions—to denote the recognition of utility as a standard, not any particular way of applying it—the term supplies a want in the language, and offers, in many cases, a convenient mode of avoiding tiresome circumlocution.

desirable as ends; and that all desirable things (which are as numerous in the utilitarian as in any other scheme) are desirable either for the pleasure inherent in themselves, or as means to the promotion of pleasure and the prevention of pain.

Now, such a theory of life excites in many minds, and among them in some of the most estimable in feeling and purpose, inveterate dislike. To suppose that life has (as they express it) no higher end than pleasure—no better and nobler object of desire and pursuit—they designate as utterly mean and grovelling; as a doctrine worthy only of swine, to whom the followers of Epicurus were, at a very early period, contemptuously likened; and modern holders of the doctrine are occasionally made the subject of equally polite comparisons by its German, French, and English assailants.

When thus attacked, the Epicureans have always answered, that it is not they, but their accusers, who represent human nature in a degrading light; since the accusation supposes human beings to be capable of no pleasures except those of which swine are capable. If this supposition were true, the charge could not be gainsaid, but would then be no longer an imputation; for if the sources of pleasure were precisely the same to human beings and to swine, the rule of life which is good enough for the one would be good enough for the other. The comparison of the Epicurean life to that of beasts is felt as degrading, precisely because a beast's pleasures do not satisfy a human being's conceptions of happiness. Human beings have faculties more elevated than the animal appetites, and when once made conscious of them, do not regard anything as happiness which does not include their gratification. I do not, indeed, consider the Epicureans to have been by any means faultless in drawing out their scheme of consequences from the utilitarian principle. To do this in any sufficient manner, many Stoic, as well as Christian elements require to be included. But there is no known Epicurean theory of life which does not assign to the pleasures of the intellect, of the feelings and imagination, and of the moral sentiments, a much higher value as pleasures than to those of mere sensation. It must be admitted, however, that utilitarian writers in general have placed the superiority of mental over bodily pleasures chiefly in the greater permanency, safety, uncostliness, etc., of the former—that is, in their circumstantial advantages rather than in their intrinsic nature. And on all these points utilitarians have fully proved their case; but they might have taken the other, and, as it may be called, higher ground, with entire consistency. It is quite compatible with the principle of utility to recognise the fact, that some kinds of pleasure are more desirable and more valuable than others. It would be absurd that while, in estimating all other things, quality is considered as well as quantity, the estimation of pleasures should be supposed to depend on quantity alone.

On Liberty

Chapter 3

Of Individuality as One of the Elements of Well Being

Such being the reasons which make it imperative that human beings should be free to form opinions, and to express their opinions without reserve; and such the baneful consequences to the intellectual, and through that to the moral nature of man, unless this liberty is either conceded, or asserted in spite of prohibition; let us next examine whether the same reasons do not require that men should be free to act upon their opinions—to carry these out in their lives, without hindrance, either physical or moral, from their fellow-men, so long as it is at their own risk and peril. This last proviso is of course indispensable. No one pretends that actions should be as free as opinions. On the contrary, even opinions lose their immunity, when the circumstances in which they are expressed are such as to constitute their expression a positive instigation to some mischievous act. An opinion that corn-dealers are starvers of the poor, or that private property is robbery, ought to be unmolested when simply circulated through the press, but may justly incur punishment when delivered orally to an excited mob assembled before the house of a corn-dealer, or when handed about among the same mob in the form of a placard. Acts, of whatever kind, which, without justifiable cause, do harm to others, may be, and in the more important cases absolutely require to be, controlled by the unfavourable sentiments, and, when needful, by the active interference of mankind. The liberty of the individual must be thus far limited; he must not make himself a nuisance to other people. But if he refrains from molesting others in what concerns them, and merely acts according to his own inclination and judgment in things which concern himself, the same reasons which show that opinion should be free, prove also that he should be allowed, without molestation, to carry his opinions into practice at his own cost. That mankind are not infallible; that their truths, for the most part, are only half-truths; that unity of opinion, unless resulting from the fullest and freest comparison of opposite opinions, is not desirable, and diversity not an evil, but a good, until mankind are much more capable than at present of recognising all sides of the truth, are principles applicable to men's modes of action, not less than to their opinions. As it is useful that while mankind are imperfect there should be different opinions, so is it that there should be different experiments of living; that free scope should be given to varieties of character, short of injury to others; and that the worth of different modes of life should be proved practically, when anyone thinks fit to try them. It is desirable, in short, that in things which do not primarily concern others, individuality should assert itself. Where, not the person's own character, but the traditions or customs of other people are the rule of conduct, there is wanting one of the principal ingredients of human happiness, and quite the chief ingredient of individual and social progress.

In maintaining this principle, the greatest difficulty to be encountered does not lie in the appreciation of means towards an acknowledged end, but in the indifference of persons in general to the end itself. If it were felt that the free development of individuality is one of the leading essentials of well-being; that it is not only a co-ordinate element with all that is designated by the terms civilisation, instruction, education, culture, but is itself a necessary part and condition of all those things; there would be no danger that liberty should be undervalued, and the adjustment of the boundaries between it and social control would present no extraordinary difficulty. But the evil is, that individual spontaneity is hardly recognised by the common modes of thinking, as having any intrinsic worth, or deserving any regard on its own account. The majority, being satisfied with the ways of mankind as they now are (for it is they who make them what they are), cannot comprehend why those ways should not be good enough for everybody; and what is more, spontaneity forms no part of the ideal of the majority of moral and social reformers, but is rather looked on with jealousy, as a troublesome and perhaps rebellious obstruction to the general acceptance of what these reformers, in their own judgment, think would be best for mankind. Few persons, out of Germany, even comprehend the meaning of the doctrine which Wilhelm von Humboldt, so eminent both as a *savant* and as a politician, made the text of a treatise—that 'the end of man, or that which is prescribed by the eternal or immutable dictates of reason, and not suggested by vague and transient desires, is the highest and most harmonious development of his powers to a complete and consistent whole'; that, therefore, the object 'towards which every human being must ceaselessly direct his efforts, and on which especially those who design to influence their fellow-men must ever keep their eyes, is the individuality of power and development'; that for this there are two requisites, 'freedom, and a variety of situations'; and that from the union of these arise 'individual vigour and manifold diversity', which combine themselves in 'originality'.[2]

Little, however, as people are accustomed to a doctrine like that of Von Humboldt, and surprising as it may be to them to find so high a value attached to individuality, the question, one must nevertheless think, can only be one of degree. No one's idea of excellence in conduct is that people should do absolutely nothing but copy one another. No one would assert that people ought not to put into their mode of life, and into the conduct of their concerns, any impress whatever of their own judgment, or of their own individual character. On the other hand, it would be absurd to pretend that people ought to live as if nothing whatever had been known in the world before they came into it; as if experience had as yet done nothing towards showing that one mode of existence, or of conduct, is preferable to another. Nobody denies that people should be so taught and trained in youth, as to know and benefit by the ascertained results of human experience. But it is the privilege and proper condition of a human being, arrived at the maturity of his faculties, to use and interpret experience in his own way. It is for him to find out what part of recorded experience is properly applicable to his own circumstances and character. The traditions and customs of other people are, to a certain

---

2. *The Sphere and Duties of Government*, from the German of Baron Wilhelm von Humboldt, pp. 11-13.

extent, evidence of what their experience has taught *them*; presumptive evidence, and as such, have a claim to his deference: but, in the first place, their experience may be too narrow; or they may not have interpreted it rightly. Secondly, their interpretation of experience may be correct, but unsuitable to him. Customs are made for customary circumstances, and customary characters: and his circumstances or his character may be uncustomary. Thirdly, though the customs be both good as customs, and suitable to him, yet to conform to custom, merely *as* custom, does not educate or develop in him any of the qualities which are the distinctive endowment of a human being. The human faculties of perception, judgment, discriminative feeling, mental activity, and even moral preference, are exercised only in making a choice. He who does anything because it is the custom, makes no choice. He gains no practice either in discerning or in desiring what is best. The mental and moral, like the muscular powers, are improved only by being used. The faculties are called into no exercise by doing a thing merely because others do it, no more than by believing a thing only because others believe it. If the grounds of an opinion are not conclusive to the person's own reason, his reason cannot be strengthened, but is likely to be weakened by his adopting it: and if the inducements to an act are not such as are consentaneous to his own feelings and character (where affection, or the rights of others, are not concerned), it is so much done towards rendering his feelings and character inert and torpid, instead of active and energetic.

He who lets the world, or his own portion of it, choose his plan of life for him, has no need of any other faculty than the ape-like one of imitation. He who chooses his plan for himself, employs all his faculties. He must use observation to see, reasoning and judgment to foresee, activity to gather materials for decision, discrimination to decide, and when he has decided, firmness and self-control to hold to his deliberate decision. And these qualities he requires and exercises exactly in proportion as the part of his conduct which he determines according to his own judgment and feelings is a large one. It is possible that he might be guided in some good path, and kept out of harm's way, without any of these things. But what will be his comparative worth as a human being? It really is of importance, not only what men do, but also what manner of men they are that do it. Among the works of man, which human life is rightly employed in perfecting and beautifying, the first in importance surely is man himself. Supposing it were possible to get houses built, corn grown, battles fought, causes tried, and even churches erected and prayers said, by machinery—by automatons in human form—it would be a considerable loss to exchange for these automatons even the men and women who at present inhabit the more civilised parts of the world, and who assuredly are but starved specimens of what nature can and will produce. Human nature is not a machine to be built after a model, and set to do exactly the work prescribed for it, but a tree, which requires to grow and develop itself on all sides, according to the tendency of the inward forces which make it a living thing.

It will probably be conceded that it is desirable people should exercise their understandings, and that an intelligent following of custom, or even occasionally an intelligent deviation from custom, is better than a blind and simply mechanical adhesion to it. To a certain extent it is admitted, that our understanding should be our own: but there is not the same willingness to admit that our desires and impulses should be our own likewise; or that to possess impulses of our own, and of any strength, is anything but a peril and a snare. Yet desires and impulses are as much a part of a perfect human being as beliefs and restraints, and strong impulses are only perilous when not properly balanced—when one set of aims and inclinations is developed into strength, while others, which ought to co-exist with them, remain weak and inactive. It is not because men's desires are strong that they act ill; it is because their consciences are weak. There is no natural connection between strong impulses and a weak conscience. The natural connection is the other way. To say that one person's desires and feelings are stronger and more various than those of another, is merely to say that he has more of the raw material of human nature, and is therefore capable, perhaps of more evil, but certainly of more good. Strong impulses are but another name for energy. Energy may be turned to bad uses; but more good may always be made of an energetic nature, than of an indolent and impassive one. Those who have most natural feeling, are always those whose cultivated feelings may be made the strongest. The same strong susceptibilities which make the personal impulses vivid and powerful, are also the source from whence are generated the most passionate love of virtue, and the sternest self-control. It is through the cultivation of these that society both does its duty and protects its interests—not by rejecting the stuff of which heroes are made because it knows not how to make them. A person whose desires and impulses are his own—are the expression of his own nature, as it has been developed and modified by his own culture—is said to have a character. One whose desires and impulses are not his own, has no character, no more than a steam-engine has a character. If, in addition to being his own, his impulses are strong, and are under the government of a strong will, he has an energetic character. Whoever thinks that individuality of desires and impulses should not be encouraged to unfold itself, must maintain that society has no need of strong natures—is not the better for containing many persons who have much character—and that a high general average of energy is not desirable.

In some early states of society, these forces might be, and

were, too much ahead of the power which society then possessed of disciplining and controlling them. There has been a time when the element of spontaneity and individuality was in excess, and the social principle had a hard struggle with it. The difficulty then was to induce men of strong bodies or minds to pay obedience to any rules which required them to control their impulses. To overcome this difficulty, law and discipline, like the Popes struggling against the Emperors, asserted a power over the whole man, claiming to control all his life in order to control his character—which society had not found any other sufficient means of binding. But society has now fairly got the better of individuality; and the danger which threatens human nature is not the excess, but the deficiency, of personal impulses and preferences. Things are vastly changed, since the passions of those who were strong by station or by personal endowment were in a state of habitual rebellion against laws and ordinances, and required to be rigorously chained up to enable the persons within their reach to enjoy any particle of security. In our times, from the highest class of society down to the lowest, everyone lives as under the eye of a hostile and dreaded censorship. Not only in what concerns others, but in what concerns only themselves, the individual, or the family, do not ask themselves—what do I prefer? or, what would suit my character and disposition? or, what would allow the best and highest in me to have fair-play, and enable it to grow and thrive? They ask themselves, what is suitable to my position? what is usually done by persons of my station and pecuniary circumstances? or (worse still) what is usually done by persons of a station and circumstances superior to mine? I do not mean that they choose what is customary, in preference to what suits their own inclination. It does not occur to them to have any inclination, except for what is customary. Thus the mind itself is bowed to the yoke: even in what people do for pleasure, conformity is the first thing thought of; they like in crowds; they exercise choice only among things commonly done: peculiarity of taste, eccentricity of conduct, are shunned equally with crimes: until by dint of not following their own nature, they have no nature to follow: their human capacities are withered and starved: they become incapable of any strong wishes or native pleasures, and are generally without either opinions or feelings of home growth, or properly their own. Now is this, or is it not, the desirable condition of human nature?

It is so, on the Calvinistic theory. According to that, the one great offence of man is self-will. All the good of which humanity is capable is comprised in obedience. You have no choice; thus you must do, and no otherwise: 'whatever is not a duty, is a sin'. Human nature being radically corrupt, there is no redemption for anyone until human nature is killed within him. To one holding this theory of life, crushing out any of the human faculties, capacities, and susceptibilities, is no evil: man needs no capacity, but that of surrendering himself to the will of God; and if he uses any of his faculties for any other purpose but to do that supposed will more effectually, he is better without them. That is the theory of Calvinism; and it is held, in a mitigated form, by many who do not consider themselves Calvinists; the mitigation consisting in giving a less ascetic interpretation to the alleged will of God; asserting it to be his will that mankind should gratify some of their inclinations; of course not in the manner they themselves prefer, but in the way of obedience, that is, in a way prescribed to them by authority; and, therefore, by the necessary conditions of the case, the same for all.

In some such insidious form there is at present a strong tendency to this narrow theory of life, and to the pinched and hidebound type of human character which it patronises. Many persons, no doubt, sincerely think that human beings thus cramped and dwarfed, are as their Maker designed them to be;

just as many have thought that trees are a much finer thing when clipped into pollards, or cut out into figures of animals, than as nature made them. But if it be any part of religion to believe that man was made by a good being, it is more consistent with that faith to believe, that this Being gave all human faculties that they might be cultivated and unfolded, not rooted out and consumed, and that he takes delight in every nearer approach made by his creatures to the ideal conception embodied in them, every increase in any of their capabilities of comprehension, of action, or of enjoyment. There is a different type of human excellence from the Calvinistic; a conception of humanity as having its nature bestowed on it for other purposes than merely to be abnegated. 'Pagan self-assertion' is one of the elements of human worth, as well as 'Christian self-denial'.[3] There is a Greek ideal of self-development, which the Platonic and Christian ideal of self-government blends with, but does not supersede. It may be better to be a John Knox than an Alcibiades, but it is better to be a Pericles than either; nor would a Pericles, if we had one in these days, be without anything good which belonged to John Knox.

It is not by wearing down into uniformity all that is individual in themselves, but by cultivating it and calling it forth, within the limits imposed by the rights and interests of others, that human beings become a noble and beautiful object of contemplation; and as the works partake the character of those who do them, by the same process human life also becomes rich, diversified, and animating, furnishing more abundant aliment to high thoughts and elevating feelings, and strengthening the tie which binds every individual to the race, by making the race infinitely better worth belonging to. In proportion to the development of his individuality, each

3. Sterling's *Essays*.

person becomes more valuable to himself, and is therefore capable of being more valuable to others. There is a greater fulness of life about his own existence, and when there is more life in the units there is more in the mass which is composed of them. As much compression as is necessary to prevent the stronger specimens of human nature from encroaching on the rights of others, cannot be dispensed with; but for this there is ample compensation even in the point of view of human development. The means of development which the individual loses by being prevented from gratifying his inclinations to the injury of others, are chiefly obtained at the expense of the development of other people. And even to himself there is a full equivalent in the better development of the social part of his nature, rendered possible by the restraint put upon the selfish part. To be held to rigid rules of justice for the sake of others, develops the feelings and capacities which have the good of others for their object. But to be restrained in things not affecting their good, by their mere displeasure, develops nothing valuable, except such force of character as may unfold itself in resisting the restraint. If acquiesced in, it dulls and blunts the whole nature. To give any fair play to the nature of each, it is essential that different persons should be allowed to lead different lives. In proportion as this latitude has been exercised in any age, has that age been noteworthy to posterity. Even despotism does not produce its worst effects, so long as individuality exists under it; and whatever crushes individuality is despotism, by whatever name it may be called, and whether it professes to be enforcing the will of God or the injunctions of men. [...]

There is one characteristic of the present direction of public opinion peculiarly calculated to make it intolerant of any marked demonstration of individuality. The general average of mankind are not only moderate in intellect, but also moderate in inclinations: they have no tastes or wishes strong enough to incline them to do anything unusual, and they consequently do not understand those who have, and class all such with the wild and intemperate whom they are accustomed to look down upon. Now, in addition to this fact which is general, we have only to suppose that a strong movement has set in towards the improvement of morals, and it is evident what we have to expect. In these days such a movement has set in; much has actually been effected in the way of increased regularity of conduct, and discouragement of excesses; and there is a philanthropic spirit abroad, for the exercise of which there is no more inviting field than the moral and prudential improvement of our fellow creatures. These tendencies of the times cause the public to be more disposed than at most former periods to prescribe general rules of conduct, and endeavour to make everyone conform to the approved standard. And that standard, express or tacit, is to desire nothing strongly. Its ideal of character is to be without any marked character; to maim by compression, like a Chinese lady's foot, every part of human nature which stands out prominently, and tends to make the person markedly dissimilar in outline to commonplace humanity.

As is usually the case with ideals which exclude one-half of what is desirable, the present standard of approbation produces only an inferior imitation of the other half. Instead of great energies guided by vigorous reason, and strong feelings strongly controlled by a conscientious will, its result is weak feelings and weak energies, which therefore can be kept in outward conformity to rule without any strength either of will or of reason. Already energetic characters on any large scale are becoming merely traditional. There is now scarcely any outlet for energy in this country except business. The energy expended in that may still be regarded as considerable. What little is left from that employment, is expended on some hobby; which may be a useful, even a philanthropic hobby, but is always some one thing, and generally a thing of small dimensions. The greatness of England is now all collective: individually small, we only appear capable of anything great by our habit of combining; and with this our moral and religious philanthropists are perfectly contented. But it was men of another stamp than this that made England what it has been, and men of another stamp will be needed to prevent its decline.

The despotism of custom is everywhere the standing hindrance to human advancement, being in unceasing antagonism to that disposition to aim at something better than customary, which is called, according to circumstances, the spirit of liberty, or that of progress or improvement. The spirit of improvement is not always a spirit of liberty, for it may aim at forcing improvements on an unwilling people; and the spirit of liberty, in so far as it resists such attempts, may ally itself locally and temporarily with the opponents of improvement; but the only unfailing and permanent source of improvement is liberty, since by it there are as many possible independent centres of improvement as there are individuals. The progressive principle, however, in either shape, whether as the love of liberty or of improvement, is antagonistic to the sway of custom, involving at least emancipation from that yoke; and the contest between the two constitutes the chief interest of the history of mankind. The greater part of the world has, properly speaking, no history, because the despotism of custom is complete. This is the case over the whole East.

Custom is there, in all things, the final appeal; justice and right mean conformity to custom; the argument of custom no one, unless some tyrant intoxicated with power, thinks of resisting. And we see the result. Those nations must once have had originality; they did not start out of the ground populous, lettered, and versed in many of the arts of life; they made themselves all this, and were then the greatest and most powerful nations in the world. What are they now? The subjects or dependants of tribes whose forefathers wandered in the forests when theirs had magnificent palaces and gorgeous temples, but over whom custom exercised only a divided rule with liberty and progress. A people, it appears, may be progressive for a certain length of time, and then stop: when does it stop? When it ceases to possess individuality. If a similar change should befall the nations of Europe, it will not be in exactly the same shape: the despotism of custom with which these nations are threatened is not precisely stationariness. It proscribes singularity, but it does not preclude change, provided all change together. We have discarded the fixed costumes of our forefathers; every one must still dress like other people, but the fashion may change once or twice a year. We thus take care that when there is change, it shall be for change's sake, and not from any idea of beauty or convenience; for the same idea of beauty or convenience would not strike all the world at the same moment, and be simultaneously thrown aside by all at another moment. But we are progressive as well as changeable: we continually make new inventions in mechanical things, and keep them until they are again superseded by better; we are eager for improvement in politics, in education, even in morals, though in this last our idea of improvement chiefly consists in persuading or forcing other people to be as good as ourselves. It is not progress that we object to; on the contrary, we flatter ourselves that we are the most progressive people who ever lived. It is individuality that we war against: we should think we had done wonders if we had made ourselves all alike; forgetting that the unlikeness of one person to another is generally the first thing which draws the attention of either to the imperfection of his own type, and the superiority of another, or the possibility, by combining the advantages of both, of producing something better than either. We have a warning example in China—a nation of much talent, and, in some respects, even wisdom, owing to the rare good fortune of having been provided at an early period with a particularly good set of customs, the work, in some measure, of men to whom even the most enlightened European must accord, under certain limitations, the title of sages and philosophers. They are remarkable, too, in the excellence of their apparatus for impressing, as far as possible, the best wisdom they possess upon every mind in the community, and securing that those who have appropriated most of it shall occupy the posts of honour and power. Surely the people who did this have discovered the secret of human progressiveness, and must have kept themselves steadily at the head of the movement of the world. On the contrary, they have become stationary—have remained so for thousands of years; and if they are ever to be farther improved, it must be by foreigners. They have succeeded beyond all hope in what English philanthropists are so industriously working at—in making a people all alike, all governing their thoughts and conduct by the same maxims and rules; and these are the fruits. The modern *régime* of public opinion is, in an unorganised form, what the Chinese educational and political systems are in an organised; and unless individuality shall be able successfully to assert itself against this yoke, Europe, notwithstanding its noble antecedents and its professed Christianity, will tend to become another China.

What is it that has hitherto preserved Europe from this lot? What has made the European family of nations an improving, instead of a stationary portion of mankind? Not any superior excellence in them, which, when it exists, exists as the effect, not as the cause; but their remarkable diversity of character and culture. Individuals, classes, nations, have been extremely unlike one another: they have struck out a great variety of paths, each leading to something valuable; and although at every period those who travelled in different paths have been intolerant of one another, and each would have thought it an excellent thing if all the rest could have been compelled to travel his road, their attempts to thwart each other's development have rarely had any permanent success, and each has in time endured to receive the good which the others have offered. Europe is, in my judgment, wholly indebted to this plurality of paths for its progressive and many-sided development. But it already begins to possess this benefit in a considerably less degree. It is decidedly advancing towards the Chinese ideal of making all people alike. M. de Tocqueville, in his last important work, remarks how much more the Frenchmen of the present day resemble one another, than did those even of the last generation. The same remark might be made of Englishmen in a far greater degree. In a passage already quoted from Wilhelm von Humboldt, he points out two things as necessary conditions of human development, because necessary to render people unlike one another; namely, freedom, and variety of situations. The second of these two conditions is in this country every day diminishing. The circumstances which surround different classes and individuals, and shape their characters, are daily becoming more assimilated. Formerly, different ranks, different neighbourhoods, different trades and professions, lived in what might be called different worlds; at present, to a great degree in the same. Comparatively speaking, they now read the same things, listen to the same things, see the same things, go to the same places, have their hopes and fears directed to the same objects, have the same rights and liberties, and the same means of asserting them. Great as are the differences of position which remain, they are nothing to those which have ceased. And the assimilation is still proceeding. All the political changes of the age promote it, since they all tend to raise the low and to lower the high. Every extension of education promotes it, because education brings people under common influences, and gives them access to the general stock of facts and sentiments. Improvements in the means of communication promote it, by bringing the inhabitants of distant places into personal contact, and keeping up a rapid flow of changes of residence between one place and another. The increase of commerce and manufactures promotes it, by diffusing more widely the advantages of easy circumstances, and opening all objects of ambition, even the highest, to general competition, whereby the desire of rising becomes no longer the character of a particular class, but of all classes. A more powerful agency than even all these, in bringing about a general similarity among mankind, is the complete establishment, in this and other free countries, of the ascendency of public opinion in the State. As the various social eminences which enabled persons entrenched on them to disregard the opinion of the multitude, gradually become levelled; as the very idea of resisting the will of the public, when it is positively known that they have a will, disappears more and more from the minds of practical politicians; there ceases to be any social support for non-conformity—any substantive power in society which, itself opposed to the ascendency of numbers, is interested in taking under its protection opinions and tendencies at variance with those of the public.

The combination of all these causes forms so great a mass of influences hostile to individuality, that it is not easy to see how it can stand its ground. It will do so with increasing difficulty, unless the intelligent part of the public can be made to feel its value—to see that it is good there should be differences, even though not for the better, even though, as it may appear to them, some should be for the worse. If the claims of individuality are ever to be asserted, the time is now, while much is still wanting to complete the enforced assimilation. It is only in the earlier stages that any stand can be successfully made against the encroachment. The demand that all other people shall resemble ourselves, grows by what it feeds on. If resistance waits till life is reduced *nearly* to one uniform type, all deviations from that type will come to be considered impious, immoral, even monstrous and contrary to nature. Mankind speedily become unable to conceive diversity, when they have been for some time unaccustomed to see it.

Conclusion

In the aftermath of the First World War and the Spanish flu pandemic of 1918-1919, the Irish poet and esotericist William Butler Yeats penned 'The Second Coming'. It is a troubling work that is as much premonition as it is poetry:

Turning and turning in the widening gyre
The falcon cannot hear the falconer;
Things fall apart; the centre cannot hold;
Mere anarchy is loosed upon the world,
The blood-dimmed tide is loosed, and everywhere
The ceremony of innocence is drowned;
The best lack all conviction, while the worst
Are full of passionate intensity.

Yeats proceeds to imagine the birth of some monstrosity—a sphinx-like creature with 'gaze blank and pitiless as the sun' slouching towards Bethlehem to be born, bringing to an end some twenty centuries of 'stony sleep'. The origin and nature of this creature are not clear, but we are left with an uneasy sense that perhaps the two-thousand year period from the birth of Christ was merely an interregnum, a temporary hiatus, sandwiched between two vast periods of time in which other metaphysical forces have been, and will be, at work—forces alien and openly hostile to the traditional order of the West.

At an interval of almost exactly one century since Yeats

wrote 'The Second Coming', his words have lost none of their immediacy: the centrifugal, anarchistic, sacrilegious forces seem—if anything—as insistent as Yeats must have felt them to be back in 1920. Arguably, though, it is the final two lines of the first stanza that ring most obviously true—and not merely in a metaphorical sense—today: *The best lack all conviction, while the worst/ Are full of passionate intensity.* For if there is a failing that is characteristic of our era, it is surely this: that those who shout the loudest and strike with the least compunction are often those whose personal virtues seem conspicuously absent, while those whose characters bloom with modest virtue shrink from public life and retreat deeper and deeper into quiet obscurity. Moral confidence walks hand-in-hand with personal lassitude while the streets burn at the whim of those whose breezy superiority has never been checked by the stern eye of self-criticism or chiselled away through the daily practice of self-discipline and self-overcoming.

The answer to social ills is not, let me suggest, to be found in more intense and more rigid moralism in the public and political sphere. Black-and-white thinking about good and evil has itself so often been a cause of evil: Milton's Satan, let us recall, thought that God was the tyrant, and himself the aggrieved party; behind the masks of the Inquisitor and the Red Guard were souls convinced of their own moral rightness and enraged by the perceived moral inadequacy of their victims. There is, perhaps, a too-little-recognised deficiency in the very notion of moral universalism in the first place. 'Act as if the maxim of your action were to become through your will a general law,' urged Kant, in a formulation that has become canonical and which appears, at first glance at least, to be unobjectionable. But this formulation doesn't necessarily lead to ethical maxims that are truly 'universal'; in fact, it may lead to maxims that only *appear* universal, while in fact merely embodying the particular preferences of a particular subjective being or group of beings. The simple fact is that there are at least as many maxims that can be willed into general laws as there are souls on the planet. William Blake put it well: 'The crow wished everything was black, the owl, that everything was white.' Nietzsche, similarly, observed that the wolf might be satisfied with a very different general law from that preferred by the lamb. Universalism coats with a veneer of moral authority what in reality may be little more than naked self-interest.

This book has charted a route through the history of Western ethics that accentuates the ethics of personal virtue as a means of self-realisation and growth. That may seem like the promotion of an inward-turning, unsocial, and unpolitical approach to ethics. Nothing could be further from the truth. From the outset, Plato was emphatic that there could be no political justice unless men could properly order their own souls. The just state was merely the just man writ large. There could be no society as such without individual justice, for it was only just men who could form and sustain a workable society; likewise, there would be no tyrants unless men were dysregulated, for the tyrant is the very embodiment of dysregulation, and, more importantly, because only dysregulated men would usher in an age when tyranny would be accepted. More than two thousand years later, John Stuart Mill harked back to the 'Greek ideal of self-development' when he made his case that it is the excellence and flourishing of individuals that heighten the respect and love that men feel for each other in society. The true foundation of society is not, then, an all-intrusive state that imposes rules upon men and herds them like cattle; it is the coming together of individuals respectful and appreciative of each others' particular gifts.

The path indicated by virtue ethics is long and arduous. There is no room for moral smugness, finger pointing, or virtue signalling. It is not simply a question of finding a moral rule that you believe you are entitled to impose on society generally

CONCLUSION

at the often minimal cost of accepting it might also be imposed upon you; nor is it a matter merely of taking actions likely to increase the overall wellbeing of those around you. Virtue ethics demands much more from you than that: it demands that you begin the long hard process of chipping away at your faults and sculpting a better self—that in order to *do* good you must first *be* good. To return to Aristotle: true virtue is virtue that has been habitualized into a virtuous disposition which experiences ethical conduct not as duty but as second nature. Nobody says it will be easy. There are forces out there—forces swirling out from 'the widening gyre' described by Yeats—that want to see you pushed and pulled by this political or social imperative or that, never grounded as your own person. The thinkers in this book offer another path. They are part of your heritage and, if you are modest enough to let them, they will guide you to places that you could never, in your wildest dreams, have imagined.

BIBLIOGRAPHY

Aristotle. *The Nicomachean Ethics of Aristotle*. Translated by F.H. Peters. 5th ed. London: Kegan Paul, Trench, Trübner & Co., 1893.

Aurelius, Marcus. *The Meditations of the Emperor Marcus Aurelius Antoninus*. Translated by George Long. London and New York: The Chesterfield Society, 1890.

Boethius, Ancius Manlius Severinus. *Consolation of Philosophy*. Translated by H.R. James. London: Elliot Stock, 1897.

Epictetus. *The Works of Epictetus. Consisting of His Discourses, in Four Books, The Enchiridion, and Fragments. A Translation from the Greek based on that of Elizabeth Carter*. Translated by Thomas Wentworth Higginson. Boston: Little, Brown, and Co., 1865.

Hume, David. *A Treatise of Human Nature*. Edited by L.A. Selby-Bigge. Oxford: Clarendon Press, 1896.

Kant, Immanuel. *Kant's Critique of Practical Reason and Other Works on the Theory of Ethics*. Translated by Thomas Kingsmill Abbott. London: Longmans, Green & Co., 1889.

Kierkegaard, Søren. *Selections from the Writings of Kierkegaard*. Translated by L.M. Hollander. Austin, Texas: University of Texas, 1923.

Mill, John Stuart. *On Liberty*. London: Longman, Green, Longman, Roberts & Green, 1864.

———. *Utilitarianism*. London: Longmans, Green, Reader, and Dyer, 1871.

Nietzsche, Friedrich. *The Complete Works of Friedrich Nietzsche Volume*

Twelve: *Beyond Good and Evil*. Translated by Helen Zimmern. Edinburgh: The Edinburgh Press, 1909.

———. *The Genealogy of Morals*. Translated by Horace B. Samuel. New York: The Modern Library, 1918.

Plato. *Dialogues of Plato*. Translated by Benjamin Jowett. 3rd ed. London: Oxford University Press, 1892.

———. *The Republic of Plato*. Translated by Benjamin Jowett. 3rd ed. London: Oxford University Press, 1888.

Schiller, Friedrich. *Aesthetical and Philosophical Essays*. Translated by Nathan Haskell Dole. Boston: Francis A. Nicholls & Company, 1902.

Schopenhauer, Arthur. *On Human Nature: Essays (Partly Posthumous) in Ethics and Politics*. Translated by Thomas Bailey Saunders. London: Swan Sonnenschein & Co., 1902

Seneca, Lucius Annaeus. *Minor Dialogues*. Translated by Aubrey Stewart. London: George Bell and Sons, 1889.

Spinoza, Benedict. *The Chief Works of Benedict de Spinoza*. Translated by R.H.M. Elwes. London: George Bell and Sons, 1883-84.

www.ingramcontent.com/pod-product-compliance
Lightning Source LLC
Chambersburg PA
CBHW021431080526
44588CB00009B/495